W9-ADF-484

GOOD FOR
A GIRL

GOOD FOR A GIRL

A Woman Running
in a Man's World

LAUREN FLESHMAN

PENGUIN PRESS

NEW YORK

2023

PENGUIN PRESS
An imprint of Penguin Random House LLC
penguinrandomhouse.com

Copyright © 2023 by Lauren Fleshman
Penguin Random House supports copyright. Copyright fuels creativity, encourages diverse voices, promotes free speech, and creates a vibrant culture. Thank you for buying an authorized edition of this book and for complying with copyright laws by not reproducing, scanning, or distributing any part of it in any form without permission. You are supporting writers and allowing Penguin Random House to continue to publish books for every reader.

Image on p. xiv © Kirby Lee; image on p. 261 © Heather McWhirter

LIBRARY OF CONGRESS CATALOGING-IN-PUBLICATION DATA
Names: Fleshman, Lauren, author.
Title: Good for a girl : a woman running in a man's world / Lauren Fleshman.
Description: New York : Penguin Press, 2023. | Includes bibliographical references.
Identifiers: LCCN 2022028016 (print) | LCCN 2022028017 (ebook) |
ISBN 9780593296783 (Hardcover) | ISBN 9780593296790 (eBook)
Subjects: LCSH: Fleshman, Lauren. | Women runners—United States—Biography. |
Women coaches (Athletics)—United States—Biography. |
Sex discrimination against women—United States. |
Sex discrimination in sports—Law and legislation—United States. |
United States. Education Amendments of 1972. Title IX. |
Sports—Social aspects—United States.
Classification: LCC GV1061.15.F65 A3 2023 (print) | LCC GV1061.15.F65 (ebook) |
DDC 796.42092 [B]—dc23/eng/20220912
LC record available at https://lccn.loc.gov/2022028016
LC ebook record available at https://lccn.loc.gov/2022028017

Printed in the United States of America
1st Printing

BOOK DESIGN BY LUCIA BERNARD

For my mom, Joyce, my first holistic coach

For Jesse, my greatest teammate

And for the athletes

CONTENTS

INTRODUCTION

The young women are getting ready to run: flexing their knees, clearing their watches, and bouncing a few times to get the feel of the track. As I approach my standard position by the start, the group of five sorts itself into a single file line.

"Are we ready?" I ask, more as a signal than a question.

"Yep!" pipes Sadi from the back. She's grinning like a kid, and I like what I see.

"Okay, how are we doing this?" I ask the group; but I'm really asking Mel, our most veteran athlete, standing in the front.

"I'm taking the first mile, then Rebecca is taking over." To Mel, a distance runner with a huge aerobic engine, this two-mile interval to kick off the track workout is cake, and everyone trusts her to set an even pace. I notice Mel is wearing her lucky top with the superhero women print on it today, which means it's go time. I'll push her a little harder at the end of the workout.

"Keep it smooth and relaxed," I say to the group. "Stay together." Mel looks at me, left foot on the line and her finger ready to press start. I nod.

"Ready . . . go," she says quietly, and the group leans forward and starts in unison, a smattering of beeping watches as they fly past me. I study them as they round the first curve onto the straightaway, Rebecca a little too close on Mel's heels. Once I'm satisfied that everyone is safely in lockstep, I walk over to the retaining wall that borders lane eight, fluff someone's sports bag like a throw pillow, and lean my back against it. I stretch out my legs in front of me and take a deep breath, letting the sunshine bathe my body. The line of women whizzes by.

"Good!" I say simply, not bothering to check the split on my watch. So much of my job as a coach is about noticing things. I can tell that the team is on pace by how evenly spaced they are, how serene Mel's face is. I adjust the bag to get more comfortable. I'll be here for at least ten minutes, and I want to relish it. The Olympic Trials are around the corner, and everyone is running lifetime bests. Their bodies are as strong as they're going to get before race day, so now is the time to coach them inward: group intervals to remind them they're not alone in their dreaming, followed by a few solo intervals to remind them of their individual power.

I love watching them run—that metronomic pop-pop-pop-pop-pop that lets each of their minds spread out—and after a few minutes of enjoying their rhythm, I look down at my own legs. I retired from professional racing in 2016. I don't miss it—I had my turn. But my body remembers the feelings of capacity and possibility that competitive sport gave me for over twenty years. I reach forward and place my hands on my thighs and give them a gentle shake, maybe in gratitude, and see that the insides of my ankles are still striped with dirt from my run among the juniper and sagebrush this morning. Even though I no longer race professionally, running will always be home for my body and mind. If I do my job well as their coach, these women will have that, too.

The synchronized footsteps get louder, and I look up to see the women approaching again. Rebecca is in the lead now, looking incredible. She is such a gamer; her desire to race oozes out of her. Like Mel and most of the others, she could have quit this sport so many times, but she didn't. Many people counted these athletes out before they were recruited to Littlewing Athletics, the professional women's running group I coach in Bend, Oregon. But I know better than to count a female athlete out based on what she hasn't accomplished by age twenty, or even thirty. I know women, and I know how poorly our sports systems nurture their talent.

I AM CONTINUALLY amazed at what sport at its best can add to women's lives, and we should never stop talking about the benefits of participation. But even fifty years after federal Title IX legislation mandated equal sports opportunities for women in the United States, we have a lot of work to do. We still haven't nailed the basics, with the bulk of public schools (especially those serving communities of color) coming up well short of compliance. But even in the places with adequate female sports opportunities, like most of the United States, Canada, Australia, New Zealand, and the UK, surprising numbers of girls who enter sports programs aren't sticking around. For those who do, physical and mental health problems occur at distressing rates, and abuse is all too common.

With female puberty framed as a threat to performance, many take measures to prevent or reverse it, often losing their periods and disrupting the hormonal function essential to building healthy bones and a healthy body. Many face pressure by coaches to achieve a body ideal that is nearly impossible during their stage of physiological development, and experience stress fractures at three times the rate of their male peers. Many learn to hate the bodies that do so much for them, and 65 percent develop disordered eating habits that compromise their ease around food, sometimes irreparably. Millions of women carry an abundance of positive memories of their time in sport, but they also carry the invisible wounds of their sports experiences. As women, we've justified these wounds as normal or internalized the belief that we were to blame.

There is something wrong with our sports systems, and deep down we know it. The sports environments we fought so hard to have equal access to were built by men, for men and boys. Our definition of gender equality has been "getting what men have, the way they have it," and it's backfiring. We fold and smash women and girls into a male-based infrastructure, and then scratch our heads when the same friction points show up again and again. Meanwhile, fundamental female-bodied experiences in sport are invisible, erased, or viewed as problems because they differ from the default male standard. The refusal to acknowledge this is causing incredible harm.

A number of committed researchers are hard at work right now identifying the myriad challenges facing women in sport, from eating disorders to psychological stress to performance dips linked to puberty; new areas of research calling for attention are emerging all the time. I look forward to the day when hundreds of peer-reviewed papers spelling out the exact issues and their solutions are available. Armed with that knowledge, we'll be even better equipped to create new best practices and policies that reduce harm and clear the way for the best parts of sport to fulfill their promise of safety, health, and empowerment. But we can't wait to address this problem.

That's why I've written this book. After twenty-seven years in sport as an elite athlete, teammate, coach, and parent, my own personal story offers more than enough evidence that something is wrong; the start of some solutions emerge, too. My story is not representative of all women and girls, and any comprehensive discussion about changing women's sports must include the voices of all who compete in that category, including women of color, women with disabilities, trans women, and people who don't fit within the gender binary. I strongly encourage people to share their stories to finally turn the tide in women's and girls' sports. We've all watched substantive change pushed to the top of the to-do pile by expressions of passion from ordinary people.

My hope is that readers might see a person in their lives—their daughter, or athlete, or patient, or friend, or maybe themselves—anew. This book is a sports story and a love letter to the running life, but above all, it's a story about a girl growing up in a world built for men, and all the friction and confusion and pain and joy inherent to that journey. It is also an impassioned expression of hope for the future.

1

THE PROMISE

You can do ANYTHING, Lauren. ANYTHING!"

My dad's callused hands gripped my shoulders and his ice-blue eyes forced mine open wider with their intensity. "You hear me?!" I tried not to blink. I was eight.

"They're just scared of you. They know you can beat them. They don't want to lose to a girl, but too fucking BAD! You go back and tell 'em you're playing, and if they give you shit, you kick them RIGHT in the balls, and drag them down here by the ear, and I'll take care of the rest." He dusted his hands together like he was about to take care of business, and added a conspiratorial wink. It was the right mix of empowering and absurd, loosening the knot in my throat and making me smile, just as he intended.

Frank Fleshman seemed to speak in all caps. He didn't turn the dial down on his personality, or language, or anything really, for someone else's comfort. He was the kind of dad who wanted sons, but he got two daughters and refused to adjust his parenting plan.

"Jesus, Frank!" my mom would reply in these situations, followed by a gentle plea for peaceful resolution. But Joyce's shy kindness had a hard time being heard over the boom of Frank's charisma or the apparent simplicity of his solutions. So I kicked the neighborhood boys in the balls. And then they let me play.

MY WORLD WAS different from my mom's in a million ways, but the one made apparent to me first was the central role of sports. The first women's NCAA championships in track and field were held in 1981, three months before I was born. Technically, my mom's time in high school overlapped with the passing of Title IX, but its promise of equal access for women and girls in sports took time to materialize.

In 1971, the year before Title IX was passed, fewer than 300,000 girls played high school sports—compared to 3.6 million boys—and my mom never met one. She did love playing ping-pong in PE class, and she had a deadly curve, according to my dad, whom she started dating in middle school. I saw it in action a couple of times at Super Bowl parties, but she was oddly shy about it, rarely playing a full game. She didn't seem to know how to claim athletic movement as her own.

My mom would have been good at sports. Dad, too, for that matter. He was too busy getting in fights and smoking weed in high school. But I could tell Dad was athletic, because he worked manual labor building sets as a propmaker and I saw him move his body powerfully all the time. My mom's body was directed to household tasks with a side of gardening, until the one time I convinced her to go for a run with me in high school. As she popped powerfully off her midfoot and lifted her knees, I almost gasped. I recognized her distinct stride as my own. Running is hard, and with no base fitness, she couldn't run for longer than a couple minutes. But I never looked at her body the same way again. Like millions of women, she carried a treasure chest of undiscovered athletic potential.

My mom's world and mine were still different, even living under the same roof. While the girl power revolution of the 1990s was swirling all around, telling girls we could have it all if we worked hard, my mom's daily reality was frozen in the 1950s. In our home, Dad got the best chair, the first serving, and the last word. He told his daughters not to take shit from anyone, then turned around and treated my mom to large helpings of his own. He represented a kind of power hypothetically available to my sister, Lindsay, and me, but not to my mom.

It would have been confusing regardless, but his alcohol abuse created a terrifying gulf between what he said and how he behaved. Every single night, we had family dinner together around the table, cooked by my mom. Most nights were fine, great even—full of compliments to the chef, questions about our day at school, and entertaining stories about the cast and crew of whatever his latest movie set was. But the possibility of an explosion always lurked, especially when he had been laid off, which happened frequently in the entertainment industry. If the Bud Light hit just right on the wrong day, he could singe any one of us to a crisp with a bolt of lightning.

Outside of the occasional spanking or head flick, I only have one memory of physical violence, when he ripped me out of my dining chair by the armpit while I was mid-bite and threw me across the living room for eating my spaghetti "like a fucking pig." I landed on my side on the sofa, still holding my fork, and curled into a ball in the far corner. My arm socket throbbing, I watched him puff up like a silverback gorilla while my mom screamed at him to stop. I watched as she laid down the only ultimatum he ever took seriously, one delivered with a cold fury I never saw in her again: "Touch either of our girls like that one more time and I swear to God, Frank, I will leave you, and take them with me."

I learned to watch him differently after that. When he stepped out of his truck after his long commute home, I scanned his hands for an empty beer can being carried to the crusher. Doing homework at the kitchen table, I kept count of the crack and hiss of aluminum tabs adding unexpected percussion to Steely Dan playing too loud on the surround sound. An interruption in the rhythm of my mom chopping onions meant he was squeezing past her in the kitchen to pull another clunking can from the twenty-four-pack on the bottom shelf of the fridge. I pretended to love using the can crusher so he would hand his empties directly to me, making it easier to keep tabs. And when the number rose above four or five, it was time to watch more closely. I learned to discern the different blinks, slurs, and seated positions. I needed to know which Dad was going to show up for dinner.

I was never the target of serious physical violence again because I learned to be perfect during those times—to observe and do what I needed to do, whether it was laughing at his jokes, impressing him with my accomplishments, or disappearing into the background.

But sometimes, despite my vigilance, my mom would slip. Dad would assert that she'd forgotten to add the cayenne to Uncle Tommy's chili recipe, or she'd put too much cream in the beef Stroganoff, or maybe dinner was too early, or too late, or too hot, or too cold. As the oldest child, I assigned myself the role of rodeo clown distracting the bull. But some nights still ended with him charging out the front door with his truck keys rattling, slamming the iron screen door behind him. Fifteen minutes later, he would walk back in, smack his paper bag full of fast food on the bar, and turn up the volume of the football game loud enough to make it impossible for us to speak, even if we wanted to.

Dad was a wild tide, but Mom was our shore. With her quiet stability grounding the family, Lindsay and I were able to absorb a lot of good from his larger-than-life personality and love. He was a bighearted, loyal person who would do anything for his friends and family—except change. And when he was sober, he shined so brightly on the people he loved that we would go to great lengths to put ourselves in the path of his light. And nothing got him shining quite like excellence. Be it John Elway's throwing arm, Bonnie Raitt's vocal power, or Arnold Schwarzenegger's performance in *Terminator 2*, when Frank felt the spirit overtaking him, he made everyone else stop what they were doing and appreciate it, too. He would rewind a scene, play a song again. He needed us to know that excellence like that was accessible to us.

"Your mom and I had nothing when we were kids," he'd say. "We had to work hard to just survive, but you can do more than that. Most people aren't willing to work hard. But you're a FLESHMAN, and Fleshmans aren't afraid of HARD WORK." He'd pound his chest twice for emphasis.

I nodded along, not only because I wanted to please him, but also because my personality drove me to work obsessively hard anyway. I genuinely loved memorizing spelling lists and multiplication tables in school. I got a thrill and felt a burst of satisfaction when I saw the star on my homework. I took my deep focus into playtime, too. While my neighborhood friends played house or Barbies, I'd hover nearby for hours, attempting to balance a peacock feather on my nose. Or extending the length of time I could sleep a yo-yo. Or learning to walk down the narrow hall and back on my hands without falling. I loved taking on challenges that required refining the movements of my body and culminated in a feeling of mastery.

But my personal drive got tangled up with my dad's drinking and overall volatility. In the ninety-minute window between when my dad got home and when his personality changed, performing whatever tricks I'd been working on became the most reliable way to bask in his affection. I'd ask Dad to hold my legs while I hung upside down from his bar, counting off sit-ups. When I began playing softball at age eight, my natural desire to learn to throw hard and accurately was enhanced by the thrill of making his hand sting so I could watch his theatrics. I got good, despite being the smallest kid in the league every year. In games, I played hard every minute of every inning, no matter how badly we were losing, because afterward I knew I'd find my dad in the bleachers with his Bud Light camouflaged in a sliced apart Diet Coke can, and he would put it down to hug me, look me in the eyes with intense love, and tell me that he was so proud of me that his buttons were busting. He would tell me I had something better than talent: I had heart.

On our annual summer camping trip on the Kern River, a slippery cliff rock loomed above the swimming hole, inviting those brave enough to make the climb and jump. Dad did it every year, but it was exciting every time. The year I was seven, we watched four kids in our group, all older than I was, climb up to the ledge one by one, only to sit down and deliberate and eventually retreat the way they came.

"They're being pussies," my dad said to me. "I bet you could do that. Just don't overthink it. Thinking kills your courage." After a minute of feeling like I had a hummingbird in my chest, I swam across the swimming hole to the rock face on the other side and climbed up as fast as I could. My kneecaps began to shake as my wet fingers pulled me up onto the slippery landing, and as the hairs began to rise on my cheeks and my mind started to race, I walked straight to the edge of the limestone and threw my body toward the darkest part of the blue.

When my head popped up above the surface, I saw my dad standing with his hands in the touchdown position.

"Did you see that?!" he yelled to his camping buddies. "My girl's got balls the size of Texas!"

Treading water, I felt repulsion, having never heard that phrase used about a girl before. Watching the grown men slap their thighs and heckle their sons to go next, saying "Don't be a pussy!" I could see that having balls was the ultimate compliment, and it was the ultimate compliment *because* it wasn't female. I didn't just have balls, but Texas-sized balls, and the kids around me had to rise to the occasion. It was striking how motivating that was for them, how much it made them squirm to have me setting the standard. And as they swam past me toward the cliff rock for another attempt, I followed them up, determined to outdo them. I was learning to see myself through my dad's eyes—through the eyes of those with power, the eyes of men.

IN SCHOOL, I heard the same promise that I could be the best at whatever I set my mind to. I was taught that boys and girls were the same, outside of a couple of small details in physical appearance and the whole "who could have babies" thing. Inconsequential. I was told that people *used* to think men were superior, but we now knew this wasn't true, and that oppression was a thing once, but now it was over. Women were just as capable as men. We could do whatever they could do. There were firsts happening for women everywhere, and there were countless more available to those who dreamed.

I remember those firsts being important to me. I colored in Sandra Day O'Connor's Supreme Court robe with a black crayon in school as we learned about the first female Justice. After Aretha Franklin became the first woman elected to the Rock & Roll Hall of Fame when I was six, my dad blasted "Respect" for us so loudly the blinds rattled. I don't remember Joan Benoit running past my waving hands outside our home in Los Angeles on her way to the first-ever Olympic marathon gold for women, but I remember my excitement when my mom told me the story. And so I dreamed myself onto the pages of history books, wondering which page I'd land on. During President Clinton's inauguration, when I was eleven, I remember my mom saying, "In your lifetime, you will see the first female president of the United States." I went to bed that night with my heart pounding with possibility, convinced that it was going to be me. I couldn't run for office at eleven years old, but I could race boys on the playground and compete with them in tetherball. Using my body athletically made me feel powerful, and I went from being someone who simply enjoyed pursuing mastery with my body to someone who wanted to use it to win—at everything. And every time I did, especially when I beat the boys, I felt affirmed that I could do anything in life.

BY THE TIME I was in middle school, I was an all-star softball player, but being good for a girl in a girls' sport didn't carry much weight. I got more recognition for being the girl who could beat the boys in PE class. And nowhere was my dominance more clear than in running. Once a week, we ran the same mile course that was marked by trees and cones placed around the outer edges of the schoolyard. The mile was completed with a lap around a dusty track carved out of the middle of weedy sports fields. Every week, at the sound of the bullhorn, I would take off with the pack, and within two minutes, I would be alone, gliding along the row of trees on the far end of the field, flying beneath the branches we were now too old to climb.

Running fast made me inhabit my body in a way nothing else could. I noticed that while my eyes scanned the terrain, if I tuned into myself, my body would adjust on its own, finding the perfect angle to round a curve without slowing, finding a landing that just missed a pothole. I would ramp up my speed until it was impossible to think of anything else but the running; until I wasn't a girl, or a middle schooler, or in PE class at all. I was just a body, limbs and blood and breath and power. The high followed me out of the locker room into the halls, and it grounded me.

Other athletic pursuits could give me this primal feeling in small bits, but only running sustained it. I never considered running outside of class. I had never seen someone running recreationally and didn't even know it was an official sport in which kids could compete. But every week I ran a mile in PE, and every week I won. And then I would wait there, picking burrs off the laces of my sneakers, watching as the others gradually approached: first a smattering, then a splash, followed by a steady stream of joggers and walkers. Rarely did someone dip under seven minutes. I was getting closer to 6:30 without really trying. Every week, the fastest runners from each class period were posted on the wall of the gym. I checked those results like some of my girlfriends checked their reflections in the windows, looking for evidence that everything was as it should be.

Then, one day after spring break, with middle school graduation just a few weeks away, I checked the list. Someone else's name was on top, and his time was almost a minute faster than I'd ever run.

2

THE SPLIT

Rocky's balls dropped, sweetie," my dad said from his barstool in the living room, swiveling both the chair and his eyes back and forth between the football game and me.

"What do you mean?" I said loudly, over the referee whistles and announcers.

"Puberty. He's turning into a man," he said, a fact as simple as the existence of gravity.

Rocky was the boy, apparently on his way to becoming a man, who'd come out of nowhere to beat my fastest race time by a full minute. I'd never seen a child become an adult before. I knew grown-up men and women looked different, but I'd been told those differences wouldn't impact anything. I thought differences in skill were based on talent, hard work, and heart. I thought we could become whatever we wanted to become.

"What, are *all* the boys going to start beating me now?" I asked. The thought made my breath go shallow, my stomach pinch.

Dad spun his stool back toward me. "Not all of 'em. You keep working hard and you'll still beat most of them, I bet."

You bet? You don't know? I was running inventory. All these kids, and no idea where I would stand in a month, in a year. It wasn't even about the winning, exactly. It was about fairness.

"What about the girls?"

"They'll turn into women. Get hips and tits and into making out behind the portables. You know."

I didn't—I knew what a woman's body looked like, but I hadn't really thought about how that body was consequential beyond appearance. Was this a joke? Boys made out behind the portables, too. What did that have to do with anything?

Mom chimed in with a truth and a lie. "Boys and girls are just different, honey. Doesn't take away from what you do."

Puberty hadn't meant much to me up until then. I had watched my neighborhood girlfriends burst into longer jeans and bigger bras. I watched them press down their breasts with their hands, complaining of soreness when playing tag in the cul-de-sac and losing enthusiasm for the game over time. Getting enough willing participants for anything more than a walk to Walgreens was proving difficult. As we walked, I heard the catcalls and studied the girls' faces as they adjusted to being seen.

My body remained unchanged, frozen in time, and the power I felt in my body when I played sports felt stable and trustworthy. My confidence as an athlete made it easier to brush off my invisibility to the boys that had crushes on my classmates. I had a body they didn't see as attractive, but I comforted myself with the fact that this body could win. But after losing to Rocky, I began to see everything differently. The fact of a girl's changing body affected my friendships and social life. And now a boy's changing body threatened my identity.

Returning to PE class, I watched the girls around me the way I'd learned to watch the beer at home. During our Presidential Fitness Test, I saw boys and girls now, where before they were just kids. During timed sit-ups, while holding the feet of a classmate, I watched her quickly check between her legs, presumably concerned about her period. As she fought for a few more efforts before the teacher blew the whistle, I noticed it looked a lot harder to do sit-ups with a weight vest worth of breasts. As we got off the gym floor to move outside for the final test, I watched the girls pull out real or imagined wedgies from school-issued shorts, adjust the unisex gray T-shirts stretched over their chests. Constant awareness of their own bodies was the new normal.

According to a 2016 study, girls in the United States are dropping out of sports at twice the rate of their male peers by age fourteen, and over half leave sports completely by age seventeen. Among Canadian teens, a 2020 study showed that one in three girls who play sports will quit by their late teens, as compared to one in ten boys. This time of life presents the largest and most stubborn leak in the girls' sports equality effort. According to the Women's Sports Foundation's twenty-five years of research, the top six reasons identified for girls leaving sports are differences in access, safety and transportation, social stigma such as being tagged "gay," decreased quality of experience, cost, and lack of positive role models. But one of the most fundamental factors in this flight from competitive sports isn't even mentioned: puberty. Little scholarly attention has been paid to how puberty is experienced by female-bodied people in the context of movement or to the reality that puberty is inadequately acknowledged or supported in physical education and competitive sports for young people.

Puberty is a fact. In female puberty, breast development is the first physical change that occurs, at the mean age of just under ten years old. Globally, the age of puberty onset for girls has moved up about three months per decade over the last thirty years, for reasons not fully understood, and within the United States, the median age of breast development has been shown to vary by race by as much as a year. A woman's breasts typically develop until age seventeen or eighteen, with some continuing to grow into their twenties. Menstruation, a misguided but time-honored marker of the beginning of puberty, follows about two years after the start of breast development, around age twelve. But by then, the show is well on the road. Girls are experiencing movement differently and have unanswered questions about how to adjust to their changing bodies. In a 2016 study of over two thousand schoolgirls ages eleven through seventeen in the UK, a whopping 73 percent of girls reported having at least one breast-related concern in relation to sport and exercise. Forty-six percent reported their breasts affected their participation. Eighty-seven percent said they wanted to know more about breast development, and half of those said they wanted to know more about breasts and sports bras in sport specifically. "I can't find the right sports bra" and "I am embarrassed by excessive breast movement" were statements linked to barriers to sport participation. Over half of the girls surveyed did not wear a sports bra.

Health class may be where you learn about the anatomy, but sports are where you're going to *feel* it. Looking at a diagram of mammary glands is wildly different from the embodied experience of jumping rope with breasts.

Movement for girls now feels different than it does for their male peers they used to run alongside, but the sexualization of girls' bodies creates barriers to adult figures talking about it. Pretending breasts don't exist is the best way to avoid being misinterpreted as a creep or worse, but breasts go on existing anyway. When a developing female does sit-ups, they are managing multiple elements: a changing body that makes the movement more challenging, their feelings about that body, and others' feelings about that body. Is movement something they will leave behind along with their child body?

IN EIGHTH GRADE, my clothes hung on my frame like a hanger, as always, and I smoothed the wrinkles out of my shirt over my flat chest. I found myself torn between feeling left behind by this pack of girls and hoping my body would stay the same forever.

In the final weeks of middle school, I tagged along with a group of softball teammates who were going dress shopping for the eighth-grade dance, and we took over the back corner of the Macy's dressing room in a flurry of satin and spaghetti straps. The excitement my friends felt as they zipped one another's dresses and admired their forms in the full-length mirrors was not available to me. Their bodies stirred a feeling of sexual attraction that made me worry I was "becoming" gay. I sensed it was a feeling I wasn't supposed to have, and not knowing bisexuality existed, I hoped puberty would help silence it. I could hide my feelings, but my body was on full display. The tops of my dresses gaped. The girls in the dressing room teased that my chest was flat as a boy's. I felt myself shrinking. I felt defective. I prayed for breasts to come, to make me normal. The body that made me feel powerful in sports was now at odds with being the *right* body, the body that qualified as feminine.

It was my first experience with a phenomenon I would see over and over again in my own life and career and those of other female athletes: the clash between the function and appearance of the female body while being subject to the dominant male gaze; the significant pressure to be both physically strong and sexually attractive. The trained body will change its appearance to meet the demands of sport, and when this body differs from the beauty ideal, varying degrees of psychological conflict can arise. Increasingly, scholars are referring to this as the "body duality" of the female athlete. But I of course had no words for that feeling as a teenager, and nobody in my life did, either.

I had trouble being consistently on time in school, but PE class was always the exception. After losing to Rocky I showed up late a few days in a row, and I faced the consequences. During the recycling revolution of the early 1990s, punishment for being tardy three times was collecting 150 soda cans. During our snack and lunch breaks, the offending student wandered from clique to clique carrying a huge black plastic bag outstretched for the humble offering of empty Dr Peppers and Cactus Coolers.

Maybe Mr. Hershberger knew something was unusual about my uncharacteristic three tardies in a row. Maybe he noticed the difference in my energy since the Rocky incident. Maybe he just wanted to win the meet. But when he delivered my verdict of 150 cans, he followed it up with an offer: to avoid my punishment, I could agree to compete for our school during the city's junior high track meet, at that point just two weeks away. It was an easy choice.

My first event was the girls' mile, except on the track it was called the 1,600 meters. The first thing I learned about track was girls and boys are at the same event but don't compete against one another; each discipline is contested twice, alternating genders. The second thing was that track appeared to be the only place in the United States where people used the metric system. Nobody could tell me the exact conversion from the mile I was used to, so I just did what the PE teacher told me: follow Ava, a girl from the other school, for the four laps of the race, and try to win at the end if I could.

I can still see her straight spine, her elbows jabbing back toward me one at a time. Ava was a tight, even knit; no movement was wasted. I tried mirroring her from behind, never having run so closely to someone else before. I lowered my eyes to the raised railing of shiny aluminum that created the inside border of lane one and watched the way Ava's left shoe almost kissed it every time it landed. She was running at that effort I had grown to love, the speed that made her feet magically find the best place to land, but I was finding myself extended somewhere beyond that for the first time. My feet seemed to be landing harder, with less predictability. My breathing went from a steady rhythm to chaotic gasps.

The sound of the bell signaling the last lap came right as I was starting to circle the drain. I was a few strides behind Ava and my conviction that I could beat any girl, anywhere, was wavering. And to my distress, so were the lane lines. Ava became a blur, rising and falling on a sea of orange tartan. A shimmer; a mirage of steam resting on the top of it all. I knew the track waving about wasn't normal. But I also knew I was nearly there, and it would end soon. When I crossed the finish line a distant second, the clock was fuzzy, but I could see it had a five in front of it.

Less than an hour later, Ava dragged me around the track behind her one more time in the 800 meters, a criminally painful event I hate to this day. Essentially a very long sprint, the 800 turns you from Wonder Woman into a nematode in the time it takes you to microwave a bag of popcorn. I finished second in both races, but I was pulled to maximum efforts and fast times I was excited about. I raced one leg of the winning 4x400 relay to close out the meet, and we celebrated our victory by cheering and jumping all over one another. I liked track, I decided. It had some of the team energy of softball, but with more individual agency.

As I was packing up to head back to the bus, a man with tight bronze skin, a buzz cut, and huge purple wraparound Oakley sunglasses approached me and introduced himself as Coach DeLong, the cross-country and track coach at Canyon High School, where I'd start as a freshman the following fall.

"Those were great performances today, pal. You've never run before?"

"No, I run. In PE. And in softball."

His eyebrow lifted as if on a string. "I meant Junior Olympic track. That girl who beat you is a Junior Olympian. She trains for this."

Well, that explained a lot.

"Have you thought about coming out for cross-country?"

"I'm going to try out for varsity softball."

He looked me over: a drowned rat with biceps the width of a broom handle. "You're a little small for varsity, don't you think?"

I wanted to say, *I'm the smallest in the league already, and it hasn't held me back.* I don't remember what I did say, but I know I felt the familiar thrill of being underestimated.

He smiled.

"Look, that girl's been running track for a few years. She's very good. And you finished close behind her in two races today without any real training. You're very talented, Lauren. I'm sure you'll be good at softball, but you could be great at running."

DeLong went on to describe a group of fun kids that would be my instant circle of friends. He described celebrations after workouts—root beer floats enjoyed in the sunshine on the infield. Field trips, like running fourteen miles one way from the Hollywood Bowl to Venice Beach, where we'd picnic and bodysurf all afternoon. And most appealing of all, a weeklong training camp at an old ski lodge at Mammoth Lakes before school started.

He spoke to me like I'd belong, and belonging was impossible to resist. I was giddy with the promise of it. Practice started in a month.

DELONG'S FIRST NAME was Dave, but everyone called him by his last name. I called him Coachie, but not until I was older, when I'd gotten so fast that I was the only athlete left to train in the post-season, him riding his bike alongside me, carrying water and telling stories to pass the miles. He was more like a second father by then, but at first, he was just DeLong, a fit thirty-three-year-old with a motivational T-shirt collection and a sunglasses tan so bad he decided never to take them off.

"Canyon High School has a long legacy of champions," DeLong

said loudly to the assembled group of new freshmen and their parents seated on the stadium steps overlooking the dirt track. He introduced the assistant coaching staff, including Tracy McCauley, who treated the girls like a caring older sister and ran with the team every day. "We have the best coaches, we know how to win, and more importantly, we know how to have fun. What we do here is special. We have a huge team kids want to be a part of, kids who stay out of trouble and get good grades, and that's only possible because of parent support."

My mom came home with a list of options for how to contribute. Parents chaperoned our field trips and training camp, fundraised to lower the cost of our uniforms and get our sweatshirts embroidered, and helped organize a year-end banquet with awards nice enough to survive an attic purge twenty years later. We were a team over one hundred kids strong, dominated by working- and middle-class families short on time and money, but DeLong got people to show up.

My first season of cross-country was like falling in love. I stood no taller than 4'10" and weighed in at seventy-eight pounds, but unlike in softball, where my size had become an impediment to getting to play at all, being a shrimp made it easier for the older girls on the team to tuck me under their wings. I got what I wanted: friends.

My first running group, the "newbies," contained all the freshmen of all genders, along with a few random upperclassmen working their way back from injuries. That first week, the veteran runners led us through two- and three-mile runs on city sidewalks that started and ended in the school parking lot. These runs were full of traffic and exhaust, with gas stations for landmarks, but I didn't care. I was going somewhere new with someone who knew the way. The older, more experienced runners would head off in another direction, returning with dirt slimed onto their front teeth from the fire roads that climbed the surrounding mountains. They looked taller when they got back, laughing together at the open tailgate of DeLong's truck, squirting water on their faces and rubbing the salt off their foreheads with their other hands. They had sports bra tan lines and pale wrinkly skin under their Timex watches, and they stepped on each other's new shoes to get the first smudge out of the way.

By the second week, when I figured out that tennis shoes weren't the same as running shoes and showed up with my first pair of ugly Asics, three upperclassmen raced over to leave the first dirty footprint on top. I'd never been happier. That was the day DeLong grabbed my shoulder and shifted me like a pawn on a chessboard from the newbie group to a JV group.

"You run with Liz today—okay, pal?"

Liz was one of the runners who went beyond the concrete, up the mountain roads. She was experienced, but her pace was accessible.

I moved to the landing where he was pointing. Five miles. It would be my longest run ever. Every day had been my longest run ever.

"How long is this hill?" I asked Liz, running up on her freckled shoulder as we climbed. It was the kind of hill you can't see the end of.

"About a mile," she said, unfazed.

It wasn't long ago that one flat mile on grass was a weekly accomplishment.

"Wait until we do hill repeats up it. That's a special kind of hell."

Liz and I climbed the rest of the hill, passing runners along the way, and turned off the noisy highway at last into a maze of unfamiliar residential streets. After several turns I'd never be able to remember on my own, we got to a dead end with an open horizon and ran from where the sidewalk ended onto a dirt trail. The trail cut through sage and tumbleweeds, dust rising underfoot. I followed Liz's line as she hopped over loose rocks and sand traps, and the trail swept left around a rusty cylindrical water tower, its ladder raised just out of reach of anyone who tried to climb. Without slowing down, she bent over, picked up a rock, and threw it at the side of the tank. It made a huge sound. "Tradition," she said. I bent over to do the same, watched it ricochet a little close for comfort, and savored the echo.

As we passed the water tower, the trail wound back to the right along a cliff not steep enough to cause serious harm, but steep enough to make my heart race, a thrill of running with a little bit of danger. This was the kind of drop that made my mom call me to her side nervously on our infrequent hikes at Placerita Canyon, and now here we were, a hundred kids running along freely without adult supervision. Beyond the cliff was a wide-angle view of the entire wash below, and beyond that, the tiny cars like Hot Wheels on Soledad Canyon Road, and beyond that, the sagebrush-covered mountains rose tall above it all.

I'd only really seen the first two inches of those mountains from the kitchen window, peeking above the rooftops of the mobile home park behind my house. From up here, they looked massive. I could see the outlines of dirt roads scarred into their sides and realized there was probably a trail just like this one that I could run on to get to the top. Maybe all those hills had trails that led to their tops. And all of them had views of my town I'd never have seen. Running was my portal to a wider world. My body felt lighter, and my face softened with awe. I wasn't flying, but it felt close.

3

GOOD FOR A GIRL

Before long, DeLong said the words I'd been yearning to hear: "Run with varsity today, pal." I hopped to it immediately, tucking in behind the pack of girls gathered at the line he'd drawn across the dirt road for our last hard workout of training camp in Mammoth Lakes.

"Fleshman the Freshman's going to join you today," he announced, delighted at his latest nickname christening.

My emergence as a front pack runner came as a surprise. Somehow, in the high altitude of Mammoth, where the air was thinnest and the trails were steepest, I found myself clipping the heels of our top seven for the first time. And now DeLong wanted to see how I fared during hard intervals. The workout was three minutes at "race pace" followed by three minutes of easy jogging, repeated eight times. Just like the race against Ava, around the halfway point

I found myself extended beyond my fitness, but I hung on to the back of the pack with pure grit.

"That's enough for you, pal," DeLong said, pulling me over to his side and giving me a high five as he sent the veterans off for their last two sets. I watched him bend at the waist, projecting hoarse encouragement to every pack of athletes, stopwatch swinging from his neck like a pendulum. As the varsity girls approached on their last interval, I tried to imagine myself keeping up and was distracted by a pack of varsity boys charging behind them. One shouted "on your left," and the girls fluidly condensed themselves to the right so they could pass. A flurry of breathless "good jobs" was exchanged. It was the first time I saw these two groups head-to-head, and the boys moved with a swiftness that surprised me. They were undeniably faster than we were, but according to De-Long's pep talks, the girls were the stronger team, the truly special once-in-a-career team, the team with a shot at winning State. Still, seeing them fly by like that, I ached to run with the boys because they were running the fastest. I was rising so quickly, a part of me wondered if I could somehow become the exception. Firsts were happening all the time. Maybe with real training, I could be the first girl to keep up with the boys.

THERE ARE NO sex-based performance advantages in sport among children. Females up to age twelve are competitive with their male peers across a wide variety of sports and disciplines and hold many age-group records. But at about twelve and a half years of age, as puberty hormones enact changes on female and male bodies differently, two distinct performance paths emerge. While both groups show improvement with training over time on average, the rate of improvement differs dramatically by sex. The hormones of male puberty create an environment for advantageous musculoskeletal changes, increased red blood cell mass, and lower fat mass. When it comes to training, males get more juice out of every squeeze. The performance gap between males and females widens with each passing year until around age twenty, at which point it stabilizes with the male advantage ranging from 10 to 50 percent, depending on the sport. This pattern is consistent, even when controlling for training, nutrition, funding, and medical care.

Nobody explained this to me—indeed, I didn't know anything about the science behind athletic performance and sex until I took exercise physiology in college—and I held out hope at first. Maybe who wins is not about sex, I thought, but about *belief*—a human failing of the imagination left over from the days of obvious gender inequality. With a little digging into horse racing at the library, I learned the Kentucky Derby had been won by fillies three times. It was rare, but it happened. Maybe we just needed the right horse—me! But every day I came to practice and got outpaced by several dozen boys, the fantasy faded a little more.

In many sports, sex-based performance differences can go relatively unnoticed by the athletes themselves because with different seasons and times of play, there is little opportunity for direct comparison. But in cross-country and track and field, girls' and boys' programs are typically combined, with athletes of all genders sharing coaches, facilities, practice times, and competition schedules. On every trail, at every race, the performance gap announced itself to me clearly, reminding me that I was a girl. Fortunately, the sting of this unfairness was soothed quickly by the salve of equal opportunity. That's what Title IX made possible in my school. As a competitive person, finding the girls' and boys' running arenas to be full of the same opportunities and rewards went a long way toward helping me find a comfortable home in sports and in my body again.

Cross-country is open to all who enter. There are no tryouts, no cuts. And the essential creed is the same in running as it is in every other sport: you get out what you put in. Effort equals results. So simple! All you need to do is show up, do the work, and believe in yourself. These "truths" make for inspiring pep talks and refrigerator magnets, but like everything else in sports, I'd later learn that they weren't created with the female body in mind.

This culture of sport rewarding effort represented everything I wanted to believe about the world. It was a different world than the one my parents inhabited, where money sometimes got tighter even when they worked harder, my dad laid off again, pacing the living room in preparation for the next phone call he would make to see if he could get some work. My father hated doing this; he was visibly agitated with shame from needing to present himself as jobless, asking for a favor. But that was how his industry operated, and it was the best he could do with the education he had. My mom's frugality helped us weather the dry spells and kept us comfortable, but there was always this feeling that it could go away; others were in control of our destiny, our security, no matter how many times Dad proved himself or how many coupons Mom clipped.

Running appealed to me precisely because it spoke to self-determination. Efforts were clearly measured, rewards fairly distributed. Cross-country teams, like softball teams, worked toward rising together, but in running there are no runs batted in. You add up all your finishing positions at the end to see where you land as a group, but the runner, measured by the immutable facts of time and distance, must cover all yards alone.

My first two high school cross-country races were against freshmen. My time for the second race was so fast that DeLong thought his stopwatch was malfunctioning. I would have been the third-fastest runner on varsity.

I WAS SHAKEN AWAKE in total darkness by a few older teammates one morning while my mom looked on with increasing concern from my bedroom doorway. With my consent, they dressed me in a vest, tutu, and wig, topped off by an abundance of scarves and plastic jewelry until I looked like a costume box had thrown up all over me. On my forehead was scribbled "FRESHMAN" in eyeliner pencil, and I was handed a sign that read "I made varsity." After being paraded around Walgreens and the donut shop at dawn, I started to feel anxious about attending school this way.

As we showed our IDs and walked through the campus gates, I was nervous and hyper-alert, like every other day, except this time I was flanked by teammates. They walked me to every class and were waiting for me at the door when I came out. They accompanied me to my locker and through the line for my pizza bagel. Every situation that could have been humiliating was turned into a statement of solidarity. They were showing me repeatedly, no matter what, no matter who has something to say about it, they would stand beside me. When my mom pulled up to the curb to pick me up after school, my posse was long gone, no longer needed.

I leaped into the passenger seat, smudged and bedraggled, but smiling with the confidence of a girl who belonged.

I learned the rituals of my team. The order of the stretches in the team circle before the run. Repeating the mantra "State champions run the stairs" on the final climb back to school. Finding one another on the starting line and forming a huddle, arms braided over and under shoulders and armpits, saying a prayer and "Amen." I didn't believe in God, but I believed in them, and I loved the way we looked into one another's eyes in that darkened cave we made together before heading off to run our hearts out. Every ritual was replaced by others at each stage of my running career, except one.

Before my first varsity race, a couple of older teammates headed out for a sacred pre-race ritual, and I followed them. We walked away from the jumble of blankets and duffel bags toward an open space under a tree and laid our track-suited backs onto the damp grass. I was instructed to close my eyes and simply "soak in the field"—no further explanation needed, apparently.

"How long does it take?" I asked.

"You'll know when it's time to get up," the team captain replied.

I took a big settling breath, closed my eyes, and felt the cool ground beneath me. There was the sound of distant laughter, people ringing cowbells off and on, cheering. I heard a pack of voices get louder and then quieter again as they ran past, oak leaves crunching underfoot. The darkness around me was textured with sounds and gave me a different perspective. This race I had been nervous about was a symphony of people, hopes, expectations, elation, disappointment, families, and teams. We'd made it all up and brought it to this park that was indifferent to all of it, a park that was here yesterday and would be here tomorrow. Someone resting in this very spot the next day would never know any of it happened.

I had a feeling of flattening out. I got heavier, like I was lying on a planet with more gravity. I was anchored in, and then I started slowly turning, like someone was screwing me into the earth with a power drill low on batteries. My worries lifted off my edges like disturbed dust, and then the turning slowed to a stop. I opened my eyes and focused on a branch above me, one of many in a web of brown and green with jagged spaces of blue. Colors and textures looked more vivid. I was calm.

Every race after that, I soaked in the field—at first with teammates, and eventually alone, on every track, in every uniform, in every country I raced in. No matter what the circumstances around me, it was a guaranteed way to return to myself.

THAT FIRST CHAMPIONSHIP SEASON as a varsity runner, I was consistently the third scorer on what would become the number-one team in California history. Winning State was a big deal. We were in the newspapers, paraded across the gym at rallies, and we shaved DeLong's legs on the school stage to fulfill a bet he made with the seniors. My mom didn't even have a team to join in high school, and now here I was, the top freshman in the state of California, standing alongside my teammates, accepting recognition in front of city council. T-shirts with a huge screen print of our team victory photo on the front were made for a fundraiser. Nine teenage girls huddled together, bursting with unselfconscious joy. My dad wore that shirt well into my thirties, long after the print resembled a Pollock painting.

I remember the bus ride home from the last big cross-country race. As we made the final left turn toward the school parking lot, kids began pounding the inside walls of the bus, yelling our traditional victory song, and I remember the thrill of knowing all the words for the first time. I remember thinking I might be born for running. It gave me a way to tune into my body and to convert the maximum effort I was accustomed to giving into something with meaning.

"You look happy," said the boys' team captain from across the aisle of the bus as we waited for the rows ahead to unload. Sam was a very cute senior, and I couldn't believe he was talking to me.

"I am," I said, too fluttery to think of anything to add.

"You know," he said, "I know you're rising fast, and it's really exciting. I hope you stay encouraged. A lot of girls run their fastest as freshmen. But no matter what, you can have fun. I hope you keep having fun."

I had no idea what he was talking about, but I nodded and said earnestly, "I will." Over the next three and a half years, I'd remember this moment often as I came to understand what he meant.

During my first track season, I was an emerging star, a budding phenom in the mile and two mile. During my final race of the year, in the 3,200 meters, I heard history being made over the loudspeakers: Kim Mortensen from Thousand Oaks nearly lapped all of us to break a long-standing national record by an astounding twelve seconds. The packed stadium had gone from cheering to silence, trying to process what they had just witnessed.

DeLong was animated when I reunited with him in the cool-down area. "She looks just like you, Lauren, but a little taller." He pointed over at her bony frame, her collarbones like a drying rack for her jersey. I heard other coaches and parents note Kim's child-like body, recall her effortless form, marvel at the lightness of her bounce. She didn't eat up the track so much as float over it.

Over two thousand boys in the United States ran faster than Kim that year, and each of the twenty-one years it took for another girl to break her record. But nobody cared that Kim wouldn't have made a dent in the boys' field—she wasn't just "good, for a girl" in people's eyes. Kim was a star, a respected athlete on the front page of the paper, headed to UCLA on a full scholarship.

Curious about the path ahead for athletes like Kim, and maybe even athletes like me, I started checking through my dad's newspaper more regularly. I didn't see any professional female athletes. This was the late nineties, but little has changed. Today women make up 40 percent of the athletes in the United States but receive only 4 percent of the sports coverage, about the same as it was thirty years ago. The front page of the sports section is more likely to feature a male sports fan than a professional female athlete. Less than 1 percent of endorsement investment in professional sports goes to women.

So, it's not surprising that until 1996, when the Olympics came to Atlanta, I had never watched pro women's sports on TV. The modern Olympics has a structure that is amenable to promoting and showcasing gender equity, should a sports network choose to. There is a women's and men's version of nearly every sport, and it is common to see coverage of both in succession. Many women's and men's sports share one governing body, like track and field and swimming, and marketing rights are often sold as a package to sponsors, eliminating the economic reasons to push one sex more than the other in the broadcast. Olympics coverage in 2021 had a remarkable 58 percent of coverage dedicated to female athletics.

The rest of the quadrennium, not so much. A USC/Purdue University study that examined sports coverage on three LA network TV affiliate stations and on ESPN from 1989 to 2014 found that only 3.2 percent of highlight shows were devoted to women's competition in 2014—and no, it didn't get better with time. The percentage actually declined over twenty-five years, even as participation rates in girls' and women's sports rose.

But men's sports? Those were always dominating the living room in my home, turned up loud enough to accommodate my dad's table saw–induced hearing loss. Football, basketball, and baseball marked the seasons more reliably than the Los Angeles weather.

We had the Atlanta Olympics on for hours every day. For two straight weeks I saw women and girls mixed into the coverage. In the pool. On the diving board. Carefully placing their manicured fingernails on starting lines of the track. When my dad saw one woman walk out to the track, a middle-distance star, a blond, white woman with a big laugh and a Crest smile, he sat up straighter and said, "Most of them are dogs. She's smokin' hot."

I paid attention to which women got camera time. Which women had stories told about them. Which women were featured in the commercials. They were pretty. They were nice. They smiled. They put effort into presenting themselves. The Olympics was a reliable avenue for a female athlete to become famous, and I wondered if I would grow up to be pretty enough or charming enough to be celebrated if I qualified. I ran my tongue over the gap in my teeth.

Still, the biggest global sports spectacle in the world had women in it, and that was exactly what I needed to see. My favorite sport to watch was gymnastics. Perhaps it was because the athletes were teenagers like me. Perhaps it was because I had loved gymnastics the one time I got to try it, but the fees were too expensive to make a habit of it. But mostly it was the gymnasts' skill—the mind-blowing tricks they did with their bodies. The way they seemed to fly. The micro-control over every movement on the beam that made me twitch reflexively. The precision. The high stakes while all those eyes were on them.

I remember wondering why the girl gymnasts wore leotards when the boys wore loose-fitting shorts or pants. Wouldn't the leotards go up their butts? Before and after their routine, they smiled at the judges. But when they were in action, they were pure power, explosive, total marvels.

Kerri Strug became a household name that summer, just three years before I'd find myself dancing next to her at a frat party in college. The all-around team competition was at its climax. Kerri busted her ankle on the first vault, clearly injured. Her coach talked to her, and she limped out for another try. The announcers seemed worried. Everyone seemed worried. I was worried. I asked Mom, "Why aren't they stopping her?" She came and stood beside me to watch.

While Kerri Strug was encouraged, as she had been thousands of times before, to ignore her animal instincts and her well-being and perform that final vault, I watched along with the rest of the world. I watched her hop on one foot on the landing, saluting the judges and then collapsing in agony. I watched her get scooped up like a child—which she was—by her coach, Bela Karolyi, who was proud of his girl.

You've probably seen this clip. It's in the highlight reel of all-time Olympic moments of inspiration. I would study it in a Sports and Society class at Stanford a few years later. And it's a moment that's representative of how we talk about the ideal female athlete. All my life, that sports highlight has been played with the musical score of a superhero movie, when it should have been played to the soundtrack of *Saw*. When the Larry Nassar case was revealed and documentaries about all the abuse showed up on Netflix, it became clear that many of the gymnasts who seemed to be living the dream were living in hell. The Karolyis reportedly shamed them for their weight and controlled what they ate, creating an environment where girls were eating toothpaste to satisfy their starvation response. Compliance was expected in all circumstances: You don't decide when you're hurt, Coach does. A medal for your country is worth any price.

A culture of compliance leads to disassociation from yourself, from your body's signals of hunger, fatigue, and pain. Today, when I see that highlight video of the 1996 USA gymnastics team, I see Kerri's incredible determination and skill, but I also see my friends and peers and countless women from lots of different sports who've shared their stories with me. I see the years of hard work required for reintegration of the self, relearning your body's hungry and full cues, relearning to trust yourself when your body says slow down or stop, relearning to trust yourself when a practitioner like Larry Nassar says he needs to put his fingers in your vagina to help with your sprained ankle. Over five hundred women and girls were sexually abused on Larry Nassar's treatment table. A culture of compliance and coachability muted the alarm bells going off inside the minds of countless parents and other adults who could have intervened.

The message to me at fourteen was that compliance, coachability, and even beauty might be more important than health and safety. As I watched the gymnastics team hold their bouquets, medals draped around their necks, it became clear what it took to be beloved.

WHEN MY TEAM gathered for summer training for a new season of cross-country, I showed up with the exhilaration of belonging and the excitement of finding out just how good I could become through hard work. But I was developing an awareness that my trajectory of success in this sport I was falling in love with might not be entirely within my control. In girls' sports, there were specific forces at play that I needed to be aware of. I needed to be coachable. I needed others to love me enough to invest in me. And I needed my body to cooperate with my plans. I had a creeping sense that my body might change and ruin everything.

| 4 |

WHO WINS

We watched a lot of game shows in my home growing up. My sister and I were rapt at the sight of normal people like us getting a chance to play a game or spin a wheel for big, supposedly life-changing amounts of money and prizes. When some people won, they simply smiled. Those people were rich, we figured. It was hard to feel excited for them. But the people who screamed? Who jumped up and down and wept and hugged strangers? Those people's lives were changed.

"How do we get on one of these shows?" I asked my parents one weekend during *The Price Is Right*.

"You've got to have connections, Lauren. Know someone who knows someone in Hollywood."

"Don't you work in Hollywood?"

"Yeah, but I'm a propmaker. If you need a good painter, or some cabinets replaced, I got you."

Translation: That kind of luck wasn't in the cards for me. But eventually, sports gave me my game show opportunity.

"You won't believe it, Lauren," DeLong said, biking alongside me on a recovery run right after State in my junior year. "Foot Locker Cross Country Nationals is like the Super Bowl of high school running. They fly all the qualifiers from around the country to the race, put you up at a fancy hotel for free, and you're treated like royalty."

He might as well have been describing Willy Wonka's chocolate factory.

"You get a bag of free running clothes, new shoes, all-you-can-eat buffets. You get to be with the best athletes in the country, all in one place. The races are on TV, and NCAA coaches are lining the course, scouting out recruits. Make it to Foot Locker, and colleges will be knocking down your door."

Weary from a long championship season for which I'd trained alone, I barely achieved the required top-eight finish in the West Regionals to earn my ticket to the big show. I collapsed afterward with the feeling of relief, and only then did I understand how much pressure I'd been under. I immediately entered a whirlwind of media and logistics, and five days later, I walked down the Jetway in my Canyon High School letterman jacket to board a plane to Disney World in Florida, leaving my family behind. Looking out the window of the plane, seeing clouds from above for the first time, I felt myself expanding into someone new, someone with control over her life.

The Foot Locker Championships were everything I hoped for. Staring in disbelief at the bounty of gear I emptied out onto my hotel bed, I slid my hand over the polyester of my first real pair of running shorts that wasn't part of my school race kit. The night before the race, we had a special banquet, and I found myself navigating different-sized forks with the fastest runners in the nation, amazed I belonged among them. I sat with my team from the west region as we watched pump-up videos compiled by the event featuring us, with clips from our regional races and interviews with some of the favorites. We were given our instructions for race day and then treated to a moderated panel of professional runners (a job I didn't know existed) who told us that they had once sat where we were now, and that we were the future of the sport.

I raced exactly like someone happy to be there, somewhere in the middle of the pack, pleased to be in the density of pedigree, slipping around in shin-deep puddles that the previous night's storm had left all over the lush grass of the Disney golf course. I was happy for the hard part to be over with, and as soon as I caught my breath at the finish, I joined a group of kids playing in a puddle as big as a city pool. I got a running start and did my best softball slide through it, a massive eagle's wing of water spraying alongside me. We danced that night at the after-party in an event room dank with Teen Spirit and CK One and, not wanting the night to end, most of us stayed up all night, backs leaned against the walls of the hallway connecting our rooms. I don't remember what we talked about, but we didn't stop until we were loaded onto the bus before sunrise and deposited at the airport, where we would stumble onto our respective airplanes and sleep at last, returning to the small ponds from which we came a little bigger. We were in this together. Foot Locker finalists. We would return home as heroes.

Foot Locker did change my life. Recruiting letters from colleges all over the country packed my mailbox like Black Friday

advertisements in the run-up to Thanksgiving. I was too busy running, studying with my best friend, and flipping burgers at In-N-
Out for gas money to read them. My mom carefully hole-punched
each letter and assembled them like scrapbook pages in a three-ring
binder. Mom was taking classes at the junior college to get her AA
degree in business, a pursuit Dad was resistant to support, for fear
it would give her the self-assurance to leave him. She wanted to
talk to me about the letters, this book of opportunities beyond her
imagination. I didn't want to discuss them. I preferred my dad's
generalized boisterous enthusiasm and pride. We knew I'd go to
college somewhere, and that was enough for now. With each letter, he'd offer his standard "That's great, honey!" unless it was an
Ivy League or a rich-kid school, in which case he'd open his eyes
big and say, "Oh, look what we have here!" Sitting tall in his chair,
as though he had a stick up his ass, he would lift his aluminum can
to pursed lips with his pinky finger extended. "It's a fahncy one."
He'd laugh, and I'd laugh and put that letter in the back of the
folder with all the ones from places I knew I'd never fit in: the too
fars, the too snowys, and the too fancys.

Our home phone rang throughout the day on July 1 the summer before my senior year, the first day NCAA coaches were allowed to call recruits, and I spent the next six months on the phone
learning about college. Having never had a glut of anything, I
didn't know how to say no to anyone. The cordless receiver pressed
against my ear grew hot from overuse while hearing about training philosophies and learning about school traditions, tailgating,
bonfires, and what the dorms were like on campuses I knew I'd
never set foot on. Coaches bragged about their recruiting classes,

their facilities, their national rankings. I didn't think to ask them about their teams' physical and mental health statistics or attrition rates, but it would have been far more useful.

I'd recount these phone calls to DeLong as we covered sixty-mile weeks in preparation for our final year together, and he'd weigh in on which colleges were more intimate, which programs were stronger, which coaches were more legendary. Too fast for the girls, too slow for the varsity boys, I found myself more and more alone on my team; every hard workout day, Coachie rode his bike alongside me, enthusiastically calling out splits he'd never seen a girl do before. I felt special, favored, all because I wasn't like most girls. I won races by larger margins, broke course records, and felt invincible in my body. There was almost nobody left in the country standing between me and the top.

IN THE LAST couple weeks before State, Dad cut off his finger at work. I've often wondered if it was because he was drunk or hungover, but he insisted it was just a bad piece of wood, a nearly petrified knot that kicked the two-by-four toward his face as he was running it through the table saw. Somehow, his finger found its way under the blade.

For those first few weeks after the accident, I'd come home from practice or races to a man I didn't recognize slumped in his La-Z-Boy recliner. There was pain, and there were pain pills and phantom limb sensations, but most disturbingly, his personality changed. He was a campfire the morning after a rain. The reaction didn't make sense to me. Frank was too big of a man to be taken down by a finger. Lots of his friends had missing fingers. They'd joked about them all my life. But then I overheard him recounting the incident to a friend on the phone.

"So, I do what they say. I bring the finger to the hospital with me. And this fuckin' guy, this white coat with hands like a baby's ass, tells me he won't sew it on. He says to me, 'Sometimes the surgery doesn't really work. If you worked in a job where you really needed fine motor control, like if you were a surgeon or something, we would give it a try.' But not for me. That motherfucker has no idea what we do. What we need our hands to do." He stood up and went to the cooler for another beer and slammed the lid shut. "He doesn't know my life."

In a moment of vulnerability, my dad's life was seen with less value. Someone who was more powerful got to decide what he needed and deserved, and he wore the evidence on his own hand. Without his finger, he knocked cans over by accident and failed to pick up his keys on the first try. As he stormed off, frustrated, I would try to help, retrieving and gently handing him the things that he wanted. This both saddened and frightened me, the idea that our future was at the mercy of others' esteem. I thought about how my running success inspired people with power to get behind me. Greatness, it seemed, offered a sort of protection, honorary membership to a more powerful class. I felt even more motivation to win.

WITH A HALF MILE to go in the California Cross Country State Championships, my eyes bore into the shoulder blades of the defending champion. There were no footsteps behind us. I'd never won a state title before, and I wanted to win so badly it threatened to erupt out of me. But as soon as I decided I'd take the lead, the mental chatter rushed in. Just like at the Kern River cliff rock, I made the leap before I could change my mind. Out front, I felt exposed, vulnerable, and brave. I held on to the feeling of bravery and let it fill me up to the brim, giving me and all the spectators lining the course the full measure of my daring. The finish line scaffolding didn't appear to be getting any closer on that long final straightaway, and I almost looked back, but I forced myself to move only forward by asking myself the question, *Is this the fastest you can go? Yes? That's all you can do. It's either enough or it's not. Who cares where the other girl is—look forward!*

The next day, around 11 a.m., I wandered into the living room rubbing my eyes. As usual, Dad had gone around town collecting all the newspapers to check for coverage of the race. He looked excited from his seat at the bar. It was clear my victory cheered him up. On top of the stack was *The Los Angeles Daily News*, with a huge photo of me winning State, eyes wild, teeth bared, fist raised mid-pump, "CANYON" emblazoned on my chest. I'd never seen myself look like that before, so completely given over to the moment, and I suddenly felt embarrassed by the crazed look on my face.

"If it weren't for your long blond ponytail, you'd look like a dyke," my dad joked, the sports page laid flat on the bar next to his coffee. I'd heard him say this about other female athletes before, a reflection of that generation's deep-down fear that letting their daughters play sports would damage their femininity or make them gay. He paused to consider the spread before him, running his callused fingertips over it. I looked at the photo again, torn between feeling proud and feeling distressed that part of winning was being photographed doing it. I had loved the way that moment felt, so animal, so purely energetic. It didn't look how it felt.

Then he swept it up and shook it toward me from atop his perch, grinning from ear to ear. "Look at this! Front page! Look at my girl." I felt my embarrassment melt down. "That's effort! That's what heart looks like! You're a Fleshman! A scrapper! That's what it takes. I'm so *proud* of you." He put the paper back down on the bar with a thwack and put his hands on his chest, puffing it out. "My buttons are busting, Lauren. Busting." And he invited me into his arms, the smell of cigarettes on faded cotton soothing me like a campfire under the stars.

ONE WEEK AFTER winning the State Cross-Country Championships, I continued on my senior tear by qualifying for Foot Locker again, finishing second at the West Regional behind the latest young phenom, Sara Bei. I'd been warned about Sara's unusual strategy that made her undefeated: she started in the back of all her races, moved up methodically through the middle mile, and burst into the lead seemingly out of nowhere to take the win at the end. Still, she went by me so fast that before I could process what happened and decide what to do about it, she was gone. It was marvelous. Next time, at Nationals, I'd be ready when she came by, and planned to hitch a ride all the way to the front.

I deplaned in Florida for my second Foot Locker Championships a seasoned runner. The veterans found their way to one another and engrossed themselves in conversations about college recruiting. Most of them already had a school locked down, while my options still lived in a binder. DeLong and I had decided to wait until Foot Locker was over to get serious about college, and I felt hungry to prove myself among all these chosen ones.

"Keep your enemies close," DeLong joked when he heard that Sara and I were roommates. I winked like I was in on it, but the term *enemy* didn't fit. Sara and I got along brilliantly. I wanted to beat her *because* I liked and respected her so much.

The day before the race, they bussed us all over to the course for a preview. DeLong had flown out to watch and support me, and as he stretched my hamstrings he seemed uncharacteristically subdued, humbled by the prestige of the event. I jogged the five-kilometer course from start to finish, and as I approached the finish line littered with camera crews scouting their spots for the next day, I imagined myself full of heart, and picked up the pace despite myself.

Beyond the finish line was a narrowing chute lined by flags, and I followed it to the corral where all the finishers would gather tomorrow, the race done and places settled. Only a handful of us would truly be able to say we'd given it everything we had and the rest would be left wondering. I didn't want to be in this corral wishing I'd dug a little deeper, been a little tougher. I couldn't control if I was good enough to win or not, but I could control that.

Walking back toward our bags, I passed the podium where the winners would be ceremoniously crowned. And beyond that was a series of posters, photographs of previous champions with laurel wreaths on their heads, huge trophies held awkwardly in their skinny arms. I stopped at the image of Kim Mortensen, the girl who had broken the national record in the 3,200 when I was a freshman, and wondered how she felt about that day now. Over the summer, DeLong had brought a *Los Angeles Times* feature on Mortensen to practice to share with me. Kim had gone to UCLA on a scholarship, just forty-five minutes from my house, but I hadn't heard anything about her since. Just a few years after redefining what was possible for a girl, Kim was leaving competitive running due to an eating disorder.

In the article, she described how the disease started with a desire to get faster, to be more dedicated. She lost weight from eating "healthier," and her times improved. When asked about her improvement at the time, she cited hard work and focus, which of course were also true. In college, though, her body began to break down. Her bones turned brittle and fractured while training. I recalled her thin frame floating under the lights that night on the track, the bony shoulders, the press frenzy. My hero was suffering, leaving the sport we loved to save her life. It seemed so avoidable.

"Why would she do that?" I asked DeLong.

"Losing weight can sometimes make you faster," he said, "but if you do it the wrong way, you pay the price." DeLong had been on a low-calorie diet to qualify for the Boston Marathon, using I Can't Believe It's Not Butter! spray on his toast.

How do you know who is doing it right versus wrong? I wondered. *How do you know if you should lose weight or not?* I didn't ask him any of these questions. I was thinking about Kim, and Kim's record, and how it might not have happened had she been healthy. And now it was in the books, likely an impossible bar to chase without hurting yourself.

It wasn't in the article, but I had a feeling I knew what Kim was trying to outrun: puberty. It was everywhere on my team, doing its work, but we didn't really talk about it. Bodies changed. Some girls ran slower despite training harder. Some got stuck in place. A few suddenly improved after a period of stagnation. The lineup shuffled around and we never made State as a team again after my freshman year. Competing as an individual instead, I had nobody to belt along to Fiona Apple with in the team van, nobody's hair to braid. When I finished as the runner-up at State junior year, I overheard random adults talking about the girls who used to stand above me on the podium but didn't anymore, pity oozing from their lips.

"What happened to so-and-so?"

"She got hips and boobs and she was done."

"She peaked as a freshman."

"Puberty is the one injury a girl can't come back from."

Back at home afterward, I remember looking in the mirror at my reflection, at the sore buds forming under my nipples. I had wanted these so badly in eighth grade, but now I wasn't so sure. What would they turn into? The tangerines of my mom or the birthday balloons of my gamy? It felt as if all of us girls were lined up for the firing squad, and only one of the shooters had blanks. Would I be the one spared from the disruption of boobs and hips? Would I be the lucky one? At sixteen, any changes in my body—armpit hair, pubic hair—I discovered with trepidation. Every race where I continued to get better was a relief. At sixteen, I still didn't have my period, and I didn't really want it. Concerned, my mom took me to the doctor, who told me a delayed period was normal for female athletes and to come back if I didn't get it by seventeen, which I eventually did. A period was a rite of passage into womanhood, and womanhood didn't stand for anything I wanted. Nobody told me there were benefits to the menstrual cycle far beyond reproduction, and that my athletic future would depend on it.

A recent study showed that 87 percent of female distance runners don't talk to their coaches about periods. Coaches, 80 percent of whom are male, report feeling ill-equipped for these discussions, which makes sense since there is no required education on female physiology, puberty, or the menstrual cycle for coaches of female athletes. A good start would be learning to say the word *period* without euphemisms. Districts confuse a natural biological process with the sexualization of all things female and often encourage male coaches to hire female assistants to handle "girl things" that come up. This strategy leans on underpaid people in high-turnover positions with "also menstruates" as their primary qualification, and it creates bogus reasons to keep women in assistant positions. Anyone and everyone working with female athletes must be able to talk about puberty and periods. They are a fact, an embodied experience shaping the daily lives of half the squad. And frankly, the stakes are too high not to.

Menstrual dysfunction has major physical and mental health consequences, but athletes and coaches are incentivized to ignore it because the greatest rewards go to those who are at their best in their junior and senior years, while females as a group are experiencing a mere 1.2 percent improvement per year, half the rate of their male peers. When puberty isn't talked about except in damaging myths, a natural and essential process is viewed as a threat, something to fear or grieve, and there is significant motivation to bypass it somehow. It's no wonder that so many girls restrict their diets, a deadly and dangerous strategy to try to freeze or reverse time and eliminate evidence of womanhood. In a 2021 Colorado study led by Aubrey Armento that looked closely at female distance runners averaging age seventeen, three-fourths of them had disordered eating behaviors or eating disorders. Nearly half had a history of amenorrhea (absence of periods) or other menstrual dysfunction, and a shocking 42 percent had low bone mineral density. Impact sports like running and lifting weights are correlated with higher bone density in the general population, but too often the competitive environments of girls' sports are doing the opposite, with lifetime consequences. Now that we can follow female athletes into older age for the first time in history, the data shows that former athletes are going on to experience higher rates of osteoporosis and bone fractures than their non-athlete peers. Monitoring menstrual health is the first line of defense against all of this harm. And again, nobody talks about it.

I looked at Kim's smile in the oversized poster on the Foot Locker course, and then I looked at her clavicles. I looked at the long line of posters of champions and wondered how many of them hurt themselves to win. DeLong had said, "There are no shortcuts without consequences. Keep your eye on the big picture. Get a little better every year. Consistency will put you on the top eventually." I wanted to believe him.

In line for the buffet at the pre-race banquet dinner, I assessed the girls' bodies around me. I wondered who was taking shortcuts and who wasn't. Everyone was smaller than average, but some of the women had very bony shoulders. Tight skin with extra hair on their arms. Thin ponytails. Oversized clothing. As I scooped food onto my plate—noodles, red sauce, a chicken leg, a roll with butter—my tongs paused over the salad, debating. I had never liked salad, but I squeezed a couple of spinach leaves and a crouton into the remaining sliver of white porcelain anyway. *Is this how it starts? Is eating salad a gateway to an eating disorder?*

The girl across from me was using the other tongs to fill her entire plate with only lettuce. She drizzled a thin zigzag of fat-free Italian dressing with careful precision, as if an alarm might go off if she drew outside the lines. Another girl waiting for her had only lettuce and a chicken breast, no dressing at all. Realizing I was holding up the line, I took my plate and sat down next to my roommate, Sara, at our team's round table. Her plate looked normal. Some kids had plates like ours, and they casually ate and talked and laughed their way through dinner. Others looked uncomfortable, like they were having dinner with a tiger. Carbs were carefully maneuvered around like they were an electric fence. One girl had only a dry roll and a couple of cherry tomatoes. These picky eaters sometimes looked too thin to my newly sensitive eye, but not always, which I found more unnerving. How would I know for sure who was picky and who was sick? Last year I hadn't even noticed them.

I felt overcome with a desire to beat every single girl who had a weird relationship with food, this strategy that made you faster for a little while—which could dictate the outcome of this race—but forced you to quit a couple of years later. I wanted to win, and I needed to know it could be done without putting myself in danger. I needed to know it was worth it to take care of my body when nobody else seemed to care. No adults at the event were addressing the issue in front of us. We had a hotel full of stars, and we were greeted with pomp and circumstance. What we really needed was an intervention.

In our hotel room that night, while trying to sleep, I watched

Sara read her Bible by booklight. I thought about how young and fast she was. She looked up to me. No matter how badly I was hurting when she caught up to me, I would say yes. I would follow. I felt I had to beat her so she'd have an older example who was healthy. She'd remember it. I was possessed by the need to prove it to her, to myself, to everyone, that you could be healthy and win.

The Foot Locker race unfolded nearly how I imagined it would. I started mid-pack and worked my way up to fifth or so with a mile to go. Sara presumably started in the very back, and when she came up on me, we exchanged a breathy "Good job." Before she went by, I looked at her face. It was turned up with the effort, leading with her chest and chin as if being towed forward by the god she prayed aloud to on the starting line. She moved by me in slow motion, and I activated the plan I'd made with DeLong. We passed one girl together, and then another, splitting apart on either side of her. My body was screaming, but it was still working. I desperately wanted to slow down, but a look at Sara's ragged form told me she was suffering at least as much as I was. I bargained. *Stay with her until that tree. Now the next one. That flag. That turn.* Ten meters at a time, I stayed.

The only runner left in front of us now was Erin Sullivan, the defending champion out of Vermont, and there was a lot of golf course between us. Too much. But Sara's chin lifted still higher. I was in awe of her. Her breathing sounded on the verge of death, and yet she pressed. The finish line appeared on the horizon, and it became apparent Erin was not going to slow down. The realization that we couldn't win hit us both at the same time, and I thought I felt Sara soften just a little. I pounced. I lost consciousness of my body, my breathing, my collapsing running form, and became nothing but atoms directed forward. I inched ahead in the final meters and held her off across the line.

Sara collapsed, physically drained and emotionally devastated. Being a champion had meant more to her, I saw, as I staggered to stay on my feet, gasping for air. Pride flowed into me along with it. I had discovered a new gear, a new level of pain, and had persisted, accelerated even.

My parents and DeLong were waiting along the string of flags bordering the finishers' area, and I hugged them one at a time. DeLong was overcome, his eyes red with tears.

My mom pulled me close and hugged me harder than usual, as though she was relieved that I'd made it to the finish without hurting myself. Last up was my dad, and I regarded him for a second before taking the last steps toward him. His opinion still mattered the most to me.

I walked into his open arms, felt them close around me, apart from one gauzed finger held slightly askance. "That's what I'm talking about!" he said a little too loudly in my ear. "Nobody's got heart like you." I stayed there an extra moment, feeling his heartbeat against my own.

5

THE GAMBLE

As I embarked on my college search, I really hoped the University of Colorado Boulder would be the one. The blue-collar vibes felt like home to me. For my meeting with Coach Mark Wetmore, I sat down on a squeaky chair in a room that could easily be mistaken for a mechanic's office, and in walked Mark in his time-worn jeans and low ponytail. I sensed a kindred spirit: He was smart, kind, and a bit odd, and loved talking about literature as much as the Lydiard training philosophy that guided his coaching. When I went on my first run in the mile-high city, my lungs were challenged by the winter cold and the elevation, and it was clear this place could harden me into something new.

I looked around me at the other athletes to get a feel for what that would be. My host was warm, but she was one of few. Outside of romantic pairings, there was a coldness to the other relationships, a competitiveness between them perhaps that seemed to keep them apart.

On my last night in Boulder, a bunch of girls showed up for a dinner at a bar and grill, and as I listened to their sharp wit and laughter, I thought maybe this could work. But when the food arrived, I felt the weight of their stares on my burger and fries. A quick scan of the table revealed that the team meal was a salad with dressing on the side. When I held a fry up to my mouth, I was watched so intensely by one woman I checked to see if there was something gross on it. A couple of my prospective teammates ate their lettuce gingerly, like it might contain bones. Whatever conversation was happening on the plates was creating static for the conversation and connection above. I didn't know for sure if these were eating disorders, but it looked exhausting. It made me value my ease around food even more, and I believed that ease was critical for my health and continued success. Colorado would be a difficult place to hold on to that.

Stanford felt different in a lot of ways. Coach Beth Alford-Sullivan was a woman, to start, which was a rarity. Even today, according to the University of Minnesota's Tucker Center for Research on Girls & Women in Sport, which publishes an annual report on gender in intercollegiate coaching, only 17 percent of women's running teams are led by women. In 1999, that number was even lower. Since I had met so few women in coaching, I assumed men were just better at it, but Beth had led the women's team to an NCAA title just three months earlier. I was willing to give her a try.

The coach-athlete relationship is a powerful way to shift gender bias. A coach, tasked with a mix of nurturing goals and imposing discipline, spans the two worlds of parental figure and professional guide. If every young person experienced a woman leading their sports team in a position of true authority, millions of people would grow up used to the idea of a woman leading their company, department, or nation.

Before Title IX, women's sport mostly took place at the club and intramural level, and 90 percent of those coaches were women. After Title IX, men took over most of those jobs, and even after fifty years of pushing for gender equity, that figure has been stuck at 42 percent for the last five years. Gender equity in leadership of men's teams seems even more hopeless: only 3 percent of NCAA men's coaching jobs are held by women. There is absolutely no justifiable reason why a woman can't lead a men's sports team, but given how ubiquitous misogynistic behavior is toward women in male-coded professions, it's hard to imagine anything changing without a massive commitment from the NCAA to create opportunities and maintain a safe environment for women to work.

Beth looked tall and relaxed in her polo shirt and androgynous haircut when she picked me up from the airport and took me to dinner at a restaurant with a salad bar, where I defiantly loaded my plate with carved meats and potatoes. After some small talk, she asked what my goals were for college, and I was direct: I said I wanted to stay healthy and I wanted to be the best. I planned to win an NCAA championship, more than once if I could. I was startled by my own words—they seemed to have slipped out from the secret place in my heart, and I wondered if it was because she was a woman.

Beth seemed startled, too. She sat back in her chair and considered me silently for a moment. I felt like she saw me. Not as a kid. Not as a girl. Not as a racehorse. As a human being. And for a second, I saw her as more than a woman, more than a coach working under the legendary Vin Lananna, Stanford's director of cross-country and track and field. I was excited to work with *her.*

When she took a bite of her arugula, I asked her about eating disorders on the team, a question that felt awkward, even verboten, leaving my lips. She acknowledged that they happened sometimes due to pressures of performance. But, she said, the Stanford team was overall a healthy one, and she wanted to keep it that way.

I didn't know enough then to ask questions about how she would accomplish that. But even if I had, there would have been little in the way of specifics for her to point to. In 2022, the NCAA still has no official policy concerning eating disorders, despite creating the ideal environment for them to propagate. The National Center on Addiction and Substance Abuse at Columbia University found that 35 percent of female collegiate athletes (and 10 percent of male ones) are at risk for anorexia, and 58 percent (versus 35 percent of men) are at risk for bulimia. When it comes to addressing the largest threat to athlete mental health that disproportionately affects women, the disease that destroys major organs and body systems, depletes bones, and has the highest mortality rate of all mental health disorders, the NCAA takes a libertarian approach: Coaches can do something to prevent and manage them, or not, and they aren't held responsible either way. Compare this to the fact that the NCAA, when confronted with concussion research and potential liability, created research-backed and strictly enforced checklists and policies for head injuries that all programs must adhere to. This pathway from concussion research to policy change shows us the way; all we need now is the will.

Beth dropped my bag and me at a dorm where my host was waiting. Maurica looked like the "We Can Do It" lady on the World War II posters with her hair tied back in a bandanna. She talked fast and was full of funny stories and answers to all the questions I hadn't known to ask about Stanford. She and the rest of the team seemed to genuinely enjoy recruiting trips as an excuse to gather. I kept being surprised that I liked them, these kids from this fancy school. Part of my identity as a Fleshman relied on who we *weren't*. We weren't *them*. I was discovering that they weren't who I thought, and I was glad to have been proved wrong.

On my last night, a group of us were gathered in a cul-de-sac under a streetlight, waiting for the last person to arrive. We had no official plans other than to be together. Maurica yelled her now-familiar "Heyo!" and a tall guy in the distance lifted up his chin, lighting half his face from the side. This guy walking toward us in his scuffed-up purple Converse had my attention. Bare ankles disappeared into a pair of tapered-leg mom jeans. He wore a North Face backpack that looked like it had actually been used in the outdoors, with a skateboard poking out the top. A Kramer-esque poof of brown curls flopped atop an olive boyish face as he introduced himself as Jesse.

Time passed easily with these new friends while playing pool in a common room, eating bowls of cereal from the dispensers, and talking about whatever came up. I was buzzing on my futon that night with the feeling that this was it. "I met my future husband today," I wrote in my journal. "I feel like I've known these people for years. I've made up my mind."

The next morning, I was taken to meet Vin Lananna on the way to the airport. I dragged my luggage through the athletic de-

GOOD FOR A GIRL

partment hallways decorated with action photos, plaques, and trophies. As the director of cross-country and track and field, Vin
had built Stanford from an outhouse into a powerhouse in a handful of years, just as he had done for Dartmouth before that. Standing up behind his desk to shake my hand, he looked like a mix of
Santa Claus and the Wizard of Oz. I felt relaxed and resolute,
ready to sign on the dotted line.

He asked how my trip went.

"I love it here. I want to make it work here," I said. "What do I
need to do next?" Stanford had been the only school that had been
vague about money and admission, and this was my last chance to
get to the bottom of it.

"Here's the deal," he said. "I believe you could be an asset to
this team."

I noticed his use of the word *could*.

"But you're quite late in the recruiting game. We already have
six commitments from athletes in your class." He listed them off,
and I recognized every name from the top of the rankings lists. He
started shuffling around in his desk drawer and pulled out a basic
calculator while I looked on, confused. After clicking a few keys,
he turned it around so I could see it.

"Here's what I can offer you right now," he said.

I wondered if he'd hit the clear button by accident.

"Zero," I read aloud slowly, searching his face for the mistake.
"I can't afford to go here without a scholarship."

I could feel him squirm a little with the awkwardness of it. He
asked what my parents did, and if we'd applied for financial aid
yet. I felt like a beggar.

"All the money is gone, but next year, we'll graduate some people, and if you do well as a freshman, I can offer you this the next three years."

He slid the calculator back to his side of the desk, hit some buttons and then flipped it back around to me.

"Eighty-eight," I said.

"Percent," he qualified.

I tried to do the math in my head.

I wondered if I was supposed to negotiate. I tried to sit a little taller, to summon the energy of my father. "Everyone else has offered me a full scholarship."

"I understand that. The thing is, they're accounted for already, and we don't really do full scholarships often, anyway. Nearly everyone on this team turns down full rides to go here."

I wondered how many of them carried around their parents' credit cards.

"We can be stronger if we spread the money out more," he said. "Think of it like an investment. To be on the strongest team, and to get a Stanford degree, one of the best in the world. That's worth putting some skin in the game."

"How am I supposed to pay for the first year?" I asked.

"Financial aid, hopefully. It sounds like your family will qualify."

I felt my face flush. He continued.

"People take out student loans all the time. Parents take out loans. There's a lot of ways to do it. This is normal college stuff for the vast majority of people. Athletes forget that."

I felt embarrassed and entitled. But I also couldn't imagine asking my parents for a single thing. I was so proud that I would be off their payroll, giving them the gift of some breathing room. I wanted to eventually pay them back somehow for the sacrifices they'd made for me—pay for a vacation somewhere amazing one day, somewhere they'd never go on their own. I couldn't imagine being a financial burden to them any longer.

I felt I should say no, and take an offer elsewhere. But my heart ached at the thought of saying goodbye to this place. I liked Vin, and the way he challenged me. I liked Beth's energy and forthrightness. I had that feeling. I *knew* it was where I should be. I had to find a way. I never asked, *What if I get injured and don't earn the scholarship?* I'd have to transfer, probably sit out a year of competition to do so, start my life over, and maybe nobody would want me anymore. I didn't know that my sports of cross-country and track made up two of the top three spots on the leaderboard for bone injuries, with female athletes accounting for twice as many as their male peers. I didn't know women's collegiate sports were full of potholes nobody bothered to fill. Throughout my long career, I'd see a trend of very few Foot Locker standouts transitioning to college dominance. But I believed I would improve, as I always had, according to the law of effort. I would prove I was worth the money.

"Okay, I'll see what I can do," I said.

WHILE I COMPULSIVELY checked the mailbox for an acceptance letter over the next few months, DeLong and Mom helped me find every obscure scholarship I could possibly apply for. Paperwork was spread across Mom's desk for weeks as she applied for federal and state grants. I kept my grades up with renewed focus, preparing to submit them to Stanford. There was no room for the senior slide.

When I got my acceptance letter, I put it under my mattress, withholding hope until the numbers came together. I'd need a campus job, but with financial aid, grants, my In-N-Out savings, my parents' commitment to do what they could, and the help of a great-aunt, it was possible. Money would be so tight I'd be sneaking my roommates' deodorant and avoiding the laundromat, and my grants were contingent on a B average I wasn't sure I could maintain, but I was going to Stanford.

The last few months of high school felt like one big victory tour. DeLong and I accomplished every goal we had for track season: The impossible "triple crown" at the California Interscholastic Federation finals, winning the 800, 1,600 and 3,200 in the same meet on the same day. Winning the state title in the 3,200 with dominance. Every honor that could be awarded to an athlete in my school, my city, my region, I won. Athlete of the Year. Newsmaker of the Year. Appreciation was piled on me, and I accepted it, deeply proud of the body of work we'd created. The shelf above my dad's bar became what my sister called "the Lauren shrine" as she fought for real estate for her softball awards, a symbol of a sibling dynamic ruled by comparison that we still haven't fully recovered from.

On the day Stanford Cross-Country asked us to report for preseason camp, I enthusiastically packed the back of my grandpa's hand-me-down station wagon with the requisite extra-long twin bedding, laundry basket, and shower caddy. I drove away with two beeps of the horn, a glance out my rolled-down window, and a wave. That's the way people in my family said goodbye on the rare occasions when somebody went somewhere significant. Now it was my turn.

My tears took me by surprise. I had been so excited to leave that I expected to blow out of Canyon Country with nothing but smiles and goose bumps. But something about the three of them standing at the top of the drive, my sister leaning on my mom, my dad's hands in his frayed pockets as he tried to keep from crying— this was the end of something, not just a stage of life, but a way of being. I wasn't coming back, not really. I sped down the freeway with the windows open while my air conditioner tried to catch up. I felt selfish. A good daughter would stay closer for college, emotionally support her mom and sister, keep attempting to predict and moderate the tides of her dad's alcoholism. But I didn't want to be a good daughter. I wanted the freedom to make a life. Riding up I-5, every song on the Joni Mitchell mixtape my dad handed me on my way out made its mark on me, songs like tattoos. A river to skate away on. Green that winter cannot fade. At last, "Free Man in Paris" boosted my resolve. Stanford would be my Paris, I decided. Nobody calling me up for favors, no one's future to decide but my own.

AFTER DROPPING OFF my small pile of belongings on one side of an empty dorm room, I parked my car in downtown Palo Alto and entered the lobby of the antique Cardinal Hotel, where I would finally meet the teammates in my class. Throughout the day, they had been gathering from around the country. We'd spend one night here before driving to pre-season camp.

Everything had a glow to it. The lack of a private bathroom in each room was adorably communal. The crooked bedpost that whacked my hip was beautifully carved: *Look at the craftsmanship!* The filigree carpet worn thin by generations of shoes was a way to touch history. Every teammate seemed to present herself to me as a future best friend. I asked them questions about their lives, looking for the reasons why I already loved them.

In bed, I stared up at the car headlights moving across the ceiling of the room I shared with Erin Sullivan, the two-time Foot Locker champion from Vermont I'd spent the last year chasing from afar, and I imagined us working our way up to dominate the NCAA as seniors, preferably me in first and her in second this time.

Before sunrise, all the women and men piled into two fifteen-passenger vans and began the five-hour drive through Yosemite to Mammoth Lakes, the home of all my high school altitude camps. These vans were full of incredible talent, big fish from every size of pond, from high schools in Florida, North Carolina, Vermont, Oregon, the San Francisco Bay Area, Wyoming, and more. I couldn't wait to show them around my favorite place. On the way, I told my new best friends about the secret clear lakes and scenic climbs I knew, and Schat's Bakery, where delicious nourishment after a good workout awaited.

But we wouldn't be going near any of those trails. We were to do all our runs from the condos, and any trips off-site required a coach to drive us, and a good reason for us to go. A good muffin from Schat's Bakery did not qualify as a good reason. A movie at the theater did not qualify. A trail run around Convict Lake that would blow your mind was nothing more than a sprained ankle risk. I'd been coming there for four years and driving myself around. It didn't matter. We were here to train and recover, I was reminded—nothing else. This was how you did things at the next level. This new family I had joined had strict parents with more power over me than my real parents ever did, and nobody seemed to mind.

Leading practice was a stranger. Coach Beth Alford-Sullivan, whom I'd been so drawn to on my recruiting trip, had left Stanford to take a position out East, leaving Vin Lananna as the head coach of both the men and the women. Dena Evans was hired as assistant to the women's team, and she came in with lots of enthusiasm but little coaching experience. Within five years, she would be named NCAA women's cross-country coach of the year, but when I met her, it seemed she was primarily brought on to do what most female assistant coaches are hired to do: manage operational tasks, execute the head coach's workouts so he could hang out with the men, and be a big sister when "woman stuff" came up.

I liked Dena. She was humble, smart, and played great music in the van. I assumed, like all of us did, that this relatively junior new hire meant Vin would be more involved on a day-to-day basis with both teams. If you're going to lose your coach, this was a best-case scenario.

But that's not how it played out. After a brief meeting with both teams, generally Vin would coach the men along with his assistant Mike, and Dena would remain with us. When someone on the women's team needed to make a workout adjustment, Dena often had to check with Vin first, causing awkward delays. It was clear who had the power and who was still in training. And it was clear which team was top priority. Only a couple of stars seemed to snag some of his valuable time, and this created tension. Some women told me that they felt invisible when they were injured, or that they weren't getting the attention they needed to get to the next level. Since I'd never faced setbacks, there seemed to me to be an easy solution: just train harder and run faster.

The end of training camp was marked by a dual meet against Brigham Young University, my first collegiate race, where I finished just off the shoulder of our biggest star upperclassman, letting her take the win.

"You looked like you could have won that," Vin said to me afterward, pulling me out of earshot of the rest of the team.

I nodded.

"So, why didn't you?"

"It didn't matter if I was first or second. Stanford had it."

"That's how our men race," he said, looking at me sideways for a beat. "Very good." He nodded and moved along on his rounds. From then on, I made his checklist of athletes to connect with face-to-face at races, and I had another male figure to rely on for affirmation.

CAMPUS LIFE WAS way better than training camp life. Andrea Jimena González Cárdenas, my assigned roommate, was bursting with energy and light that matched her wild mane of highlighted curly hair. She broke into dance spontaneously, always with two hands open, insisting I join, and she is the reason I can sort of move my hips in any direction besides forward. If it hadn't been for Andrea, my collegiate experience would have been limited to the forty or so people on my team. With twenty hours of practice a week and traveling to races every weekend, a collegiate athlete can easily miss everything "college" about college and increase their risks of negative mental health outcomes by having an identity entirely tied to performance.

But Andrea dragged me out of my room for every significant school tradition. She made sure I kissed a stranger at Full Moon on the Quad, heckled the opposing football team with the famously petulant school band, and participated in at least a few dorm activities. At Stanford, being an athlete didn't gain you the preferential status I'd heard about on other campuses. If anything, it had the opposite effect, casting a pall of doubt that you really belonged in the classroom. My team sweats worn straight from morning weights gave me away to professors, and travel made me an undesirable partner for group work. As I took furious notes, I marveled at the brains around me that absorbed difficult academic concepts the first time around. They could do with their minds what I could do with my body.

At training, I could finally breathe. My teammates and I worked together to execute challenging sessions, speaking the same physical language in silence as we took turns leading the pace. During our rest intervals, I watched in awe as the huge pack of men moved together like a school of fish. Training was the highlight of my days, and the races were even better. Every weekend, we boarded a plane somewhere new to race: Indiana, North Carolina, Arizona. I felt rich; we were handed keys to hotel rooms with two queen beds and ate at restaurants where someone else paid the bill. We got a daily rate of cash in envelopes to cover incidentals. Life had never been so frictionless. The assistant coaches drove the same white rental vans to a grass expanse somewhere outside of town with a course marked by triangle flags on a string. Sometimes it was hot. Sometimes it was cold. I never even bothered to look at the weather, or the course map, or the competition. Knowing as little as possible made my job simple: soak in the field, get off the line strong, run alongside Julia, Sally, and Erin up near the front, and finish on empty. The races were a blur of maximal exertions that lasted fewer than twenty minutes. The rest of the time, our bodies were smashed together on planes or spread out on lobby floors, casually interweaving our lives.

My first NCAA championships were the weekend before Thanksgiving break. Stanford was ranked number one, and our top seven runners lined up with 250 of the nation's best. I felt ready, like I was doing what I was made to do. When the official said "runners set" into the bullhorn, I remember the metal spikes that lined the bottom of my shoes sinking into the damp grass for traction, loading my body like a spring. I remember the deep silence of waiting for the starting gun, and when the air finally cracked, the expanse of women to either side of me sprinting straight ahead. I pulled myself even with them before being funneled by narrowing flags into a massive snake of runners ten feet wide and several hundred feet long.

Sally, Julia, Erin, and I found one another around the halfway point of the race as we had every other week, this time in around fortieth place. The competition was deep, and physical, and being near my teammates in the mass of strangers helped me relax. I loved not being alone in this place. Erin's confidence as she pulled up alongside me was quiet, like a smirk. Before the race, she said to me, "You know what keeps me calm? They're just girls." Erin saw all of them as vulnerable and bowed to nobody. Remembering this, I blurred my vision slightly and tried to see the women as nothing more than bodies to move through.

Erin and I found ourselves side by side, working our way into the top ten with a mile to go. And then we kept moving up until, with only a half mile left, there were only a few bodies left between us and the wide-open course. Those seven or so minutes of running alongside Erin, I thought, *This. This is why I came to Stanford*. I knew in the moment how special it was, and I glowed, even as my insides burned. I was becoming the best by putting myself among the best. I was competitive; I wanted to beat Erin. And I wanted Erin to be at her best when I did it. I wanted to be the top freshman in the nation.

Erin and I embraced in the finish chute while runners staggered around us, and, arms linked, we walked to the recovery area to wait for our team. I finished fifth and she seventh in the entire NCAA Division I as freshmen, a remarkable showing for both of us. Our team was spread out behind us more than usual, and we wound up a disappointing third, with several teammates visibly upset with their performances; some had finished well behind their placing a year earlier. They didn't understand what happened, why they felt they had no strength on the day, as if their bodies had betrayed them. I didn't understand it, either: I had run great, and we all had the same coach. The men's team had performed well, too. I figured it was probably the pressure of defending the team title, and I could feel empathy for that. But it wasn't that. The pattern would continue. In the photo I've kept of Erin and me from after the race, noodle arms draped around one another's shoulders, proud grins below our cheekbones, we didn't know it was coming for us, too.

———

THAT FIRST WINTER of college, with a successful first quarter of school and sports behind me, I experienced collegiate sports at their best. They gave me a structured arena to explore my athletic potential and built-in mentors in my teammates. The team also gave me a secure base in a challenging academic environment where I'd have been likely to drift. Training added predictable structure to my weeks and instilled in me the physical and mental benefits of daily exercise. I felt engaged, purposeful, curious, alive.

The anchor of my personal college sports experience became the Sunday long run, where I fell more and more deeply in love with running—and Jesse Thomas along with it. During the first few months of freshman year, I'd gotten very close with the cute guy I remembered from my recruiting trip. Jesse wasn't happy staying on campus patching together fourteen-mile urban loops on concrete. He grew up running the single-track trails of Bend, Oregon, trails that climb buttes, snake through burn forests, and zag along rivers; in the face of brutal engineering courses and fighting to make the travel squad, trails were how Jesse stayed connected to himself. Every Sunday, he'd offer up the bench seats in his filthy green minivan to teammates and drive into the Santa Cruz Mountains. We'd unfold our cramped bodies and open our strides, forgetting what any of this training was for besides play after a mile or two. On the way home, I'd flip through Jesse's case of CDs for clues as to who he was before I met him. He loved running in a way that made him want to share it with others, just like I did.

The crush started out fun and quickly became insufferable. Andrea and I would hash out our unrequited loves over bowls of

Lucky Charms consumed on our dorm room floor, practically nose-to-nose, plotting how to get them to see us as more than friends. Jesse and I studied together regularly now, but he remained aloof, treating me in a way that was clearly platonic. It was the first time in my life I resented being viewed as one of the guys.

Then Jesse surprised me by asking if I had plans on Valentine's Day. Andrea and I were giddy. "This is it!" she said. I wrote him a card professing my crush, stuck it in my back pocket, and went over to his place to pick him up. No plans had been made beyond hanging out in the apartment, which we did, not touching, like usual, and the card sat in my pocket. As the evening was wrapping up, he brought over a small bonsai plant to the table along with a card of his own. It was written on aged Garfield stationery that essentially said, "Thanks for being a good friend. From, Jesse." I walked out the door and into the parking lot headed for home, overtaken by anger and disappointment. He ran out and stepped in front of me under a lamppost, holding me by both shoulders so I wouldn't run away. I told him I didn't want to be his friend, and that you don't ask a friend to hang out on Valentine's Day. I didn't want to waste any more of my time. "You're not, trust me," he said with a crooked smile.

It turned out he had bigger plans a couple of days later, and he had been "building suspense." He picked me up at my dorm wearing a suit complete with a tie and cummerbund from his high school jazz choir and invited me to go for a drive.

As we sailed up the 101, he nodded toward the back seat; Andrea had given him a formal dress and shoes on the sly for me to change into, which I did while the van rocked toward the city lights on the horizon. Arm in arm, we walked up stone slab steps and through enormous doors revealing the San Francisco Symphony hall. I smoothed out the front of my too-short dress. This was a room I never even thought to imagine myself in. When the music played, my eyes blurred with emotion, not just from the propulsive energy of the piano solo, but from the improbability that a space full of people could be silent enough to hear every single note.

We drove through Golden Gate Park in the dark afterward, with no plans and no money left, prolonging the date. A brightly lit museum appeared on our right with formally dressed people walking past security two by two.

"Want to check it out?" he said.

"Check what out?"

"The party. We would fit right in in these clothes."

My heart beat out of my chest. "We'll get caught!"

"Nah. We'll act like we belong and walk through talking to one another," he said. "If you look like you know what you're doing, people rarely question it."

I sat there, considering.

"Worst-case scenario, we say oops, wrong party!" he continued.

"Okay, fuck it," I said, bursting out the van door, pretending I was going to run in without him. He ran up and grabbed my hand.

"I like you," he said. "A lot."

Together we walked straight past the bouncers dressed in tuxedos and into what turned out to be a Republican Party fundraiser. We were the youngest people by about thirty years. It was too late to turn back. We wandered through the museum looking at art, grabbed prosciutto-wrapped melon and petit fours, and joined the business elite on the crowded dance floor. If someone looked at us, we gave them a thumbs-up and danced harder. I felt like we'd gotten away with a heist. We left the party after a few songs and wandered through the park back to the van, elated. I willed him to kiss me, but he didn't.

Two weeks later, Andrea reminded me that I was a modern woman, and I made a plan to kiss him myself. His birthday, Leap Day, only comes once every four years, and he'd been talking about it—and how much he loved Oreo cookie mint milk shakes—since we'd met. I stashed a cooler of milk shake supplies on the bank of the lake on campus and brought him out there for a stroll as midnight approached. We stumbled upon the cooler and loaded it onto the wooden platform people pushed around the lake like Huck Finn. Once out in the middle, we crushed Oreos into plastic dining hall cups and mixed our milk shakes by hand, delighted with ourselves. It began to rain, and as our milk shakes flooded with water and our hair plastered itself to our foreheads, we shared our first kiss.

Our relationship quickly deepened. It felt good to love and be loved, to have someone who understood the other's drive. I felt right in my body. Love was a performance-enhancing drug.

Vin didn't see it that way at first.

"Jesse?" Vin said incredulously. "What are you doing with that guy?" I couldn't tell if he was kidding or not. He liked Jesse. But Vin seemed to view a relationship as a potential threat to my future performance. "Just don't lose focus," he told me.

Kicking acorns on the way back to my dorm, I thought about all the examples of men accomplishing things, and the women behind them in supporting roles. I thought of my parents. I thought about Vin working long hours and traveling most weekends while his wife, Betty, raised their children and managed the household. I thought about how nearly all the famous coaches and top professors I knew of were men in similar positions. Women made great men possible. What made great women possible? Avoiding the vortex of a man's ambition? Being alone?

After that meeting with Vin, I went back to Jesse with my antennae up a little more. I guarded my heart, sensitive to any sign that he was going to get in the way of my dreams. Jesse had also internalized that a romantic relationship was the one thing that could distract him from his path and potential.

Because we both feared that romantic relationships weren't compatible with our goals, we practiced barricading our intimacy from one another. Afraid of losing ourselves to the other, we let our support out in doses, expecting the other person to handle their challenges mostly alone. In the home I'd come from, there was only room for one person's needs in a relationship; I worried if I set the expectation of prioritizing Jesse's, I would get swallowed up.

We were on and off romantically, but we always had our Sunday long run. Jesse's van collected so much forest detritus from our adventures together that mushrooms grew out of the floor mats; the van became widely known as "Swamp Thing." Those runs were the reset button I looked forward to after every competition, and they became more important as freshman year wore on and managing stress inevitably became a challenge. On Sundays, I flexed my independence and returned to the kind of running I initially fell in love with, one of connecting to my body through exploration and play. Every other day my body was being forged into a tool for winning, and the racing and travel schedules were relentless.

A collegiate runner has cross-country in the fall, indoor track in the winter, and outdoor track in the spring. Each sport culminates in its own NCAA championships overlapping with finals week. Because I was under nineteen years old, I was also eligible to compete on the USA's junior national team, which involved additional qualifiers and championships. These took me to exciting places like Portugal, where I stuck my toes in the iron-rich sand of the Algarve, and Denton, Texas, where I ate at a Waffle House (these were equally exciting experiences at the time).

"What a year," Vin said to me from across the desk in his office, toying with his white beard. This was my much-anticipated end-of-year meeting, and I was completely drained. My station wagon was parked outside, packed with everything I'd emptied out of my dorm that morning, ready to head home.

"Your consistency is fantastic. You train like a guy. You compete like a guy. You've accomplished more as a freshman than most collegiate athletes do in their entire careers," he said.

I had really stood out on the women's team that year. I was one of few who qualified for indoor and outdoor NCAA championships, and not only did I advance to the final of the distance medley relay, the 3,000, and the 1,500, I was an All-American every time I raced, bringing my total to four. I even anchored our indoor relay to an NCAA Title, helping earn us our first plaque on the Wall of Champions. In the spring, I broke the American junior record in the 5,000 meters on the track my first time running it, and qualified for the Olympic Trials while doing so.

"You have a lot of exciting running ahead of you, Lauren." I beamed at his approval. "I'm granting you a full scholarship for the rest of your time here. You've earned it."

I had done it. I was thrilled, but even more than that, I was exhausted. Every cell of my body felt tired. I was overtaken by the intense urge to sleep.

I WANTED TO stay home and take a long break, but I didn't. The Olympic Trials were six weeks away, and I was required to return to train with the select group who had qualified. I was exhausted, and I expressed it, but I was encouraged by both Vin and Dena to push through to gain the experiences that would help me make the Olympic team the next time around. After a weekend visit with my family, and a visit with the DeLongs at the hospital, where their son Justin was being treated for leukemia that would take his life in July, I was devastated to leave. But I returned to Stanford.

I struggled to hit the paces in every workout, but I enjoyed the intimacy at the track with only a handful of women and men there. When I finished my set, I'd stay and watch Vin work with the men, taking notes for a future coaching career I didn't know I was going to have. Vin created strange workouts that mixed the top men from different training disciplines, athletes that were generally siloed due to having completely different training needs. "Excellence benefits from working alongside excellence. That matters more than any specialized workout at this point." They'd take turns using their unique strengths to pull the others along, and it left me buzzing in their wake.

Whatever they were doing worked at the Olympic Trials. The

women were mediocre; I finished last in my semifinal, feeling heavy-legged, as I had for weeks. The men flew. When my teammate Gabe Jennings took the lead with five hundred meters to go in the 1,500 meters, a stupidly long finishing kick that simply was not done, a collective gasp emerged from the crowd, and he crossed the finish line first. Our teammate Michael Stember qualified for the Olympics right behind him, and team captain Brad Hauser qualified in the 10,000. This unseating of professionals by these kids in college jerseys had everyone talking about the Stanford program. The men's team, with their identity of "The Machine," got it done. I decided that if I wanted to become truly great, I'd need to pace myself for a long season, and choose my role models among the men's team.

6

THE FEMALE PERFORMANCE WAVE

It was hard to know when it started—that summer, maybe, or that fall of my sophomore year—but my body began to change. I rarely weighed myself, and the numbers meant little to me, but my boobs got bigger, my thighs touched more, and my Levi's 501s fit differently. I wasn't worried about it at the time, perhaps because things were going so well. In school and in life, I was thriving in ways I now understand were related to adequate food intake through female developmental changes. My human biology core curriculum was demanding, but I felt a sharpness and vibrancy exuding from me in class. My retention of the material was strong. The hallways of Toyon Hall, the all-sophomore house where I shared a tiny bunk room with two other women, were full of pranks and flirtation and deep conversations I happily put myself in the middle of, and when alone, I could be found learning guitar in the courtyard or making art. I'd never felt so creative, playful, and embodied, like I was becoming who I was meant to be.

The only place I felt tension around my new body was in sports. In practice, paces didn't come as easily as they had the year before, and the new freshman phenom was clipping my heels. Caitlyn was springy in her childlike body, while my own form sank a bit. My competition briefs rode up my ass when I raced, and I experienced the chafing my teammates jokingly described as "chub rub." The same curves I enjoyed seeing in my dorm mirror drew my eye differently in the hotel mirror before I headed to a racecourse. The tight, minimalist uniform made it tempting to compare myself to others, and in an attempt to hold on to my confidence, I'd move my gaze from my undefined thighs to my eyes and remind myself of the strengths others couldn't see.

Nobody competes like you, Lauren. My dad's voice echoed in my ears. *You're a Fleshman. You've got HEART.*

It worked. In the early-season races, I'd have to dig way deeper than I used to, but I willed my way to the front. I got a thrill from beating competitors who were thinner than me. It made me feel like all this fear of changing bodies was overblown. I'd been aware that that fear was threatening to tear my team apart. The latest star athlete to join the squad arrived deep in the grips of an eating disorder. It was clear from the first week of pre-season camp that something was off. Caitlyn would show up to practice carrying an open textbook in the group huddle, and Vin would awkwardly ask her to put it down. The book also served as her social repellent in the condos while the rest of us bonded. When the team sat down for our communally prepared dinner, she would sit slightly back from the table with a container full of something unusual, like raw spinach leaves or frozen okra, and eat it painfully slowly. She'd disappear to the bathroom for long periods after meals. I heard her ravage the pantry late at night from my bed in the loft. Before long, people stopped trying to connect with her. She was there but not there, cautiously observed, but mostly ignored, like so many people exhibiting signs of mental illness in view of others.

While the men's team—The Machine—bonded over Wiffle ball in the parking lot, several women were entering a flurry of destabilization. Some were triggered by the behaviors, picking up old disordered eating habits they had left behind in high school, slowly snacking on grapefruit segments, drinking pints of water to trick their bodies into feeling full, and talking about wanting to lose weight. I talked to Vin and Dena about what was happening, as did a few other women on the team, but I was met with noncommittal responses, some version of "Yes, we know. Leave that to me to worry about. You need to focus on your running." The subject was taboo for some reason, and it was clear that nobody knew what to do. Caitlyn kept coming to practice, despite getting sicker and sicker. I felt sorry for her at first, but eventually I got angry. I just wanted her to stop. I didn't understand the psychology of eating disorders, the way the illness can take over your entire life, with the number on a scale becoming more important than family, than God, than life itself. I just hated what it was doing to my team.

As the top performer on the women's team, I tried to lead by example, eating with the ease more characteristic of the men and being vocal about it. I had the cookie. Enjoyed a second helping. I ate when I wasn't hungry sometimes to prove a point.

But then I stopped winning.

At Pre-Nationals, a dress rehearsal on what would be the NCAA

Championships course with deep, competitive fields, I got absolutely destroyed. Halfway through, the grass felt like quicksand under my feet, and no amount of grit could power me beyond a ranking in the seventies, with 25 percent of the field passing me by in one year. I grabbed onto my splotched thighs in the finish chute, absolutely gassed and shell-shocked. This was a completely unacceptable performance. These were the same athletes I'd raced at Nationals the year before, when I'd come in fifth. Vin waited to talk to me about it until we got home.

"How's your weight?" he asked. Seated across from Vin at his desk, I bounced my leg. "Fine. I don't know, maybe I gained a little."

I remembered overhearing other women described as "sloppy" and "unfit" and wondered if anyone was saying that about me.

"Hmmm. Well, you need to be careful. Are you eating healthy?"

"Mostly, yeah, I eat normally." I thought of the chocolate chip banana bread I had in my bag. "I could probably do better."

"You need to be mindful about your diet, just like getting your sleep, or getting in your mileage," Vin said. "Weight is a factor in performance. What's your race weight?"

"I have no idea." *Race weight* was a term I'd heard my teammates throwing around, and I wondered if they'd had meetings like this.

"What were you last year at NCAAs when you were fifth?"

"I think about 122."

"What are you now?"

"Maybe 135?" I had a vague memory of a gym scale at some point.

Vin raised his eyebrows and said nothing for a moment.

I could see there was a problem.

He suggested again that I eat healthier. I asked if he had any tips and he got squirmy. "I'm not the right person to ask. You know the basics; eat your vegetables, cut down on the junk. Look at the food pyramid. There's a thing called the Zone Diet you could check out. You'll have to look into it." These are the tidbits I remember being tossed around. The only words I recall him saying exactly were "Just don't do anything stupid, Lauren."

I stopped bouncing my leg when he said that because that sentence was so much louder than anything else. So much clearer. The message behind it was *Don't get an eating disorder.*

I swallowed, nodded. "I won't."

He continued, "I want to be able to talk to you about this like I would talk to the guys. Don't. Go. Crazy."

"Okay."

"I mean it."

"Got it."

I THOUGHT I was different from the other women. *You're not like the other girls,* men I looked up to had always said to me. *You compete like a guy. You think like a guy.* Because I had competed like a man (predictably, linearly) I had been spoken to like one. To be viewed as one of the boys came with a special kind of privilege—being adjacent to power, hearing what men really thought of women. I liked that access, and I was afraid of losing it. I didn't want to be one of the girls, but it was coming for all of us eventually. My body needed to be fixed.

Research tells us that the majority of female collegiate athletes are unhappy with their bodies, and 90 percent of those feel they need to lose weight, an average of thirteen pounds. Given that they are top performers in their sport, one might assume female athletes have higher body satisfaction than their nonathletic peers, but it's the opposite. Not only are they subjected to the cultural forces that associate Western beauty standards with personal worth, there is an even tighter standard within sports: an ideal weight, an ideal body shape, one that almost nobody achieves without harming themselves. If so few are reaching it, how can it be valid? Where does it come from? Athletes aren't asking these questions, at least not out loud. Instead, we google "how to lose weight," and enter the diet vortex.

Or we look around to see what our friends are doing. Copying one's peers is a fraught strategy full of bad ideas, and in the running world, it's what leads to a tableful of people ordering the same salad with dressing on the side and glaring at the person with the burger. Teams tend to copy the fastest person, or the person whose body most closely matches the "ideal" that coaches praise, but rarely is that person healthy, let alone trained in nutrition. She's often made harmful choices and she's about a year away from a string of injuries, but for now she's the example. Next year, there will be someone new to copy.

These forces were present to some degree on the men's team, too, which I knew intimately now. Jesse had been a multisport athlete in high school; over time, in response to pressures to change his larger frame to match the ideal, he had developed bulimia that caused him to isolate himself from everyone, including me. The stigma of being a male with an eating disorder made seeking help even more difficult, because eating disorders were considered a girl problem.

I chose my example carefully. I settled on copying the 800-

meter star on my team, Lindsay Hyatt. It was easy to eat around Lindsay. She made knowledgeable choices without being rigid. She looked strong and athletic without the warning signs of being veiny or sinewy. Plus, she was fast. Lindsay was one of the few women on the team who consistently made it to Nationals like me. When I told Lindsay I wanted to learn from her, she started packing two of all her snacks, simple things like yogurt and fruit or Ziploc bags of animal crackers and pretzels, for our long days in the human biology core, making it easy for me. She taught me the basics: don't go long periods without food, don't get to the point of feeling starved or stuffed, and learn to enjoy more nutrient-dense foods, like romaine lettuce instead of iceberg. I never remember feeling distracted by hunger or deprived. If you're going to be sent to the Wild West to lose weight as a female athlete with no instructions or professional guidance, you are almost never going to get lucky as I did.

I learned a lot, but I didn't end up losing much weight. Over many months, I settled into my stable woman's body, which was bigger than the year prior, but missing the bonus couple of pounds I'd gained from performative eating. I felt good about my improved nutrition habits, and my overall health was outstanding, but running was still hard. I missed my lighter frame and wondered if racing would ever feel good again.

For the first time in my life, I wasn't moving up the ladder. When I got passed by competitors I'd defeated previously, I'd question why I was putting myself through so much pain to get a worse result and feel tempted to give up. Losing was made more difficult by the revolving door of women willing to starve for a chance to finish first. When I called DeLong to vent, he was sad and his

advice was grim. He reminded me to keep the long view, that anyone not eating enough wouldn't last and I would be the last woman
standing. I tried to stay as close to the contenders as I could. I
earned a reputation for being a "gritty bitch" and people liked to
comment on how "healthy" I looked. *Healthy* was code for *fat*; *fit*
was the compliment everyone valued most. I tried not to hold on
to any of it, but I grew tired of needing to be so gritty to do what
was once so natural. As I eked out All-Americans and watched my
teammates ride the turbulent waves of their seasons, I watched the
men's team deliver again and again. When they won the conference title in outdoor track for the first time in history, I envied
them. They were focused on battling the competition. We spent
so much of our competitive energy battling ourselves.

Nobody told us what was normal, or how long the period of
discomfort would last. The truth is, nobody knows. A plateau can
last a year, like mine did, or two or three years, or it can become a
fall from a cliff you never climb back from. When you look at a
woman's performance trajectory year over year and consider its
dip or plateau, it is difficult to parse which parts of that are due to
biology and which parts are due to how those biological differences were met by their environments.

I began to feel stronger right at the end of my sophomore year.
I qualified for the NCAA championships in the 5,000 by matching
my time from the year before, and unlike the women who had
been depleting themselves, I showed up to historic Hayward Field
in Eugene, Oregon, healthy and on the upswing for the final meet
of the year. In my pre-race workout, I finished with a 400 in sixty-
one seconds, much faster than expected, surprising the coaches

and giving myself goose bumps. It had been over a year since I'd felt power like that in my legs.

Dena took it upon herself to keep me relaxed before my race, and offered to take me on the running history tour around Eugene. I couldn't believe there was a city that loved track the way other places love football. We ate at Track Town Pizza, a restaurant with walls covered in track memorabilia, the vast majority of which showcased men. We ran on an iconic trail system named after a famous runner from the '70s. I learned that Steve Prefontaine wasn't just a runner, but a working-class, gritty runner like me. We visited Pre's Rock, a shrine dedicated to Prefontaine's legacy, which was littered with race numbers, track spikes, and love notes. In just twenty-four years of life, this mustachioed tough guy had earned a plaque to his memory and moved a generation.

People loved Pre not because of what he did, but how he did it. He famously said, "A lot of people run a race to see who is fastest. I run to see who has the most guts." For Pre, this meant taking a daring lead, pushing the pace into places nobody wanted to go. For me, it had meant something different this past year, but it still applied. It takes guts to put yourself out there when your body doesn't match the ideal, and to keep doing your best when your best isn't what you hoped for, or what others expected. There was value in that. I wish teams celebrated this more.

When Vin sat down with me the night before the 5,000-meter final and asked me what my plan was, I surprised us both when I said I wanted to try to win.

Vin smiled and stroked his mustache. He already had a plan.

"Stay on the rail for the first ten laps, invisible in the top five or so. Never lose sight of the leaders. With six hundred meters to go, you take the lead and make a big, decisive move. Approach it like it's an all-out four hundred, and then keep going. I know logically it seems like you won't be able to continue, but trust me, you'll find a way."

My stomach dropped. A lap and a half is an abnormally long kick. The craziest kick I'd seen was five hundred meters, run by my teammate Gabe Jennings, and the pain looked otherworldly. It would feel like standing on hot coals and counting to one hundred. I couldn't imagine a more painful way to do it. I had wanted an easier way to win. But his plan demanded boldness bordering on recklessness. The thought thrilled me.

In the final call room, waiting for the official to lead us out from under the west grandstands into the packed stadium, I looked around. I noticed that nearly everyone looked skittish and tightly wound, and I remembered the final call room of indoor nationals. The future winner had stood there completely calm while the rest of us wiggled around in our seats and fussed with our shoelaces. She must have known what she planned to do, the risk she was going to take. *Where did the calm come from?* I had wondered at the time. Now I knew. It was a resolve to execute the plan without attachment to the result. It was about valuing the guts more than the win.

I remember nothing about the race until seven hundred meters to go, when I made the decision to follow through on the plan. From there on, I remember it viscerally. I came off the rail to move up onto the shoulder of the leader. I could have easily not made the next move. But I found I wasn't afraid of losing. With exactly six hundred to go, I shot out into the front like my ass was on fire. I ran so fast that I later heard people thought I had miscounted the laps, but when I passed the ringing bell marking one full lap remaining, I kept going full-out.

I heard the stadium screaming, and it was almost too much. I focused on looking forward. Everything forward. When I finally came off the final curve and saw the finish line in the distance, I remembered the way the track waved in the heat and delirium of my first-ever race and how badly I wanted the end to come.

With eighty meters to go, I didn't know how I would make it to the end. My legs had no pop left, the major muscle groups leaden with lactate. I was paying the price for the big early move. I felt myself recruiting my forearms, my kneecaps, any body part that could help make a final push, and when the crowd roared louder, I briefly feared I was being passed.

Just do your best. The words of my parents, who were seated in the east grandstands, came to mind. I made every quicksand step my best, and it turned out to be enough.

I stood on the podium with my teammate Sally, who finished an incredible fourth in our race, right after finishing as the runner-up in the 1,500. My teammate Jonathon Riley won the men's 5,000, and he told me that I had inspired him. I couldn't believe I had inspired someone on The Machine.

Afterward, I put on my trainers and jogged my cooldown along Agate Street, running my hand along the backside of the east grandstands rising to my left. The oversized image of Steve Prefontaine hung there with the quote, "To give anything less than your best is to sacrifice the gift." A Nike swoosh dashed below it.

In all that time since his death, it was still Pre we were given to look up to. I thought about how Sally and Brad inspired me just as much or more. I wondered who made the decisions about who gets to be a role model. I wondered what it would take to become a person who inspired like that, and when the world would be ready for a face of the sport to be a woman. Someone would do it. Why not me?

"DO YOU KNOW what *integrity* means?" Vin said from his uphol-stered chair in the coaches' condo at Mammoth.

The audience was the entire women's cross-country team, squished like a line of peas on the sofa, seated cross-legged on the living room floor. We'd been at camp in Mammoth for a couple of days, but this annual meeting marked the official start of the sea-son, and every season had a theme.

Someone raised their hand and said, "Doing the right thing?"

"Well, yes, but it's more specific than that," he said. "Integrity is doing the things you say you're going to do."

Our women's team had an integrity problem, he continued. For example, a woman says she is going to start a race in the top twenty and move up from there, and then she finishes 135th. A woman says she is going to run the prescribed sixty miles per week, but she gets caught running extra miles late at night, and then gets injured. A woman doesn't eat properly and gets injured. A woman says she is going to be committed to running, but then she doesn't get fit. Of course, being fit in the running world meant being thin.

"I've heard some of you say the men are treated differently than the women, and that's why they are having more success. That's simply not true."

The Machine had just won the outdoor NCAA track and field

title as a team, which is almost impossible with mostly distance runners. They were making history. We were underdelivering.

"You are every bit as good as the men. The men's team is more successful because they run with integrity. They do what they say they are going to do. It's that simple."

There was nothing overtly inappropriate about Vin's integrity talk. All those observations were true to some extent. At the time, I felt smug knowing that he wasn't talking about me. I was the exception. *Finally, someone said it!* I thought. *It's not that hard, people.*

What makes me cringe now is Vin's—and my—inclination to place blame on the women, without any acknowledgment of the forces at play for us. The outcomes he described—eating disorders, self-harm, self-sabotage—predictably show up on teams all over the world. But instead of asking why, we shake our heads in frustration and continue to blame the women. These behaviors look like personal choices, but they are choices made within a particular sporting environment that women had to fight to get access to but did not get a chance to create.

As a coach, I still use Vin's basic definition of running with integrity as a tool for my athletes to develop trust in themselves. At the core, that's what he wanted us to do. He knew that every time we said one thing and did another, a little part of us died. He preferred an athlete to say that her goal was to get fiftieth and then finish fiftieth than to say she wanted to get tenth and end up fiftieth. It's frustrating for everyone when an athlete can't get an accurate read of what's going to happen. On a team, not showing up the way you said you would erodes team culture. All of that was true then and is true now.

But for my college teammates and me—and as I've learned

since, for young female athletes across the board—it's hard to set accurate goals and make good decisions. These women don't understand why things feel like they are falling apart. It is not fair to place that burden on the athlete while you are misleading them by saying they can and should be improving and performing just like the boys.

The team that got the integrity talk was probably our most promising team yet, as far as rosters go. Even after Sally graduated, we had four Foot Locker champions and three runners-up—plus enough Foot Locker qualifiers to fill another van. We just needed seven women to keep it together and run with integrity, and we'd finally win the NCAA cross-country title.

Julia was off the grid managing another injury, determined to maintain her fitness by using the StairMaster in her living room. Caitlyn was missing, and the coaches were cagey about why. Even so, we had a wicked front pack at practice. Jean had battled bulimia in secret and suffered related injuries from malnutrition but seemed to be healthy and engaged now. Malindi Elmore, a former high school star out of Canada, was returning from her third or fourth unexplainable stress fracture with real momentum. Beyond them, Erin and a group of upperclassmen were more adjusted to their women's bodies now. Pretty much all our experienced athletes seemed to be on their way up from a rocky road at the perfect time.

And the freshmen—wow. They were good. Dena was coaching more confidently and had recruited an amazing incoming class, highlighted by my old friend and Foot Locker roommate Sara Bei (now American record holder Sara Hall). I knew her racing style would be a huge asset to the team and would push me to another level. As a team captain, I tried my best to shepherd everyone together.

"Look, I know most of us are not in the place we'd imagined we'd be right now," I said. "We were all used to winning in high school, and now the competition is so much deeper. But even if where you are as an individual isn't super motivating to you personally, we can do something amazing as a team if everyone can get excited about doing their best on the day for each other."

That was easy for me to say. The performance dip I had experienced as a sophomore was brief and didn't involve injuries that required starting over from the back of the pack, an experience that is far more psychologically challenging. Staying engaged and remembering you matter while in twentieth place is easier than doing so from the anonymity of 120th place.

We won the conference championship and Regionals as a team, but lost the individual titles to a woman from a rival school who had lost so much weight from the year before that you couldn't help but stare at her exposed hip bones in horror. I watched her isolate herself from her teammates at the event and felt lucky we didn't have that bad of a problem.

We traveled to the NCAA cross-country championships ranked number one, and I was one of the favorites for the individual title. As we rode the van to the course on race morning, we passed around a pen and wrote a mantra on our hands to remember to do our best for one another, no matter what. I got off to a good start in the race and found myself in the lead pack in what I hoped would be an exciting battle for first. If it came down to a kick, I liked my chances.

But then, with half the race still ahead of us, the same thin woman on a winning streak pulled away from the lead pack with an ease that made me feel helpless. Anger and frustration started pressing in on me. She was killing herself and she was going to win the thing, like so many others had over the years. And every athlete, and every coach, would see that and add to the pressure to be thinner. In my mind, that coach who was allowing that athlete to compete while severely ill was hurting her—and the rest of us, too.

As I climbed up a hill with a half mile to go, I was struck by the fact that I might never win the NCAA cross-country title because I was healthy, and I began to lose emotional steam. Just like when I lost to Rocky and learned I was a girl, my frustration wasn't just about winning—it was about fairness. I wanted to give up. But then I saw Shalane Flanagan, another top-ranked runner I deeply respected, who would go on to win the NYC Marathon and an Olympic silver medal. Shalane was getting swallowed by our lead pack as she shuffled up the hill, and I recognized the look of defeat on her face as I came up alongside her. I had been moments away from the same fate. I ran alongside her for a few strides and encouraged her to keep going, to not give up, and doing so strengthened my resolve. I dug down and fought for every place I could.

I crossed the line in third, my best finish ever. I wondered how my teammates fared in their own personal battles behind me. I waited and waited. They trickled in, looking battered. We finished a disappointing fifth, our worst finish as a team yet. Vin avoided us, clearly agitated and probably sensing that he should cool down before interacting with us. Dena stood beside us under our tent as we changed out of our racing shoes and put on our sweats, offering small bits of encouragement. We were all bewildered and disappointed, and it was unclear who, or what, to blame.

I loved my teammates so much. I felt like I was failing as a leader. The problem was so nebulous, and I didn't know how to make things better. But I started to feel pretty sure it wasn't a failure of the women's efforts or spirits; it wasn't our fault. Something else was going on. My teammates were women of integrity. They were people who followed through in life, in school. They were brilliant and fun and hardworking . . . and often struggling to get the results they wanted in running. But we had no language for why.

COLLEGIATE SPORTS WERE built by men for men and boys in the early 1900s as an arena for promoting traditional ideas of masculinity. Competitive sports used battle terminology and focused on aggression to keep studious men from going soft; so many athletes died that an organization was created to protect the health and well-being of collegiate athletes. That organization is the NCAA, now a behemoth with over a billion dollars in annual revenue. Protecting student athletes is technically still its purpose, though I was about to learn how much it was failing to do this for women.

The NCAA does not have any female-specific policies or best practices for the issues that disproportionately befall them within the collegiate sporting environment, at least none that I could find. In the bylaws and policies, sex is minimized to the point of erasure. Caroline Criado Perez discusses this ubiquitous cultural pattern in her prizewinning book *Invisible Women*, explaining how a gender gap in data perpetuates bias and disadvantages women. The assumption of sameness naturally prioritizes the male body as the default. But during the ages of eighteen through twenty-two, the fact is that underneath the skin, the male body is doing something entirely different from the female body. Expecting the same performance trajectory is not only dense, it is harmful.

For males, ages eighteen through twenty-two are the years of peak testosterone, maximum training capacity, and robust recovery power. (These are the same years young men are recruited to be soldiers.) Men are in an unprecedented physiological prime for athletic improvement at exactly the years they are of age to be pursuing a collegiate degree. It makes sense that a sports industry built for eighteen- to twenty-two-year-old male bodies would have a body ideal of leanness—and an expected trajectory of steady performance improvement.

Meanwhile, the body of the eighteen- to twenty-two-year-old female is continuing the change into the body of a mother. We may not be focused on reproduction at this age, but our biology is investing in peak fertility. High circulating estrogen wants a woman's body to be softer, to hold more body fat and fluids. The body builds and invests in tissue that has no direct value to sport, such as breasts and uterine lining that will shed after making us feel bloated, and our weight will fluctuate on a monthly cycle. These natural shifts in body composition are not immediately compatible with a male standard of steady, linear improvement. They also make the idea of an ideal race weight totally absurd. As female athletes allow their tendons, ligaments, muscles, and bones to adjust to their new strength-to-weight ratio, they are likely to experience what I was experiencing: a performance plateau or dip. This is normal and healthy, but sport hasn't been taught to see and respect difference.

Every time I speak to young female athletes, they are surprised to learn that they actually *need* to allow this plateau to happen, that it is a true rite of passage that should be welcomed, because they will never reach their ultimate potential without it. Nobody has told them that the record holders and medal winners are grown-ass women, not girls, all of whom had tough years once upon a time, and that their own best years will truly begin in their midtwenties. Instead, my inbox regularly pings with calls for help from young women worried that body changes are ruining their careers, while coaches and parents look upon them with disappointment.

I know Vin and Dena cared deeply and did the best they could in a system that sees the normal female performance wave as problematic, and they have certainly grown since, as I have in my coaching. You don't know what you don't know. My college experience certainly provided stories to learn from, but it could have been far worse. Unlike other coaches I've heard about (and who still have jobs), mine didn't shame me outright. They didn't put me on a highly restrictive diet. They didn't police my food order on team trips. They didn't create a team policy that required weekly weigh-ins to control women's bodies. They didn't employ skin-fold tests, didn't pinch my lower belly and inner thigh and read the number of millimeters of fat out loud in front of my teammates. They didn't talk about my weight in front of the team, either. They didn't train me through an eating disorder until I broke my leg and withhold medical imaging so they could make me race. They didn't threaten my scholarship. These are all stories I've heard from young women in the last year.

What my team needed was to be seen. We needed our coaches to be educated on female physiology, to affirm our body changes as normal, and to safeguard our healthy menstrual cycles. We needed them to identify the predictable landmines of negative body image and eating disorder culture. We needed language to talk openly about these issues without stigma. We needed athletic departments to be armed with official policies for preventing and treating eating disorders to maximize full recoveries. We needed staff to be measured and rewarded based on the mental and physical health of the athletes in their care, and the number of women who graduated college still loving to run. Instead, we were told that we lacked integrity.

My teammate Julia, the extraordinary star I'd looked up to since high school, had always been in and out of the team with injuries, and nobody had known what was going on. All I knew was she trained with unmatched discipline, and she always had an incredible physique that set the bar for what an ideal distance runner should look like. Lean, strong, tan, and beautiful, she never gained weight, even when she was injured.

But then Julia fell off her skateboard riding to class one day, and two compound fractures and a spiral fracture broke her tibia into hundreds of tiny pieces. The injury exposed that she had osteoporosis and had never gotten her period, facts she shared with me without emotion as she sat in the golf cart she was now using to get to class. I examined the torture contraption on her leg, a halo of metal suspended in the air by over a dozen thick gauge pins going from the frame through the skin to hold her bone together. She was upbeat and positive about her injury, explaining that she was being taken care of by the doctors and feeling supported by the coaches. Fosamax, a drug linked to an increased cancer risk she didn't want to dwell on, was going to hopefully build her bone density back up. Julia had always been a joyful, energetic teammate, and when she was healthy, she was always down to drive somewhere far and fun for a trail run that ended at a waterfall. Our running chats were always full of mutual encouragement. I had no idea she'd never had her period, leaving her exposed to the forces of running without the estrogen levels needed to build bone density. I wondered if anyone had ever asked her about it or cared.

Like Kim Mortensen, who set the national high school record for the 3,200 before disappearing from the sport, the fallout of Julia's accident left me with a lot of questions. I searched for which personal choices and behaviors led to this fate, but there was nothing obvious. She was a little obsessive about exercise, sure, but it came off as steadfast dedication to being the best she could be with the best attitude possible. There hadn't been the same warning signs I'd seen in others, no obvious body wasting, no personality changes. I felt angry *for* Julia, not with her. She was the first athlete who opened my eyes to the fact that when it came to poor outcomes, we had an attribution problem. I felt anger at an outside force, something I couldn't quite name yet, something I'd have to face myself before I would understand. When Julia drove away in her golf cart, I stood there haunted by the thought that all along, under those four distinct quad muscles we all coveted, her bones were full of holes.

In my sport, I was the rare woman matching the male standard of excellence, justifying the standard's existence. I was praised for doing what so few women did: transitioning from high school dominance to college excellence, competing consistently at the top and improving year after year. I was the bar my teammates were compared to, or who they compared themselves to, who they used as proof that the system worked just fine. But I was a rare outlier.

At Mammoth, preparing for my senior year, I found myself alone with Jean in her condo, and found evidence of her purge in the toilet. She admitted to her eating disorder for the first time.

"Jean, you're so talented," I said. "You're just as good as I am. You just need to stay healthy. Stop hurting yourself."

"You don't understand. You shine such a bright light, it's blinding. There's no light for anyone else."

I felt like she had punched me in the stomach. "No, that's not true—"

"Don't act like you get it. You don't."

"We need you. We can't win without you," I pleaded.

"The truth is," she said, "I'd rather be skinny and injured, than healthy and running fast."

We sat there in silence, and after a moment I got up to make a cup of tea, ending the conversation. I couldn't fathom how to respond. Neither, it seemed, could the adults in charge.

WHAT I COULDN'T OUTRUN

What kind of legacy do you want to leave behind on this team?" Dena asked us at the season kickoff meeting at my final Stanford training camp. "I want you to take some time to think about it, and then we will share as a group."

I loved this question. I loved the way it prompted many to stop making comparisons with their high school selves. I loved that it was open-ended beyond performance alone. I loved that it empowered each person to own their story.

Even as many members of our team still struggled with the weight of expectations and the coaching staff's endorsement of developmentally inappropriate leanness, Dena's leadership was beginning to have a positive impact in other ways. She not only had some experience under her belt now, but also increasing confidence and power to put it to use. A primary coach who was empowered to make decisions helped assuage feelings that we were the B squad to The Machine; by asking us what kind of mark we wanted to make as individuals and as a collective, Dena made us feel like we were building something of our own. The younger athletes on the team were all recruited by her and truly deferred to her, and while I still relied on Vin as my primary authority figure, Dena showed me on a daily basis that a woman could lead. I watched her navigate her career through pregnancy, birth, and early motherhood, as well as the challenges of being a woman of color leading in a predominantly white male field. She would say herself that she wasn't perfect, and that she would do some things differently, but watching her grow on the job was what later influenced me to coach before I felt ready and to have compassion for myself as I made mistakes.

Thanks in no small part to Dena's leadership, we almost won the NCAA team cross-country title that year. In fact, for two minutes, the unofficial results declared us the winners and we jumped all over one another in the finish area, crying and smiling so big our cheeks ached before they made the correction over the loudspeaker. Then we stood silently, watching BYU perform the same celebration fifty feet away. The disappointment didn't last long, even as we watched the men's team claim the title. The fact was, every single woman on the team performed well that day. While leanness was still emphasized and we weren't all holistically healthy, none of us were injured, and Dena gave us a lot of time and encouragement that boosted morale. I finished fourth, just behind Alicia Craig, but I didn't mind. Alicia was exceptional, and the team's future was in good hands. I never won the individual title, but I had capped off the best cumulative cross-country career of any athlete before and maybe since, and past experience told me I'd climb my way to the top by year's end.

There was just one problem. Shalane Flanagan, the woman from UNC who won the individual crown in cross-country that year, was the real deal. Unlike so many other top cross-country runners, she was rumored to be healthy, and therefore was probably going to stay a pain in my ass for the rest of my senior year. Shalane was a thoroughbred, with two professional runners for parents. Her mom got one of the first-ever athletic scholarships for women after Title IX was passed and had once held the world record in the marathon. I was a little intimidated at first, but I decided to let her inspire me to raise my game. I scheduled a meeting with Vin.

"I'm ready to do what it takes," I told him. "Just tell me what to do to be the best, and I'll do it." I really felt like I would do anything the man said. I would be coachable. I would be perfect if I needed to be.

"Okay. There's no secret to the training we do. Keep doing what you're doing there, and I'll push you a little more. But you're going to have to do the right things when nobody is looking. Stay focused. No distractions. You need to eat healthy, sleep nine hours, take naps, stretch, do all the little things."

"Done."

This discipline excited me at first. I began to orient my entire life around performance. Jesse and I had been discussing getting back together after our most recent breakup, and on the day he came over to reunite, I surprised him by saying no, that I needed to focus on myself. I'd always hated naps, but I closed my eyes from 2:30 until 3:15 every single day. I aligned my classes as closely as possible to my goals, creating a personalized area of concentration for my major in human biology: "women's health and athletic performance," with advanced coursework that included exercise physiology and sports nutrition. I pored over the material, hoping to learn how to optimize my body.

A famous exercise physiologist was visiting campus around this time, and Vin set up lab tests for the top runners on the team to help optimize their training. When I showed up for mine, I was nervous. A VO2max test has two parts, both done on a treadmill with a clip pinching your nostrils together and a mask strapped to your face, controlling and measuring your air flow. The first part of the test determines the effort level, or "threshold," at which your body shifts from using its more sustainable aerobic system to the anaerobic system, the one that makes your legs feel like lead and leaves you bent over your knees, gasping for air. During the test you take ten-second breaks every couple of minutes to get your fingertip stabbed by a needle, measuring the lactate buildup in your blood along the way. The result of this test is a snapshot of your fitness at that very moment, which training can improve dramatically. Part two of the treadmill test determines your VO2max, or the maximum oxygen-carrying capacity of your body under stress. This test culminates with you running on the treadmill up a steeper and steeper incline until you reach failure. While you rip the tubes off your face and desperately drink air into your lungs, the physiologist puts a bunch of numbers from your test into a formula. Your prize is a number called the VDOT, and that number roughly correlates with your ultimate performance potential. The only other time I'd had this test done was in high school, at the Olympic Training Center, where young talent was tested and identified, and my results had been unremarkable.

As an athlete with big dreams of being the best, I hoped for a better result this time, one that proved my high school test was a mistake. Maybe I'd turn out to be truly gifted like Lance Armstrong. But the physiologist did not leap out of his chair when he got the results, which were almost exactly the same as four years earlier. I watched him slide his finger down the VDOT chart. My predicted potential in the 5K was only about ten seconds faster than I'd already run. I didn't even know if that was enough to hold off the young runners nipping at my heels at practice every day, much less defend my outdoor title in the 5K against Flanagan or indulge my fantasy of becoming Shefontaine. It was impossible to hide my disappointment in front of him.

"Is there any way to raise VO2max?" I asked.

"Not really, genes play a huge role, and you've already been training at a high level for years. But the number is calculated as it relates to kilograms of body weight, so a person can change the number if they change their weight."

I'd heard so many people remark over the last couple of years that I didn't look like a distance runner. No matter how successful I was, there were people who were surprised because I didn't look the part. "Imagine how fast she'd be if she lost some weight," I'd heard an assistant coach say when he didn't know I was listening.

"What if I lost five pounds?" I asked him.

"Well, that would put you on this line here," he replied. The times looked much more exciting. "But the number only changes if you lose nonproductive weight. You can't lose muscle. Only fat."

Nonproductive weight was a term that instantly brought to mind all the body changes that happened during puberty, all things female. "If you're fit, when you jump, nothing should jiggle," was the motto of a rival coach in the conference, and a myth I still hear repeated among female athletes.

In researching body fat in my sports nutrition class, I learned that it had essential human functions, such as offering a layer of protection under the skin and around the organs in case of impact. I didn't plan on slamming into things, I reasoned, so I didn't need much of that. I learned that it helps people survive in a famine, giving you stores to draw on when food is scarce. I didn't need backup fuel; there was a dining hall open twenty-four hours. I learned fat was essential for normal menstrual function and fertility. I had no interest in babies, but I didn't want amenorrhea, the total loss of periods that could lead to osteoporosis and stress fractures: the dreaded condition known as the "female athlete triad." I didn't want that. But I could miss a few—four periods per year was the cusp of alarm, according to my ob-gyn (this has since become an outdated benchmark). Between my physiology class and my nutrition class, I developed a plan to outsmart my body that I felt wouldn't have consequences. It wasn't black-and-white, but a shade of gray—the very space Dena had told us all elite athletes reside in. It was meant to keep us from stigmatizing and pointing fingers at one another's habits, but more than a few of us took it as an endorsement for disordered eating, believing it was safe territory.

When I decreased my fat intake and began reading food labels and keeping a food log with calorie counts, adjusting my habits according to my interpretation of nutrition science, my period became irregular. Reproductive hormones are the first line of defense in times of caloric restriction. Since I read it was typical for athletes to have irregular periods, I took it as evidence that the plan was working.

I was often hungry, but I never starved myself or skipped meals. I never threw up or binged in my closet. I never avoided team meals or packed okra in a container to eat when everyone else was ordering off the menu. I would eat according to the science, trying to make the best choices even if I didn't desire or enjoy them. Often unsatiated, my body craved fat and sugar. In what I would have called a moment of "weakness" at the time, I'd buy a cookie at the snack cart on campus and then, after wrestling with myself whether or not to eat it, I'd give it to a friend in class to make it disappear. I didn't recognize this food pushing as the sign of disordered eating it was. It was the kind of control you see modeled in sports movies, the boxer swallowing raw eggs, the noble removal of pleasure, intuition, and community from the act of eating.

In scrutinizing my reflection for signs of change to justify the nutritional diligence that was taking up so much headspace, I noticed my body more. I noticed everyone else's bodies more. I got a thrill anytime someone commented that I looked fit, and I noticed when they didn't. I praised teammates who lost their "baby fat." I am haunted now knowing that during that year, I contributed to eating disorder culture on my team with my body talk, my perfectionism, my recitation of nutritional insights and eating strategies. In obsessing about the scale and how I looked, I was outsourcing my confidence. Even if I had a bank of amazing workouts in my training log to tell me I was race-ready, I found myself looking for confirmation in the hotel mirror the night before the competition, dressed in my race kit. I liked what I saw.

———————

THE FIRST TIME I got to line up against Shalane Flanagan, we were the anchor legs of our relay teams at the Penn Relays. I lacked pop in my legs and couldn't summon my typical responsiveness when she made her move. Not only did I get smoked decisively, I ran a slower time than my fitness would have indicated. Back on campus, I didn't feel like I was recovering between workouts. I got my ass kicked by several of my teammates on a session of kilometer repeats that was normally my bread and butter, a session that prized my normal strengths of pain tolerance and grit. It was more than the expected decreased energy from eating less. I felt more sensitive to the discomfort of the intervals, and unable to catch my breath between repetitions. New research shows that decreased pain tolerance and compromised recovery are hallmark effects of menstrual dysfunction.

Vin confronted me after the terrible track workout and asked me what was wrong. I didn't know. He asked if I was eating enough. I said I had been working hard to be disciplined and was almost to my race weight. He reminded me that championship season was upon us, and the most important thing now was to get myself psychologically ready to race; whatever weight I was now was good enough. It was a relief to hear this from him. It felt like he'd burst the door open on a cage I had been living in. I started eating more and curbing my obsession with control.

My energy improved, but I still felt scattered, and without a center. I had been leaning too much on external factors to give me confidence, a path I'd watched many people travel down and fail on before. I had to get my shit together.

For my last long run before the NCAA championships, I went running alone on a decommissioned road too full of potholes for anyone else on my team to bother with, a place I sometimes went to clear my head. As I ran, I tuned in to my chest, my lungs, the rhythm of my footsteps. I listened until my steps and breath combined to make a kind of music. Finding my way to the middle of the road, I closed my eyes and imagined myself in the middle of the race. My footsteps were now on tartan track, the sun was now a tower of halogen bulbs. With each step, a force of gravity built up in my core and pulled all the parts of me back to center. I felt compact, dense, no loose bits vulnerable to a snag. I saw the finish line moving closer and closer to me, nobody else around. I raised my arms in victory and felt the expansiveness of a supernova.

"Nice finish," a voice said, and I opened my eyes to see a cyclist buzz past, disappearing around the next corner.

I laughed out loud, embarrassed to discover that I had really lifted my arms and not just imagined it. But after a few minutes of running alone again, I changed my perspective: I had gotten caught dreaming. Maybe I had given him a gift.

Three weeks later, I put six seconds on Shalane in the final three hundred meters of the 5K to win my third consecutive NCAA title, becoming only the second woman to ever do so. I was so happy, so in my body, that I missed it when the announcer said I'd broken the collegiate record. It was the highest-stakes race of my life so far—I stepped right into the pressure, kept it fun, and I came through. I felt so proud of myself.

For most of my life, I've looked at that last year of college as a close call. I didn't have a clinical eating disorder or the female athlete triad, I've told myself—I was just buckling down, being disciplined; I had pulled back to safety just in time. In the photos, Shalane and I look almost identical physically. I don't look unhealthy to me. I don't look like I "went too far." In fact, I don't look much different from the year before. But you can't determine someone's health by what she looks like, and I wasn't out of the woods yet. In a state of low energy availability, there is so much going on below the surface that nobody can see: bones are losing density, muscle tissue isn't healing as quickly, the reproductive axis is being suppressed, metabolism is slowing. . . . I thought I'd pulled back in time, but it wasn't that simple. That last national title would come at a cost, but nobody knew it yet.

I walked out of the stadium triumphant: a five-time NCAA champion and fifteen-time All-American, one for every time I stepped on the line at an NCAA championship race without fail. As I approached the gate to the cooldown area, the sports agents—and with them an utterly new phase of my career and my life—were there waiting for me.

8

GOING PRO

I started to feel like a pro athlete when the first big box of Nike gear arrived at my parents' house. By then I'd already traveled to four countries, ridden luxury buses escorted by police convoys to compete at enormous stadiums, and raced some of the best distance runners in the world, but now it was sinking in. As I unwrapped bag after bag of technical sports gear from a cardboard box the size of a coffee table, I kept one eye on my dad's reaction. He walked around the living room in his new extra-large USA jacket I'd traded someone for in Paris, oohing and ahhing over each item I held up. His daughter was a professional athlete. A Nike athlete. The brand of Michael Jordan and "Just Do It" commercials.

"You're hot like SIXTEEN motherfuckers!" he nearly shouted. I glowed. Sixteen was as high as the scale went. Nobody knew why. "Look at you, a Nike athlete traveling all over the world. Give you another year and you'll be kicking all their asses!"

"Dad, I have a ways to go," I said. I was worried that he didn't grasp how big the leap was from collegiate to professional running, that he'd gotten used to me winning all the time. "But I'm going to go for it."

"Of COURSE you will! You're a FLESHMAN! Ain't NOBODY got a heart like you."

His praise felt amazing, but the truth was that I was overwhelmed by what would come next. In pro track and field, there is no professional infrastructure. Unlike in soccer, basketball, or other team sports, there is no team to join. There is no league that has minimum salaries or benefits negotiated by unions. All those postcollegiate athletes representing Team USA in the Summer Olympics are spread out all over the country trying to patch together individual support systems as independent contractors, an employment designation that leaves them without essential protections and benefits. The living of a professional track athlete is made through prize money from events she fronts money to travel to, essentially placing a bet on herself. The only viable way to make track and field a full-time career as an American is to secure an endorsement deal with a major sports brand. Athletes must make the case for why they are a worthy marketing investment or hire an agent to do it for them. I couldn't have set myself up better, and agents were coming to me, but I was about to learn that there was a big difference between being the best, and being the best girl.

VIN HAD JUST mentored multiple men on my team through the process of going pro and expected I'd make low six figures. (I had to ask him what that meant, never having heard the term.) In preparation for my agent meetings, he insisted I ask them what they thought my market value was. "They're not going to want to, but make them commit to a dollar amount. Then they'll fight harder for it."

Every meeting was essentially the same. "Normally I'd say I could get you twenty-five, maybe $30K a year," prospective agents would tell me. "But you've got the look they like, which helps, so maybe $45K." I felt disappointed that the estimates were so low to begin with, and I attempted to gauge how attractive I was based on the numbers they gave me. I thought about how many people had called me cute over my lifetime rather than beautiful. Would a different woman double or triple her base value by presenting herself as more feminine or overtly sexual?

When I came back to Vin with the numbers, he was appalled and paced the room, red-faced. "That's not enough," he said. "That's insulting." My male teammates had gotten offers of two to three times that.

I decided not to get an agent and instead represent myself, figuring nobody could sell me better than me. I carefully honed my pitch: Over the next five years, I would improve gradually to put myself in a position to qualify for the 2008 Olympics and become the greatest American distance runner of all time. It would take some patience at first, but I wanted a brand to stick with me to get there the right way. Along the way, I wanted to launch a campaign to combat the massive problem of disordered eating and injuries plaguing high school girls and college women. It seemed that every year there had been a new female phenom plastered across websites and running magazines with skin stretched over sinew, only for her to disappear mysteriously and be replaced by the next one. We needed to be talking about it and modeling a different way forward—a longer view of success. Nobody was talking to female athletes this way, and I was willing to work hard. My ask was $60K.

Every sports marketing executive I met with was a cisgender white man. Two asked if I had a boyfriend, and when I said no, they said "Good." I was a more valuable marketing asset as a single woman. When we got to the topic of marketability, I presented my vision for helping change girls' sport and reach a female audience in the process. They acted like my ideas were cute. The audience that mattered wasn't girls. One said, "Men are the ones that watch sports, not women. The female athletes worth watching are the ones that appeal to men. It's gross, but it's the way it is."

"Do you know where the best seats to watch women's track are?" another one asked.

"Where?"

"The starting line of the women's 1,500. Do you know why?"

I shook my head no.

"Think of the view. The best bodies in the sport are all lined up, in little more than bathing suits." I tried to hide my disgust, but my face must have betrayed me. "What? I'm not saying that's how I feel, but that's just the reality of every young guy watching women's track. My job is to get them to buy shoes."

Then and now, these market forces, based on the presumed tastes of straight white men, influence the entire landscape of women's sport. They determine who gets to be a professional at all. Those standing on the podium aren't necessarily the best talent—they are the best of those who fit an image, or the best of those who can afford to keep doing it.

The offers I was negotiating on my own weren't any better than the agents had promised. After my meeting with Nike, John Capriotti, the global head of track and field sports marketing whom everyone called "Cap," refused to negotiate with me at all. The moment I pushed back on his offer of $30K and asked for a salary of $60K, he told me to get an agent. He said that athletes shouldn't hear the things executives say about them in negotiations.

Vin was deeply disappointed to hear about my experiences. But he was also a realist. "If I were you, I'd get an agent and give Nike one more chance. I bet Cap will come through. Nike is the brand with the budget to create change when they decide they believe in something. But know this: This change-the-world stuff? They won't do anything unless you win. So focus on that first."

I hired Ray Flynn as my agent. He was a trustworthy, legendary Irish miler, his tall frame softened some by years on the road. Ray did the dirty work while I focused on being likable and charming, and soon after, I had my $60K offer from Nike in a tall stack of legalese. For all that talk about marketability, the focus of the contract was performance. To maintain my salary, I needed to make USA teams and achieve high national and world rankings. Bonuses were available for the biggest stages and fastest times. If I fell short of expectations, or went too long between competitions, my salary would be reduced by up to 50 percent, and there was no way to get it back. I wasn't thinking about having a child anytime soon, but pregnancy was conspicuously absent. Behavior viewed as a poor reflection on the brand could result in termination; such terms were intentionally left vague.

The message was clear: Win or perish, and be a good girl. I could do that. The Olympics were a year away. I needed to learn how to win at this level as soon as possible, so I flew to Europe for the track and field racing circuit that happens every summer, putting myself among the best in the world. My agent got me a spot on the best starting lines he could. I don't remember where I stopped first; maybe Ireland. Maybe Belgium. That summer and every summer after is mostly a blur of planes, trains, buses, subways, hotel duvets, buffets, dining tables full of athletes grouped by language, laughter, flirting, races, calling cards, and training runs through cobblestone alleys.

I learned from the races, but I learned a lot more in the spaces between them. The most valuable information came during long talks over coffee, killing time until the espresso dregs hardened inside our illy cups. The most successful and impactful athletes on the track were six to twelve years older than me. Nearly everyone I met was generous with their experience and advice. Most had seen their pay reduced after a bad season at some point, never to recover. Most were now experiencing ageism from their sponsors, who offered them less money at contract negotiation time despite having just set personal bests. This seemed especially unjust for the women, whose physical prime was later than the men's, but everyone was valued according to the male performance timeline. I was aware that this ageism freed up budgets for young talent like me, and that I'd face the same fate unless I could somehow make myself indispensable.

My last stop was at the World Championships in Paris, and I had one more conversation that shaped the economic landscape for me. In the computer lab of the athlete village, I found myself seated next to Jon Drummond, a Black male sprinter and one of the team captains. Jon was kind and charming, especially for someone who had just experienced failure and public humiliation on the global stage. Jon had inadvertently moved his foot in the blocks before the starting gun went off, and a new false start rule disqualified him from the competition for the first offense. He lay on the track, refusing to leave, holding up the entire meet for several minutes. Viewers, primarily older white people, labeled him disrespectful, an embarrassment.

"You're lucky. You're a cute white girl," he said. "You'll be fine. Me?" He spun his chair to face me and leaned back, pausing as his expression turned from skeptical to defiant.

"You get paid. I'm gonna guess fifty, sixty, $80K? For what? Potential? Don't take this the wrong way, but you haven't done shit yet at this level," he said with pain behind his laughter.

"Fair enough," I said. Like all the other Americans in my event, I had failed to advance to the final.

Jon explained that it had gotten old seeing distance runners, who were mostly white, getting paid well to get knocked out in the first round, while sprinters, who were mostly Black, were being told to win or starve.

"You distance people need to make teams to keep your jobs. We need to be the best in the world."

"That's unreasonable," I said. "How can you expect to win medals every year in this sport?" I had just been beaten so badly I was having a hard time imagining ever winning one at all.

He lifted his hands in a shrug.

"You tell me," he concluded, and went back to his email.

One definition of privilege is who gets to make mistakes, and Jon and I would be treated very differently for not qualifying out of the rounds. I had been so upset about being paid less than the men, but now I knew there were people who had it worse than white women in pro sports. Back in my room, I felt relieved to be born who I was. I also felt upset hearing Jon describe the racism he had encountered, but I didn't think I could do anything about it. I didn't think that was my job. I know better now. But I came from the kind of broader community that says "all lives matter." The kind of working-class white people who get the short end of the stick enough times to not want to hear about the long ones they have, viewing what feels like a rare advantage as fair game. Sports teach you to exploit any advantage you have and silence your protests of injustice with reminders of your disposability. To make a mark on the world stage, I had a long way to go, and only three years to do it. I needed to stick to running. It would take several years of witnessing bias and sport activism in action to develop the courage to become an active ally.

IN MOST INDIVIDUAL SPORTS, the objective of a pro athlete is clear: Make Olympic teams. That's the standard of success universally understood and expected in our culture—and valued financially. And all professional runners in the United States know what they need to do to qualify for the Olympics. It isn't political or subjective; there is no panel of judges. You simply have to achieve a certain time standard at some point during the season to be considered eligible for the Games, and then, on that one day in summer that comes once every four years, you line up and compete your heart out at the United States Olympic Trials, and the top three athletes with the qualifying standard get to go. Catch a cold, get injured, get tripped—too bad. Our country's talent pool runs so deep that you can't afford a bad day—there's always a stable supply of hungry athletes ready to take you down and claim their own Olympic dream.

So I set my life up to stay at Stanford to work with Vin. I enrolled in a master's program at Stanford's Graduate School of Education, extending my scholarship, and signed on as a graduate assistant coach. This would allow me continued access to all the same training facilities and still-enrolled teammates to train with. When Vin broke the news that he was moving to Ohio to take a job at Oberlin College, I panicked. I had already signed a lease on a cottage with friends and bought my textbooks. But then we settled on a plan for him to coach me long-distance through March, with Dena agreeing to assist in our objective of getting fit and avoiding injury. I would cram all my coursework into the first two quarters, appeal to the School of Education to work on my master's thesis remotely during third quarter, and move to Oberlin for the twelve-week lead-up to the Olympic Trials.

During those six months at Stanford, I thought of nothing else, did nothing else. I kept a meticulous training diary, closely measuring my training with notes on distance, pace, terrain, and weather for every run. I added columns in the margins for hours of sleep, weight, and calories consumed. What you choose to pay attention to changes your behavior, and I gradually found myself obsessing over the things I recorded, moving workout days or times around the weather, adhering to a strict sleeping schedule that isolated me, and eating perfectly measured portions of the "right" foods. If I was unable to achieve the prescribed paces of an important workout, it would create so much stress that my chest would tighten, flaring up my asthma.

If there was one thing I should have been recording and obsessing over, it was my menstrual cycle. I no longer trusted the medical recommendations given to women now that I knew how little research was done on them. I convinced myself that as someone on the cutting edge of high performance, I knew better, and having lower estrogen levels that more closely mimicked those of a man had more immediate benefits than nurturing my fertility as a twenty-one-year-old. It felt freeing not to have to deal with bloating, cyclical weight gain, and emotional swings on top of a rigorous training schedule. Never getting my period meant that every day of the month was a good day for a key workout or race, which reduced the mental load only my female peers had to deal with. If there had been intentional space made in sports for menstrual health and symptom management by coaches and staff, I would have viewed my cycle as something to learn from and work with, instead of as a limiting inconvenience that made me resent my female body. The decision to ignore my absent period felt like taking agency over my performance outcomes. I convinced myself that the warnings about amenorrhea in textbooks were likely overblown, and I considered myself healthy because I ate the wide variety of foods recommended by my dietician. But following a measured meal plan was disconnecting me from my body. I trusted the calorie calculations in my log more than the growling of my belly or the thermostat of my hormones.

On the surface, enough things were going well to make me believe my perfectionism was serving me. I had a 4.0 GPA in my graduate courses. The Stanford women finally won the NCAA cross-country title and gave me a championship ring for assistant coaching. Most importantly, I was fit: In my final test before driving across the country to Ohio, I raced the World Cross Country Championships in Belgium and finished in the top twenty-five and as the second American behind Shalane Flanagan—a good sign I was on target for my goals in the spring.

When I arrived at Vin's humble office at Oberlin College, I tossed my bag of athletic gear and box of books on the worn linoleum floor, gave him a hug, and then flopped into a cracked plastic chair opposite his desk to hear his plan with an eager smile. He'd found me a free place to stay in the attic of an eighty-three-year-old retired sports reporter named Dori Sturges and secured a training partner in a male grad student named Colin. I felt like Rocky Balboa, ready to disappear into the training cave, away from all the usual distractions. I would transform myself and emerge unstoppable.

Routine came quickly. Every morning, I padded down the attic stairs, laced up my shoes, and went for a run with Colin around the patchwork of agriculture fields. Four to six miles later, I'd arrive home to Dori passing me a helping of her daily breakfast: a small slice of an Entenmann's Danish and a cup of Folgers. We'd sit in her vintage kitchen at the square Formica kitchen table set for two and chat about our plans for the day. Hers involved tennis, socializing, some Hawaiian dancing, and household chores. Mine included training, writing my thesis, resting, and completing physical therapy exercises on the living room floor. She marveled at how motionless I was around the house when I wasn't training, and I would marvel at her buzzing about fixing gutters and hoisting pool covers like a person half her age. Dori insisted on cooking for me, so I insisted on being her assistant and cleaning up. We'd talk about life over triangles of tuna sandwiches and neat squares of hamburger casserole. Dining and talking with an elder sports pioneer filled my soul, but eating like an octogenarian sent me to bed at night starving.

I could have bought more food. Dori offered me a cabinet of my own and free reign of the kitchen if I wanted to cook something different. But a shadowy part of me saw this situation as an opportunity. The daily calories I was recording in my training log were firmly in a weight-loss zone. It would be far easier to copy Dori than make fifty daily decisions in an attempt to lose weight on my own.

I didn't *need* to lose weight, but I didn't know that. All I knew was my body didn't match the ideal of the top professionals in the sport, the women I needed to become as quickly as possible to succeed at my job. When I googled the athlete bios of the fastest women in the world, mostly women from Kenya and Ethiopia, my height and weight were so dramatically different that I wondered if I was built for global success at all. But when I searched for the fastest woman in the world who looked like me, I found Paula Radcliffe. Paula was from the UK and was the only white person who was consistently competitive with the athletes from East Africa in recent years. Not only had she won world cross-country titles, she had also recently broken the world record in the marathon. I watched a video of her bravely leading the women's 10K on the track at the World Championships only to be outkicked for a medal in the final stretch. She didn't buy into the limiting beliefs I heard from a lot of white distance runners, that we couldn't be competitive on the world stage. Paula was from the same part of the world as my ancestors. She was five feet, eight inches tall, exactly like me. And her bio listed her weight as ten pounds below mine, which immediately became my goal race weight. It never dawned on me that the weight listed on athlete profiles could be inaccurate, or experienced once for a couple weeks, or recorded during a year that ended in injury. I didn't know that a woman's body could perform at a world-class level at a diverse weight range. I wish someone had told me, but I don't think anyone knew.

My weight dropped quickly on my senior-citizen diet. Vin noticed right away and commented that I looked fit—which felt like a drug to hear—but also said to be careful not to lose too much. I said I wasn't an idiot, and I wouldn't take it too far. But after I'd struggled to move the scale two pounds in college the year before, the ease with which the numbers fell now was intoxicating. I liked how it felt to move the little weight along the metal bar of the scale in the gym until the pointy end found level, the number getting a little lower each time. Strangers commented on my body in the coffee shop and the gym, many lacing their compliments with self-deprecation. "You're so thin! What do you do? You must be a runner. Tell me about your diet. I've been trying to lose this gut for years." There was a kind of cheap confidence acquired in these interactions, knowing my body's appearance communicated "fitness" and "expertise" simply by existing. I'd carry that with me to the locker room mirror before my workouts and pinch my lower abs, my obliques, my inner thighs, and marvel at the tightness of the little roll of skin where there used to be softness. The day that the scale settled at my goal weight, I felt I had left the younger me behind and was finally a professional. It took only six weeks.

At exactly the halfway point of my three-month Olympics-or-bust camp in Ohio, I hopped on a plane bound for Stanford for my first real test. The Payton Jordan Invitational had a stacked field of women looking to hit the Olympic standard of 15:08, and provided a pacesetter to pull us through even splits. I had one job: get the standard out of the way. Then, all that would be standing between the Olympics and me was finishing in the top three at the Olympic Trials.

"YOU LOOK THIN," Dena said when I showed up to our run date the day before the race.

I watched her eyes scan over my body and saw the worry plain on her face.

"You look on the edge."

I heard her words, but there was a louder voice inside me now. *It's working,* the voice said. *Don't listen to her. She doesn't understand what it takes.*

"I just got to my race weight," I said, picking up the pace to make conversation harder. "I won't lose any more, don't worry."

"I'm just saying be careful. It's a big change, and I don't think you need to be that lean."

She doesn't really want what's best for you. She's just jealous.

On the night of Payton Jordan, the track glowed under the lights, and the air was brisk and still: ideal 5K conditions. Teammates lined the backstretch of the track with their homemade percussion instruments made from empty Gatorade bottles, trash can lids, and other found objects. Every lap of the race, I would feel their rhythm in my stride and in my breath when I passed them. For ten of the twelve and a half laps I was right there with the top established Olympians. Someone made a move and I went to match it. My breathing wasn't labored, but my legs couldn't *go* for some reason, and three competitors ran away from me. My focus turned from competing for the win to securing the Olympic standard time. Some quick math at the bell told me I just needed to run one minute and twelve seconds for the last lap, a slight acceleration, but nowhere near the speed I usually finished, yet still I couldn't manage to do it. Even as the Stanford crew pitched their bodies over the fence, yelling their encouragement with a half lap remaining, I found myself stuck in one speed, missing the Olympic standard by one second.

On the cooldown jog, I heard Dena's words in my head and wondered, *Is it the weight? Did I lose my power?* No, my weight was right, I concluded. My body matched those of the best in the world. I just needed to go back to Ohio and do some speed work.

The next morning, I went to the thesis presentation event that concluded my master's program. Once passionate about my classes and determined to earn A's, I now stood beside my slapped-together-last-minute poster presentation feeling embarrassed. My classmates were spread about the room at their own stations, animatedly discussing their work with the professors drawn to their colorful pie charts and graphs. In the short time I'd been away, I had become a cliché: the jock doing the bare minimum to float through. Feeling shame rise up, I told myself it didn't matter. Nothing mattered more than making the team.

As soon as the clock on the wall reached the formal end of the event, I took my poster and walked out the door, stuffing it into the nearest trash can. On the way to my car I ran into my teammate Katherine, her eyebrows knit with concern.

"Did you hear about Jesse?" she asked.

"No, what happened?"

"He broke his neck in a bike accident yesterday. He's at Stanford Hospital getting emergency surgery."

"Who's with him?" I asked.

"His mom flew in. Give her a call; it's not good. You should go visit him."

Jesse lay supine in the hospital bed with a neck brace digging into the bottom of his chin. He turned his eyes as far as he could when he heard my voice, but he couldn't quite see me. I walked right up to the side of his bed and looked down at his face, all the Italian brown drained out of it. His blue eyes looked scared and sad. I learned about the Jefferson fracture: his C1 vertebra had broken into five pieces and had been put back together with hardware. I learned about the hangman's fracture, which occurs when the head is snapped violently forward, and how the surgeon fused his neck bones together. I heard his mom describe the way doctors had been passing through his room that morning, in disbelief that he wasn't paralyzed or worse. The recovery would be long. Prompted by the nurse, I pushed his IV tower alongside him as he took his first wobbly steps, cracking jokes to make him smile. When I said goodbye, I felt sick inside. I'd been telling myself he'd always be there, but I almost lost him. I thought life could wait, but what if it couldn't? It would have to.

On the flight back to Ohio, I felt shaken from the last twenty-four hours. Between the race, my academic embarrassment, and nearly losing Jesse, I wondered if these were indications I was losing my way. But the Olympics are full of stories of sacrifice, and I determined that my commitment was simply being tested. I ignored my hunger and called it discipline. I ignored my lost period and called it adaptation. I ignored my loneliness and called it independence.

A FEW DAYS back into training, on a run around the soy fields with Colin, I stopped to take a rock out of my shoe and couldn't find one. I put it back on, made it a couple of steps, and took it off again, examining more closely this time, sticking my hand inside to check the insole. There was nothing there. I finished the loop, limping by the end.

At the Cleveland Clinic, an orthopedist examined my foot and laid out the possibilities for what I was feeling, the worst of which would be a stress fracture. He ordered an MRI to rule it out, and I came in for a follow-up to get the results.

"Have you heard of the female athlete triad?" he asked, a little uncomfortably.

"Yes," I said. "It's when you have disordered eating, amenorrhea, and osteoporosis."

"When was your last period?"

"January." It was May.

"Are you normally regular?"

"No, I've had oligomenorrhea off and on. But I get about three or four per year."

"Okay, so no amenorrhea. How are you with food? Have you ever had an eating disorder?"

"No."

"History of stress fractures?"

"No. I've never been injured."

"Hmm, and no memory of specific trauma to your foot: falling, dropping something on it?"

"No, it just started feeling weird on a normal run."

The MRI showed increased blood flow in the area of my second metatarsal, a long bone on top of my foot. Not a stress fracture, but a "stress reaction." We caught it early, but it still required a boot and crutches for at least a month.

I managed to hold in my tears until I got to Vin's office and told him the news. He called the doctor and paced the room while asking questions, his soles squeaking on the linoleum during the long silence while listening to the doctor's replies. At last, he hung up.

"Here's the plan," he said with his hands on the desk, towering above me and willing me to make eye contact. "Hey," he said. "Lauren, listen to me." I cried harder. "This isn't the end of the world, I promise. And we still have time. Have you heard of Joan Benoit Samuelson?"

"Joanie," as she came to be known, was famous for winning the first-ever Olympic gold in the women's marathon, the one I'd watched from my mom's hip when I was nearly three. The image of her little white cap perched on her short hair, USA across her chest, waving to the fans in the Los Angeles stadium is an iconic Olympic moment of triumph recycled every four years during the broadcast.

"Did you know she injured her knee several weeks before the race and had to train in the pool?"

I didn't.

"Well she did. There's still time. Bones take four to six weeks to heal. If you do everything you can to heal on the short end of that, and cross-train diligently in the pool, there's a chance. It might be a long shot, but if you want to try, I'll write the training."

"But why did this happen?" I asked. "I did everything right."

"I don't know," he said. "The doctor didn't know, either. But this is the situation we're in; it's not the end of the world, and we're going to get through this."

The conclusion was that the injury was a fluke. I added my name to the long list of teammates who had similar flukes, injuries that fell short of the diagnostic framework of the female athlete triad. Many, if not most, of these could probably have been attributed to relative energy deficiency in sport, or RED-S. That "elite athlete lifestyle" of continual caloric restriction and control that was encouraged to keep our bodies lean shifted the hormone levels in our endocrine systems, impacting our bone health. During the small window of years through age twenty-six when women's endocrine systems are responsible for building the entire bone bank we spend the rest of our lives drawing from, so many of us are creating an environment where we're barely able to maintain what we have.

What likely happened to my foot was that the conditions of low energy availability from restricting my diet disrupted the hormones responsible for bone building. My bone density was still technically "normal" overall according to a DEXA scan, but according to a previous test from a few years earlier, it was trending downward at the time of life when it should have been doing the opposite, especially since running is an "impact" sport, which should further build high bone mineral density. Areas of higher stress that absorb more forces, like the bones of my foot, weren't able to fortify themselves the way they had in the past. This fluke, without the modern framework of RED-S to guide my coaching and medical team, left me to continue on a dangerous path. Instead of leaving empowered, I left confused, without a clear idea of what to do differently to avoid a similar fate. So I puzzled it out on my own, suspecting the culprit was my diet. I'm not sure if I met the criteria for a clinical eating disorder at that time, and I was never referred to anyone who could guide me, but I made the decision to turn down the dial on my restriction after that, taking a wild guess at what would be enough.

WHEN I WASN'T cross-training twice a day in the pool, mimicking running form in the deep end and executing intervals and sprints that left me gasping on the side of the pool, I was eating calcium chews and dairy with every meal. I approached the injury like an overachieving Stanford student, optimizing every facet of my life. I spent as much time as possible resting, visualizing tiny elves reconstructing my bone, sending positive vibes. Dori was impressed and horrified by my massive salads in a mixing bowl filled to the brim and the entire rainbow of colors I ate with dinner. "Vitamins!" I said. "Gotta give the body everything it needs to heal!" I was recovering harder than anyone had ever recovered—ever!

When it came time to test the foot on land, two weeks before the Olympic Trials, it felt even worse than before. Where my second metatarsal was, it felt like someone was slowly breaking a wooden pencil, the splintering shards rubbing on one another. "Phantom pain, perhaps," said Vin, my physical therapist, and my massage therapist. Nobody wants to face a hard truth when a big race is on the line. The truth kept bubbling up inside me, saying, "Your foot is broken, let go, it's time to rest." But I kept silencing it and returning to the noble work of believing in myself.

Then, one day, I couldn't do it. I crutched to the edge of the pool for a workout, sat down, and took off my boot as usual, but I simply couldn't get in. I sat there for twenty minutes watching swimmers doing flip turns, put my boot back on, crutched back out to the parking lot, and sat on a curb and cried. I wanted someone I could be small with; I wanted Jesse. I'd helped him walk; maybe he could help me.

"Why is this happening?" I asked, looking for somewhere to wipe my tears and snot and settling on the inside of my T-shirt. "I don't understand how I did it. This is the worst timing ever."

I always felt like an injury was the result of bad choices. I judged people who got injured. Had I made bad choices? I didn't know. I thought I was making good choices. I was doing what I thought a professional was supposed to do to reach the standard of success set for my sport.

"Sometimes bad things just happen, Lauren," Jesse said. "Even when you're a good person. Even when you try to do all the right things."

I didn't want that to be true.

In the Sacramento State stadium where the Olympic Trials were held, I watched the women's 5K race from the very top row of the metal bleachers, leaning on the pads of my crutches. It had taken a lot of courage just to show up, and waiting for the gun to go off, I felt like my intestines were twisting together. During the first two miles, my muscles twitched as the runners passed. I was supposed to be down there with them. When the leader made her move, I watched the women behind her turning themselves inside out to hold on. Dreams came true and dreams shattered before my eyes. Only three made the team, but so many more deserved it.

Maybe I would have made it, maybe not. Until recently, I had convinced myself that I was exceptional, that I possessed unusual physical talent and judgment and intuition that made me bullet-proof. I didn't want to believe I was vulnerable like everyone else. Trapped in perfectionism and my own echo chamber, I had blown it. I thought I needed to get light when I really needed to get strong. I thought I could go it alone, but I needed friendship in my life, teammates, maybe even love.

9

THE BATTLE WITHIN

S ee this crack here?" said Dr. Fredericson as he traced his finger along a clear line on the X-ray that ran diagonally through my second metatarsal. "This is why your foot still hurts. It's broken clean through."

"I don't understand," I said. I was back in Palo Alto, and it had been six weeks since my initial diagnosis in Ohio. The first four of those weeks I had done everything the doctor told me, never once letting my foot touch the ground. The fracture had been so small at first that an X-ray couldn't even detect it; only an MRI could. Now here it was, a fault line.

"How much did you run on it?" he asked.

"Nothing for four weeks, only pool running, like my doctor said. And the last two weeks before the Trials, I barely ran at all. Maybe six short runs total."

"That is strange," he said, looking at the X-ray. "Maybe your body needs a break. Can you take some time off?"

After pushing so hard for so long, it felt unnatural to stop, but I did. Stillness forced me to process my botched first year as a pro, since I couldn't use cross-training my brains out as a lifeline or delusion anymore. Being with my family helped. That unkind voice inside me was hushed by the familiar sounds and rhythms of home. My foot took twelve weeks to heal in the end, twice as long as it should have.

I noticed how much better I felt when I gained weight and stopped cross-training. I felt strong in my body, my immune system was more robust, and my inner voice was gentler. I wondered if cross-training to maintain my fitness and weight had slowed my healing, but rigorous cross-training was the norm for competitive runners; new ways of not resting were being invented all the time. My intuition at the time was correct. It would take ten more years, but a consensus paper published by the IOC (International Olympic Committee) in 2014 to update the 2005 statement on the female athlete triad would introduce the world to RED-S, which is defined as "impaired physiological functioning caused by relative energy deficiency" and includes, but is not limited to, impairments of metabolic rate, menstrual function, bone health, immunity, protein synthesis, and cardiovascular health. The underlying cause of RED-S is low energy availability; in other words, the gas isn't in the tank when you need it. This deficit could be the result of consistent diet restriction, but it could also arise more innocently: poor meal timing that prolongs the state of post-workout depletion in order to adhere to standard cultural meal times, increasing training loads without increasing energy intake, underestimation of the energy demands of cross-training, or limitation of nutrition out of a fear of gaining weight while injured. I likely developed RED-S with a mixture of all of the above. Restrictive eating habits and cross-training for weight management were—and still are—conflated with discipline. But they've also shown themselves to be killers of careers.

The comeback was tough. In the fall, after building basic fitness with DeLong and the varsity boys, I returned to Stanford to do a training block with the team. I was supposed to be the professional in the group, and yet I couldn't keep up on a basic set of 1K repeats. As the top women began to pull away, their shoulder blades sharply visible on their toned backs, my attention was drawn to my thighs rubbing, my ill-defined abs, my squishy sides pinched by the elastic of my shorts. These college women looked more professional than I did. I was angry at myself for letting my body change this much and overwhelmed by how long it would take to get back to where I was. Finding it hard to breathe, I stopped mid-interval, and tears came out despite my efforts to keep them in. Dena found me, and I told her what was going on.

"Look, so you gained some weight. You were injured. That's normal. It's okay! You needed to! You're healthy, and that's what matters. You don't need to be in peak form right now. You can't be that way year-round. It's just not necessary."

"It was so hard to lose it. I don't want to go through that again."

In truth, it had been easy, but I would never do it that way—would never go to those extremes—again. *Dropping weight quickly is what got me injured*, I thought. I'd have to lose it slower, more sustainably, which I presumed was healthier. To me that meant "watching it." Restriction. Living with the feeling of hunger. Diligent (but not obsessive!) monitoring of my body. I wanted to be free from all that. *But that kind of food freedom is reserved for those who are the "right weight" more naturally,* I thought. I still felt like there was some magic number I needed to reach, a perfect race weight where I'd race fast and stay healthy, if only I could figure out what it was.

After the training block with Stanford, I moved to the next training camp in Boulder. And the next in Albuquerque. Each one was with different people I'd met through racing. My VW pop-top camper van gave me a home on wheels, and a place to crash on the long drives. With no stable residence of my own, I forwarded all mail to my parents' house. This instability wouldn't work for most people, but I thrived. I loved the independence my van offered me, and the way I could build community everywhere I went.

The running community is generous and hospitable, happy to share their hard-earned local intel. All you have to do is say you're coming to town, and you'll more than likely get a list of favorite local trails, coffee shops, a reference for a massage therapist, and an enthusiastic invitation to a Sunday long run. Pro athletes are often spread out, lonely, and eager for company on hard sessions, and since Vin believed deeply in the power of putting talent with talent, he helped me adapt my training plan to utilize training partners. Workouts were so much more fun with another woman or two, striking that balance between collaboration and competitiveness to help redefine my limits. Most of what these people did for training was minor variations on the same themes: tempo runs, speed work, hills, long runs, gym. Different athletes had different strengths and weaknesses in different kinds of workouts, but all of us ended up racing within a few seconds of one another. It removed the pressure to be perfect at everything. And it helped me see that nobody had a magic formula for success that Vin and I didn't have.

Nearly all of the professional female athletes I trained with had stories to share about disordered eating and injuries on their college teams. The stories were heartbreaking, and there was a shared feeling of helplessness. Looking back on the places we came from, thin, sick girls continued to lower records, win Foot Locker, succeed at NCAAs for a season or two, and then disappear. All of us had somehow gotten through that gauntlet, but we carried the insecurities with us. Most of us talked about our bodies a lot; most of us had a lighter weight we strived for. Orthorexia (an eating disorder characterized by rigidity around eating only foods deemed clean and healthy, with no flexibility) was common, though I didn't know it had a name at the time. Fortunately, there were enough fast women still willing to have a cookie to keep me on the good side of the line. The more I heard the same stories about high school and college running, the more convinced I became that something needed to be done to free young girls of the pressures that lead to so much harm. How could something be this ubiquitous and still have no counterattack? In my alone time, I filled notebooks with ideas for talks I could give at schools, or ad campaigns Nike could do that would help change the culture. And then I'd train with my sights set on becoming a national champion so I could have a platform to do it.

I busted back onto the scene by qualifying for the World Cross Country Championships in France, where I finished eleventh, leading the USA team to a bronze medal. In the USATF Outdoor Championships in 2005, I finished second behind Shalane Flanagan and qualified for the World Championships in Helsinki. In the Nike hospitality suite, I picked up my swag and was relieved to find myself back in the good graces of Cap and the Nike marketing team, who took time to joke around with me. They told me how fit I looked and praised my season. All felt right in the world.

In preparation for the World Championships, I traveled overseas for the European racing circuit and ran on some of the biggest stages, lowering my 5K time to 15:02 in Rome. The best part of racing the European circuit, and the best part of my job, was getting to know the other athletes. I began recognizing people moving hotel to hotel, and in a sea of international strangers and rotating languages, any familiar face became a friend. I formed bonds while lining up at the meal buffets, taking the bus to and from the track, and of course partying after the meets. I had been mostly isolated for ten months a year, feeling invisible to the larger sports culture, and reminding myself that what I did for a living was real. Now, suddenly, I was surrounded by people just like me, and we were moving together like a traveling circus, being treated like actual professional athletes, competing in full stadiums, being asked for our autographs, and having our races broadcast on international TV.

Racing professionally was an amazing career, I decided. Thanks to health and community, I felt like I'd connected with myself again. The only time I felt something missing was after a race, at the usual after-party for the participants. I envied the ease with which people took pleasure around me, whether it was in letting loose at the bars, finding someone to get tangled up with for the night, or gushing to a romantic partner back home from the floor of a phone booth. Week after week I watched my peers debunk the myth I'd created that love and sex were incompatible with success.

One night, a gorgeous steeplechaser I'd been attracted to all summer started giving me attention in the bar, but when he went to the bathroom, I slipped out into the cold London air and walked back to my hotel alone. Rolling over to the empty side of my bed the next morning, I thought about Jesse for the hundredth time that summer. I was accomplishing my goals alone, but I wanted to be capable of love, too. It had been a year since we'd last spoken. He had a girlfriend, he'd told me. I wondered if he still did, wondered if he still thought about me, wondered if we had grown up enough yet, if we were ready for one another. I suspected we weren't. I needed him out of my mind so I could love someone else, so I could loosen up and join the summer party all around me.

I wandered down to an internet cafe in London and I sent him an email with the subject "you are ruining my life." The body of the message simply said "grrrr." His reply came within minutes: "I miss you too."

AS THE SUMMER came to an end, the traveling circus thinned down to those who had qualified for Worlds, and I connected myself to a training group from Australia I'd gotten to know. I loved the athletes in the group, but their team culture around food and weight was unsettling. Comments about fellow competitors' bodies, regardless of sex, were sharp and frequent. Bluntness around food restriction made me question my own plate.

Old habits of body-checking resumed: lifting my shirt up to see my abs in the mirror, glancing at my profile in store windows, and pinching the softer areas to determine if all was as it should be. On a bumpy bus ride back from a track session with the team in Helsinki, the last workout before Worlds, I remember looking at their star female athlete's bare abs as she sat. While I could feel my belly jiggling every time the bus bumped, hers remained taut. I sought out a scale as soon as I got to the athlete village in Helsinki, and the number made my heart race. Images of croissants I had enjoyed were now linked to shame.

It was only two pounds, and it could have just been the time of day or time of month, but that level of obsession is the danger of the concept of "ideal race weight," of hanging your confidence on appearance instead of function. All other signs from the summer pointed to me being in the best shape of my life, and I was. But by the time I got to the start line, I saw myself as someone who had fucked it all up. Vin had flown out for the race and he dismissed my weight concerns, saying all the right things to boost my confidence. But the internal chatter was too loud. In that critical moment about two-thirds of the way through the race when you're hurting more than you've ever hurt before, your job is simple: You say yes. You don't worry if you can maintain it. You say yes and extend the game a little longer, and a little longer, giving yourself a shot. At that critical moment with a mile to go, my confidence was preoccupied with a heated debate as to whether I belonged there at all. It sucked all the power out of my legs, leaving me shuffling along toward a distant last.

I was disappointed in myself before I even made it to the finish line. As I changed out of my spikes, Vin stood over me speculating what went wrong, blaming his training plan that peaked me too soon, or international travel preventing consistent quality gym work. But I knew what it was. I knew, but I didn't tell him because I was ashamed. All that hard work so easily neutralized by lack of body confidence. What a waste. I vowed to never let it happen again.

Ethiopia swept the top four places in the final, only the second nation in history to accomplish that feat. Meanwhile, none of the American women made it out of the rounds. Talk of the need for formalized American middle-distance training groups was everywhere now, and Mary Wittenberg, the CEO of New York Road Runners, committed funding to champion the concept. When I heard a group was starting in Mammoth Lakes, my favorite place on Earth, I knew I had to give it a try.

SOMEWHERE EAST OF San Francisco, from the captain's chair of my VW camper van while driving toward my new home, I dialed Jesse's number.

"Hello?" Jesse said.

"Hey."

"Hey."

There was a long pause, a farm of windmills slowly spinning on the horizon out my window.

"I still love you," I said.

"I still love you, too."

We laughed.

"Coffee? I can be in San Francisco in a couple of hours."

"Yes please."

I turned the van around.

Like two boxers coming together after far too many rounds, we flopped into cushy seats at a high-ceilinged cafe near his apartment in the Mission. His neck was fused, and he had to turn his whole body in the chair to see me. I felt flooded by the memory of almost losing him. As we filled each other in on our lives, the buzz of our connection was unmistakably there below the conversation. He was working on a fuel cell startup and had picked up a couple patents, a dream of his. I told him about the new training group, a dream of mine, and the chance to train alongside veterans Jen Rhines and Deena Kastor, thirty-year-olds in their prime.

Eventually we ran out of avoidance strategies.

"So . . . are you seeing anyone?" I finally got up the courage to ask.

"No, not anymore. I compare everyone to you," he said.

"Yeah, it sucks, doesn't it?"

He laughed. "What about you? Anyone in your life?"

"Nope, same deal. You keep ruining it."

"Well, glad I can return the favor." He smiled, and we paused a moment.

"We should probably stop fighting it and just get back together," I suggested with a fake sigh.

"Yeah, I mean, why fight the inevitable?"

We were feigning resignation on our faces, but we broke into laughter. We were both elated. We'd found one another again.

Jesse was the best part of that year. We had grown out of a lot of our bullshit. He wasn't acting distant in the face of my drive, or resentful of my success. He had an identity at work that gave him confidence outside of sport. He was showing up in real ways to help me. And humbled by the injuries and losses I'd experienced while we were apart, I was a more empathetic partner. I allowed myself to soften around him. We were both living extreme lives in different industries, but we had confidence in ourselves and in one another. At twenty-four, there was no rush to force our day-to-day lives onto the same path, but we visited one another any chance we could and fell in love all over again.

The training group turned out to be a bust for me, and I wasn't alone. While the two veteran stars thrived, almost all of the younger athletes in the group sustained injuries or experienced declines in performance. Many of us ended up leaving. With the benefit of years of reflection, coaching experience, and emerging new research on female athletes, I'm confident that RED-S played a big role. The training schedule, designed to make American women competitive with the Ethiopians, was relentless and built around the older athletes in the squad. There was rarely a day that was truly restorative, and nearly every day required multiple training sessions. Not being able to meet the goal of the workout was a regular occurrence, and we were encouraged to soldier on undisturbed, like Jen and Deena did.

The young athletes on the team struggled with RED-S symptoms more than the older ones, and we were far more likely to have menstrual dysfunction. This could be because Jen and Deena met their nutritional demands better; they seemed to have healthy relationships with food. But it could simply be attributed to age itself. Though this topic is underresearched, one study showed that a controlled decrease of energy availability for just *five days* was enough to decrease the sex hormone responses of all adolescent females (aged approximately 20.5 years) but did not impact the older female athletes (aged about 28.7). Those first fourteen years or so of menstruation are the most sensitive. This matches the trend I noticed throughout my career: Older athletes were more likely to have a more robust menstrual cycle even during times when they were restricting their diets. Sports performance physiologist and RED-S researcher Dr. Trent Stellingwerff has also noticed this trend, which suggests that RED-S manifests differently not only among individuals, but also potentially within the same individual depending on their stage of life.

A similar principle applies to weight management, for reasons largely related to endocrine activity. Every single female athlete I have ever talked to has said that by her late twenties, her body naturally leaned out. Making small changes to their bodies—losing or gaining a couple of pounds at different times of the year—was easier. In my early twenties, losing a couple of pounds felt almost impossible. If I didn't feel noticeably hungry all the time, I wasn't losing weight. This was a running joke among the women's team at Stanford, who marveled at the stubbornness of the scale even while continually depriving ourselves. But in my late twenties and thirties, just cutting out beer for a couple of weeks, or getting busy and forgetting to fuel properly every now and then, changed my body. My body now responds more like what I've seen in men all my life.

THE TEAM IN Mammoth broke down in different ways. One teammate stopped being able to do anything besides easy runs; if she attempted any kind of higher heart rate work, she would feel the sensation of being stuck in mud. Another runner's race times got slower and slower, with no obvious explanation. One found herself feeling flat in the late stages of races, unable to access her finishing speed. Others, like me, broke bones. Sometimes bones just break when you're training hard, but stress fractures are four to five times more likely in athletes suffering from RED-S.

For my part, I sustained a stress fracture in the same foot, but in a different bone. The coach did everything he could to get me access to an underwater treadmill so I could maintain as much fitness as possible. Losing faith in my ability to remain healthy in the new program, I stayed behind when the team packed up to train elsewhere for the spring, and Dena agreed to oversee my return to health. The bone took several weeks longer than expected to heal, again from too much aggressive cross-training and not enough rest. It wasn't until I took time off completely and gained some weight that it healed. It wasn't the weight itself that made me more healthy—you can be healthy or unhealthy at a wide variety of weights—it was moving from low energy availability into energy balance, which rebooted my menstrual cycle and allowed for normal bone growth. With only a couple of months left to prepare for the USATF Outdoor Championships, I felt behind. But Dena encouraged me to embrace where I was. Within a matter of weeks, I was not only making progress, I was also enjoying running again.

Later, when I would become a coach myself, I would fully appreciate the one-on-one time she spent with me running along the Baylands that form the water's edge of Silicon Valley's epicenter in Mountain View, California, or after-hours at the Stanford track. With two kids and a career to manage, Dena didn't need another job. I insisted on paying her. This formalization of our relationship, plus her increased confidence that came with experience she gained coaching at Stanford while I was away, made her someone I trusted with my life.

It was different working with a woman. Or at least this woman. There was space for all emotions and feelings with Dena, and we were training in a way that wasn't putting me back in RED-S territory. She maintained this bubble of belief that I could overcome and succeed all the way up to the morning of the USATF Outdoor Championships. But then when it came time to warm up for the race, surrounded by all my competitors who hadn't missed any training time, their lean bodies floating along while my feet stuck to the ground like wet garbage, I had a meltdown.

"I think I should withdraw," I told her with tears in my eyes. "I missed half the season injured, and I'm not ready." I was afraid of going out there underprepared and getting beat by half the field after making Worlds the year before. And, aware that my place of work was also a pageant where commentary on the female body was its own sport, I was afraid of being out there in my race kit looking less fit than usual. That's the thing about track: You cannot hide. Your reality will be revealed to everyone. I thought it was better to not race than to be seen failing.

"You don't know what you can do," Dena said. "You don't know yet."

I looked to her, hopeful, and made myself take a deep breath before spilling my insecurities out at her feet. I told her I felt fat. I told her I didn't want to be thinking about that, because I knew those kind of thoughts would ruin my race.

She listened, and I found that allowing her to be a witness to my worries defused them, whereas trying not to think about them had made them louder. "Forget everyone else," she said. "Do this for *you*. You know who you are. Let's keep it simple and figure out how to create the environment for *your* best race. That's all we need to do."

We decided on a plan: I would start in the back of the pack, move up gradually, stay open to feeling good, commit to a best effort no matter what, and just see what happened.

I soaked in the field by lying on the track. I felt myself screwing down into the earth below, and when it slowed to a stop, I opened my eyes. I stepped to the line at peace. My best turned out to be not only way better than I'd expected, but the best I'd ever been. I battled for the win with Kara Goucher, who was soon to become a two-time Olympian, down the final straightaway, my eyes wide with wild desire to get to the line first. And when I broke the tape across my chest, I felt like I radiated energy far beyond my physical self, in awe of what my body just did. And then I softened in surrender to the lack of oxygen, falling onto my knees as the tidal wave of bodily discomfort finally overtook the adrenaline. I was finally a United States national champion. Winning had never felt so hard-earned, and the pleasure buzz lasted all summer.

WINNING EARNED ME a trip to Athens for the World Cup, where I finished fifth. My family got to watch me. Taking them on vacation was a dream realized, and we spent a week being tourists afterward: pebbly beaches, crumbly ruins, real Greek salad, broken plates, ouzo, the whole thing. For once, I could take care of them.

My contract was up for renegotiation, and with the good work of my agent, a bidding war between Nike and Reebok resulted in my getting a six-year deal from Nike for $125,000 per year. The reduction clauses were huge, and I had to make the 2008 Olympics to keep my salary, but the fear of holding on to it was nothing compared to the sound of my dad's voice booming in excitement through the phone at the news. "Well, look at you, you rich bitch!" He began speaking in a "rich lady voice," which sounded exactly like his Julia Child impression, and we both carried on about beef bourguignon for a while, cracking ourselves up.

Everything was coming together. Jesse and I got engaged over Christmas. Then Vin called me up out of the blue. One of our favorite ways of connecting when I was in Oberlin was sharing dreams for the reinvigoration of the sport we loved. He told me that he had taken a job at the University of Oregon and had a vision for reviving TrackTown, USA, in the post-Prefontaine era, and he wanted me to be a part of it. There was a budding pro team I could race for called Oregon Track Club Elite. If I moved to Eugene, in two years I'd be racing the 2008 Olympic Trials right there at Hayward Field, on the same track where I practiced every day. I could fight for a spot on the Olympic team at my presumed athletic prime in front of a hometown crowd. I could see it playing out perfectly, like a sports movie.

In December of that year, Nike brought the top distance runners on their payroll onto their campus for a special appearance: the Nike Cross Nationals. It was to have the prestige of Foot Locker Nationals, but it was built entirely around celebrating the best high school teams instead of individuals, since cross-country is a team sport. The concept was incredible, the brainchild of some marketing guys I really liked, including Josh Rowe and John Truax. Similar to Foot Locker, there would be pro athletes on-site to act as team captains and provide advice. I'd just returned from doing this at Foot Locker and found that I loved the role of mentoring young runners. There were still so many girls who were sick or on the verge of it, and I felt like I had made at least a little bit of a difference for the ones I worked with. Now I was back at it on Nike's campus, high-fiving kids in my head-to-toe Nike street style the marketing team kitted me out with, sitting down with teams over meals, being invited as a guest to team meetings. The kids got heaps of swag, customized shoes, and access to endless teen-friendly activities. Vin was right: When Nike decided to put their money behind something, they could do it better than anyone.

Before leaving the Nike campus, I made sure to schedule time with the marketing team to talk about my ideas for changing the culture of eating disorders and promoting health for female runners. This time I thought they would take me seriously. I was a four-time World Championships team member, a bronze team medalist in cross-country, and the reigning 5,000-meter national champion.

My passion had only intensified in the three years since I'd first pitched them. At both high school national events I went to, the problems were as bad as ever, if not worse, and I had now experienced some of the scary forces at play myself. Campaigns empowering female athlete health were good for the sport, and good for business. Nike could make caring about your health cool. They could call out the damage of the thin ideal that robbed so many female athletes of the full measure of benefits that sports can offer. Nike's famous "If You Let Me Play . . ." campaign with young girls advocating for themselves could be redone with "If you let me develop . . ." There could be a "Just Don't Do It" for sacrificing your health in the name of short-term success. A version of "This is your brain on drugs" for eating disorders. Millions of women were runners, and the sport just kept growing; this would get their attention for the right reasons, and they'd think of Nike as the brand that cared about women and girls. I looked for enthusiasm reflected back at me from the room and saw none.

"If you have something to say and want people to listen, your best bet is to focus on making that Olympic team and bringing home a medal," one of them said. As good as I believed I could be, I knew the odds of getting a medal were slim, and even *if* I got one, it would be years from now. How many girls would it be too late for? I didn't understand why they didn't get the urgency, or see the bigger picture, or want to. I was burning, but I tried to keep a neutral face. This was the same guy I'd heard criticize the body of a "big" female runner while watching a race beside him, even though she'd won. He was part of the problem.

I considered the power they had over my career and finances and was afraid to challenge them. Instead, I said simply, "Well, keep me in mind if anything changes. Female runners could really use role models right now."

10

OBJECTIFY ME

Back at the apartment Jesse and I rented in Eugene, the Nike women's catalogue arrived in the mail and I brought it inside. In 2007, Nike poured significant resources into a marketing catalogue exclusively for women. This felt like a crucial turning point because it meant the market share of women buying activewear now must be significant—big enough to matter to a brand like Nike. With men dominating the sports industry and women depending on big brands to endorse women's sports for them to survive, this kind of investment elevated women's sports as a whole.

But as I walked through our apartment flipping through the catalogue, I stopped moving when I couldn't find any professional athletes in it. No Sanya Richards, the brilliant Jamaican American sprinter and recent Olympic medalist; no Suzy Favor Hamilton, the most recent face of American women's track. There were, however, lots of thin models with perky breasts; I was holding, more or less, a sporty Victoria's Secret catalogue. I turned to a page I found particularly offensive and held it up to Jesse, enraged.

"This catalogue is for athletic wear and it's full of this!"

He came over and looked. A gorgeous woman posed on a spin bike, stick-thin arms shaved smooth and perfectly tan—arms that had likely never lifted a dumbbell—gently propped on the handlebars, a perfect little wisp of hair out of place and some fake sweat on her brow.

"She looks hot," he said jokingly, pretending to grab it away from me.

I swatted him with the pages. "She looks like she wants to fuck the photographer."

I felt tied in knots all afternoon and into the evening. Of course, I knew the world sexualized women to sell things. I'd grown up seeing it in fashion magazines and billboards and TV ads. Western beauty standards were part of why I got paid, and why many other people were overlooked. If you were fast, cute, and white or lighter-skinned, you got paid. If you were just fast, maybe you got paid—but you'd better be *really* fast. Nike had an entire roster full of champion athletes, and a lot of them were attractive. But muscled or sturdier-appearing bodies weren't attractive enough to be fully celebrated in the women's catalogue for the brand that paid us.

That's what I stewed about until the middle of the night, keeping Jesse awake with my tossing and turning and muttering. "Okay," Jesse finally said. "You need to do something about this, or you'll never sleep. And neither will I."

"What can I do? The sports marketing people don't care. Nobody gives a shit."

"Didn't you just meet the CEO? You said he was friendly."

I'd met Mark Parker recently on Nike's campus, at the cross-country nationals event where I'd mentored the country's most promising young runners. When I approached him to introduce myself, I was surprised to learn that he knew who I was; his wife, Kathy Mills Parker, had been an elite runner, briefly holding the world record in the 5,000 meters in 1978.

"Why don't you email him and ask to talk to him about it?"

I laughed. "Sure, I'll just email the CEO."

Jesse pushed at my shoulder. "Why not?"

A few minutes later, I took an educated guess at his email address and fired off a message. Around 3 a.m., my impassioned email now on its way to Mark, I got into bed and stared at a spot on the ceiling while my nervous system settled down. I was proud of myself for doing something, for saying something. It released a knot inside me. I finally fell asleep. The next day I got a reply to schedule an in-person, one-on-one meeting with the CEO of Nike.

MARK PARKER'S OFFICE was perched up high, with walls of windows overlooking the beautiful landscaping of Nike's enormous campus. We made small talk as we settled in to the time together, and he showed me some sketches of what Hayward Field would look like when it was remodeled for the upcoming Olympic Trials. It was a thrill to be in the room where decisions and plans for the cutting edge of my sport were being made. And as much as I wanted to excel on the track—increasingly, it felt like, even more than that—I wanted to contribute to those conversations.

"Your email was very powerful," he said as we sat down. He

spoke for a while about the history of Nike and its ties to athlete input and activism. "We care what our athletes think. I want to hear what you have to say."

I told him that I reached out because when I met him, I got the impression he really cared about the sport, and that since he was married to a female athlete, I thought he might understand what I was talking about better than others had. At Nike, I'd noticed, the company's female athletes weren't seen as suitable enough to model the women's clothes. Nike was withholding marketing until someone came along who fit an existing ideal, like Maria Sharapova or Gabby Reece. Someone hot enough for *Playboy*. The standards of Western beauty for women at the time were noodle limbs and cleavage and thigh gaps, and it was frustrating to see that damage perpetuated in sports through the women's catalogue. When someone opens a catalogue, she's often aspiring to be what she sees inside, even if subconsciously. *What are you telling people to aspire to with your casting?* I wanted to know. I told him about the eating disorder culture pervasive in running, which he was familiar with, and how strongly I felt about combatting it. I told him that Nike's marketing was exacerbating the problem.

Track and field, I explained, is a sport primed for combatting bias: It offers an event for every body type and racial and economic diversity, and every spectator who buys a ticket ends up watching both men and women use their bodies in powerful ways. You go to a sporting event to see what power looks like, and seeing women there expands your definition of both power and women. You go to a magazine to see beautiful people and things, and if Nike used their professional female athletes in their catalogue, it would expand the narrow definition of beauty. Seeing such examples would make women and girls more likely to embrace their strength.

"Do you think athletes would want to do this?" he asked.

"Yeah, for sure. You've got to have at least a hundred athletes already on payroll sitting on a shelf, and all of them have mandatory appearances in their contracts they need to fulfill."

"I'm going to think about this," he said, standing and dusting the wrinkles off his pants. I stood to leave.

"I'm sorry if my email seemed angry. It's just so frustrating to see this problem getting worse, and I can't seem to get running marketing to care. They say you need to have an Olympic medal for anyone to listen."

"Do you agree?" he asked.

"No."

He put his hands in his pockets and looked at me. His eyelashes were so long I wondered if he was wearing mascara. "I'm not sure I do either," he finally said. "I think this is a larger conversation than running. I've got a few people I want to talk to about it."

I wondered over the years why Mark made time for me. It could have been my connection to Vin, who had influence there, or my race and event discipline. But there were also real business reasons to pay attention to my message. While women were outspending men for the first time in history in the category of sports apparel, they made up less than 20 percent of Nike's sales. In 2002, Nike created a sub-brand, Nike Goddess, to address this hole in its business. In a *Fast Company* article covering the brand move in 2002, Mark Parker said, "Nike Goddess is the manifestation of us getting our act together."

A flagship Nike Goddess store was opened specifically for

women and rather than have a woman design it, they sent their best guy out to do research on what women wanted. "Women weren't comfortable in our stores," John Hoke, the renowned designer behind the store concept, explained. "So I figured out where they would be comfortable—most likely in their own homes. The [women's] store has more of a residential feel."

The stores have since evolved and consolidated, and despite far better ideas in recent years, Nike's efforts to market to women have often been overshadowed by news of the company's poor treatment of actual women; in the twenty years since the founding of Nike Goddess, the women's apparel category accounts for only a few additional percentage points of their total business.

Within a couple weeks, I was on a flight to Kauai to shoot the next Nike women's catalogue with pro track athletes Kara Goucher and Sanya Richards. We stayed in the Princeville Resort, and after I threw my bag down in the hotel room, I browsed the colorful welcome materials on the desk and saw that the basic rooms were priced at seven hundred dollars per night. I hadn't even known such places existed. We worked with famous photographers and makeup artists, men who sprayed us with fake sweat and tucked away our loose hairs and directed our faces toward light bounced off silver disks. We ran back and forth along private dirt roads in the mountains. We learned how to time our steps to float airborne at the right moment, our faces relaxed, our lips parted, our gazes directed off into the distance.

The photos appeared not only in the Nike catalogue, but also on advertisements in store windows. They sent the message that athleticism could be beautiful. I felt proud to have played a role in a change like that at the time. But we weren't thinking big enough.

We were expanding what beauty could include, barely, but we were still centering the male gaze. It would be best if women weren't socialized to think of their bodies as things to be looked at at all, but I wouldn't reach that level of understanding until later.

I GOT A CALL in the spring of 2007. It was Josh Rowe, the new number two in Nike sports marketing.

"I've got some good news!" he said.

"I love good news!"

I also loved Josh. Before his recent promotion to becoming Cap's Mr. Smee, he'd worked on marketing to high schoolers, and I was always eager to help with his events. He was part of the visionary group that created the high school nationals event that competed with Foot Locker.

Josh had great ideas. We were both hardworking dreamers who were desperate to use our time and skills to help build the sport we loved and felt was undervalued. But his impact had been mostly limited to youth events. His promotion gave me hope for my sport.

"Nike has been working on the first true women's-specific running shoe," he told me.

At first, I was a little hesitant to believe that men's and women's feet were that different. Men's shoes had worked fine for me. But I remembered how many sex-based differences had come up in my anatomy, physiology, archaeology, and osteology classes and asked for more details. "The Kitchen," a laboratory on Nike's campus where shoes were developed, was full of leaders in innovation.

"Running shoes are made on a last, which is a mold that shoes are built around," Josh explained. "That last that running shoes are made on is designed around the male foot, so women's shoes are really just men's shoes in different colors. 'Shrink it and pink it' is the industry joke. But these are the first shoes designed around modern biomechanical research on the female body and built on a women's last."

"So, do you want me to test it?" I asked.

"No, it's been tested. It's ready to go. You don't understand. I put your name forward to Nike Brand and they want you to be the face of the campaign."

"For the shoe?"

"Ads, poster, a commercial, the whole thing. They want you. It's an incredible opportunity. Expect an email soon with the details, okay?"

My first call was to my dad, and he reacted like I knew he would. Fuck yeahs. Buttons busting. Unbridled joy. Affirmation that I would do a great job with the campaign.

"I'll do my best," I said, pacing the kitchen of my apartment.

I hung up and stood in the kitchen in silence. For the first time, I asked myself why I still felt such urgency to call my dad when I accomplished something. Jesse and I were set to be married in six months, after the track season ended, and I was an adult with a six-figure income. I hadn't needed anything material from my parents in years.

Dad was a great hype man, yes, but it wasn't just that. When I heard pride in his voice, I felt like I was giving him what he couldn't give himself. I wanted him to see that *we* had it in us, the Fleshmans. He had it in him, too. He was good enough, even if he didn't have the same opportunities I had. I carried this childish idea that my success could somehow save him. If he could see my victories as extensions of himself, maybe he'd see he didn't need to beat himself up, to slowly kill himself with alcohol.

WHEN THE EMAIL ARRIVED from Nike Brand, I was on the couch eating an apple, killing time between workouts. A creative brief described the campaign, the asks, the timeline, and an example of the look and feel.

"NIKE OBJECTIFIES WOMEN," the title read in big, bold black type on a white background, impossible to ignore. It made my hair stand up on my neck, as intended. Below that was copy explaining what they really meant. Nike carefully studies women, with the purpose of creating a shoe for women's anatomy and biomechanics. It went on to explain the research and the specific features of the shoe. It was a thrilling moment that would make readers appreciate that the new dawn for women's running was upon us; Nike had come to the rescue, finally seeing women as worthy of a highly technical shoe of their own.

But when I looked at the next piece of the campaign, my jaw clenched. An attached image was an example of the look and feel of what they had in mind for the photo shoot: a recent ad that featured the soccer player Brandi Chastain naked, bent over a soccer ball. It was tastefully done in black and white, from the side view, with all nipples and cracks obscured.

Brandi Chastain was an absolute icon in women's sports. Why was I bristling at this? I asked myself. To be used in a comparable way in advertising should excite me. But why did she have to be naked? Why did *I* have to be naked?

I went for a run to process what I was feeling. Was I afraid to be naked? No, that wasn't it. It would be a little scary, for sure, but I could do it. But *why* do it? Why was appearing naked—or in lingerie, or in a swimsuit issue—the ultimate sign that you had made it as a female athlete?

As I ran along the woodchips of Pre's trails, memories came back from my Sports in Society class at Stanford. I remembered learning how female athletes were treated differently in media—that they were more likely to not only have their physical appearance commented on, but also be addressed by their first names, be more harshly judged for displays of aggression and competitiveness, and be asked questions about their dating lives. Women's uniforms were designed to show more of their shape and skin to be sexually pleasing. They were expected to smile, assure audiences of their uncompromised femininity.

I'd known all this and disliked it, but I'd accepted it as a temporary necessary evil. The people with power and money to make my sport popular (or not) were men; the people who watched sports were men. Men were basic little Neanderthals who only thought about sex, according to pop culture, so you did what you needed to do to get them to care. Being a feminist was counterproductive to me. Men didn't like feminists. Being sexy was something I struggled to portray on my own—deep down, I was a tomboy, and I felt most comfortable being playful and creative. But Nike could do the work for me, I decided. I'd do the campaign, more people would know who I was and like me, and then I could use that fame to change things in a bigger way, later.

But as I ran farther and pondered this ostensibly incredible opportunity in front of me, I felt the discontent stirring and getting louder. I tried picking up the pace to return to my body. Seeing the Willamette River appear to my right from behind the trees, I felt drawn to it. I pulled off the wide trail onto a rough offshoot path through waist-deep foliage until it ended, and sat on a rock on the water's edge, alone. The river swirled around a rock a few feet in front of me, and I stared at it for a while.

I wanted to be recognized in an ad—I was a performer with an ego, after all. But I also wanted to be a role model to younger girls. I wanted to inspire them to feel powerful and worthy without any-one's approval. To be more free than I was. Having a poster of me naked on their wall as an object of male sexual approval, no matter how clever the copy below it, would be me contributing to the same cycle. This wasn't just a shoe poster. It was a statement to young girls of what success looked like.

I walked home and talked to Jesse about the decision I faced for hours. Jesse felt the ad wasn't very creative, or purposeful, and that I could do better. In the end I decided that I would risk my likability, and the opportunity itself, and propose an alternative campaign.

I sat down at my computer, nibbling what was left of my finger-nails. *Who is this ad for? Girls. Women. What do I want them to see?* I got up and filled my water bottle and sat back down. I hit reply to open a blank email, and after staring at the angry skin around my nub nails and resting my fingers on the keyboard for a minute, I decided to just be myself.

I conveyed my disappointment after seeing the ad imagery. This ad, I argued, needed to be an expression of female power beyond sex appeal. I proposed we flip the copy into first person. Why not tell Nike to objectify me, on my terms? I challenged Nike to be a leader in presenting women differently. I saw no reason to participate in this ad any other way but by being myself: standing up straight, with running clothes on.

I spent hours reworking the email, choosing every word just right. I was scared to contradict this prestigious ad agency and to ask Nike to do better.

The email sat in my drafts folder for a sleepless night. If there had been more women in the marketing room, I might not have felt this way. I was doing the least likable thing imaginable, expressing myself assertively, asking too much. I wasn't an Olympian; I wasn't Serena Williams–level good. I wasn't good enough to be a diva, to be able to wave my wand and have people do whatever I said, something I wasn't sure even existed in the women's sports space. I felt like I had to choose to be compliant and grateful, or I'd be labeled a difficult woman. Difficult women tend to face consequences. And then I pressed send.

To my shock, Slate Olson, the project's talented and brash brand leader, who had a tattoo of Steve Prefontaine's face on his rib cage, replied with support, thanking me for my ideas and feedback and promising to advocate for them with the ad agency. He told me the ad would be so much stronger this way and threw out some dates for the shoot. "This is why we need more women in the room," he said. I couldn't believe it.

I rewrote the copy for the campaign. An experienced team from the prestigious advertising firm Wieden+Kennedy came to Eugene for the photo shoot, and, wearing my standard sports bra and iconic tempo shorts I ran in every day, I stared down the camera with my arms folded across my chest. I didn't smile.

The campaign received industry recognition, and the poster featuring my defiant stare hung in locker rooms and bedrooms across the United States. The commercial aired briefly on TV, to the delight of my family and friends back home. Occasionally, I still get approached by current and former Nike employees who reference it as a campaign that made them proud to work at the company. The ad struck a chord with women employees in particular, hundreds of whom marched in protest of the company's treatment of women at its headquarters in 2019.

My mom recently moved out of my childhood home and called me to see if I wanted the box of leftover posters from the garage. I told her to recycle them. If I want to see one, I know where I can go.

When the poster came out in 2007, I brought a cheaply framed copy into Track Town Pizza in Eugene, the tourist restaurant with photos of famous track and field athletes all over the walls. Since my first visit there in college, little had changed. Most of the photos were of Prefontaine, or other famous white men, with a few female athletes scattered among them. I pulled two oversized pushpins out of my pocket, twisted them deep into the wall behind the salad bar, hung the poster up myself, and walked out the door.

That poster isn't about fame or athletic accomplishments to me. Its existence is a reminder that speaking up is scary, and when you have a lot to lose by doing so, you are likely to deliver your message imperfectly, or overcompensate with anger or rage that you need to speak up at all. I'll never know if I'd have been listened to the same way had I not been white, thin, and aligned with Western beauty standards. The more marginalized your identities, the more obstacles you face in your attempts to be heard, and the less grace you may be offered by those in power when your tone doesn't assuage their egos. The poster, to me, is a reminder to allow anger to exist alongside advocacy in the world around me.

11

THE FAVORITE

Running along the dry riverbed with DeLong biking beside me, I felt like the star returned home. "Queen of Nike," he teasingly called me, not-so-secretly proud of the sudden visibility of his protégé and friend. My ego responded by picking up the pace. "Queen" was a bit of a stretch, but I had become Nike's go-to runner for multiple campaigns lately, the kinds of campaigns I'd clipped out of *Runner's World* and taped to my wall in high school. In the last few months I'd been featured alongside NBA and NFL stars in the "Quick Is Deadly" campaign; brought in to consult on the development of Nike+, the company's state-of-the-art online fitness tracking program; and worked several youth event booths signing posters and race numbers.

I gulped down the attention, but it left me feeling empty. It wasn't based on anything real or lasting, and deep down, I didn't

feel I deserved it. I felt the pressure to back up my national championship win, to prove myself worthy of the spotlight. And now
there was even more on the line. I had just purchased a home in
Jesse's hometown of Bend, Oregon, just a two-hour drive away
from Eugene, and filled it with renters who only covered half the
mortgage; the economy plunged into a recession four months later.
Buying a home with an income that depended on podium finishes
during an economic collapse activated childhood stress around
scarcity. It wasn't just a home; it was a stake in the ground for our
future family. It wasn't just running; it was the thing everything
else depended on.

One photo shoot was planned the day before a 5K race where I
planned to get my Olympic time qualifier out of the way, but after
draining my physical tank for hours to get the perfect shot, as well
as my emotional tank trying to be likable to the crew, I ran out of
gas with a mile to go, fell short of the time standard, and got my
ass kicked by Kara Goucher on my home track. After that, I felt
behind, and pre-race anxiety grew out of control.

"You've gotta cut this out," Vin said after I broke into tears in
the warm-up area before a 1,500 race and tried to negotiate with
him to let me withdraw. He paced without looking at me, shaking
his head. "The photo shoots, all the travel, you need to tell them no."

I didn't know how to say no, and I was afraid to. I was worried
it would all go away. Professionals managed to train and market
themselves at once all the time, and I needed to figure out how.
But I was running out of time—to get fit, to get to race weight, to
make this upcoming World Championships team. I asked my agent
what he thought would happen if I didn't make the World team.
Nike was looking for ways to save money, laying off employees

like crazy, and he felt I should stop doing the appearances and focus entirely on racing to be safe. I told him to go ahead and turn any future asks down.

Those months under pressure are some of the most miserable memories of my running life. Instead of feeling anchored and powerful on my runs, I felt scattered and desperate. More and more frequently, while struggling to breathe, I couldn't finish a key workout Vin had prescribed, and I'd break down in tears. At races, instead of walking into the final call room ready to run through a wall, I felt like a cow being led to slaughter. I felt weak and ashamed and wasn't comfortable talking to Vin about it for fear he'd think I couldn't hack it as a professional athlete and was letting my emotions win the day.

At Nationals in Indianapolis in June, where the World team would be selected, Vin and I made a race plan together. He reminded me that I was the defending champion, and that we'd come so far together. When anxiety started rushing through my veins during the warm-up, I made no space for my feelings. I tried to be a machine. When I tried to soak in the field, nothing happened. There was no sensation of grounding down and connecting deeply to the core part of me that had always been waiting there. It was like opening your front door and finding the furniture gone and the walls bare, making you wonder if you'd mistakenly gone to the wrong house. I felt self-conscious lying on the track, stood up abruptly, and got myself to the line.

During the race, I found myself in a lead pack of four women with a mile to go. We were pushing harder than anyone else could manage, creating a sizable gap on the rest of the field. I was in that part of the race where the pain accumulates and bulges and threatens to spill over at any moment—the part of the race when I had always thrived, the part when I'd hear my dad's voice in my head, egging me on.

But his voice was gone. I didn't feel scrappy or powerful. I felt distracted—and physically exhausted. It took everything I had to stay connected to the back of the three other women. If I gave them an inch, I knew I would pop off like an untied balloon, so I ran right up on the third-place woman, close enough to reach out and touch her shoulder without breaking stride, trying to focus on only that. Her shoulder. This last mile would be full of decisions. *Do I stay in this excruciating pain a little longer?* The answer always needed to be yes. That was how you won the 5K. Say yes as long as possible, and then when you don't think it's possible, say yes anyway.

For anyone watching who knew me, the race was setting up perfectly. Any other year I would be licking my chops, thinking, *This is perfect, all I have to do is beat* one *of these women, and I'm on the team.* But instead, all I could think was, *What if after all this effort and pain, I'm the one who doesn't make it?*

I was ashamed of even having this thought. Then it grew louder. So loud I wanted to cover my ears. I began to imagine ways out. I could trip on the rail and pretend it was an accident. I could fake an asthma attack, and pretend my inhaler was expired. Grab my side and fake a terrible cramp. Anything that could explain not making the team that didn't mean I wasn't good enough. I knew I was collapsing under pressure, but I couldn't do anything about it.

Lit by the stadium lights, the line marking six hundred meters to go began to reveal itself to us. Instead of making my signature long kick for the win, I pulled off into lane three and stopped entirely. Standing there, out of the corner of my eye, I watched the lead pack zoom away around the bend.

I was stopped for thirteen seconds, but it felt like time was moving in slow motion. As I was looking for an exit into the stands, a young Stanford runner ran by in a distant fourth place, leading the chase pack. She was running toward fourth place, not away from it. It was a much-needed slap in the face. I remember asking myself, simply, *Can you physically run? Is anything actually wrong with your body?* The answer: *no.* I made my second crazy decision and ran back into lane one and started sprinting at full speed.

I was later told I was running so fast all alone I looked like I'd lost my mind. But really, I had relocated it. I flew past the fourth-place runner, reclaiming my previous spot, and kept going. It was like I had somehow reinhabited my own body, and all I cared about was expressing it as fully as possible. I knew I wouldn't finish in the top three, but I stubbornly didn't care—*even more of a reason to push,* I thought, when it mattered just because. I sprinted past the bell and pushed until my legs screamed and my arms were numb, and my chin lifted toward the sky in desperate search for more oxygen. When I crossed the finish line, I took in the sight of the three women who made the team ahead of me embracing and felt the ache. I knew I wasn't really battling them; I was battling myself. Having managed to tap back into who I was for that final lap, I quickly grew furious that I had ever lost her and was determined to never do so again.

In the media zone, with digital recorders waving around the face of the defending champion who choked, I answered the questions of puzzled reporters. I told them the truth: that there were loud voices in my head fighting against me, telling me to drop out, and that they had overwhelmed me. I explained how I turned it around. To me it was a revelation, a comeback moment, and while I could have hidden in shame at not making the team, I had decided to speak honestly about the feelings I had been ashamed of before. I naively believed that sharing the truth might be helpful to someone out there.

Vin gave me a hug and said he was proud of me for getting back in there. Alberto Salazar, the head coach of the Nike Oregon Project, another elite training program, came up to me later in the stands, told me that he believed in me, and offered up the services of his team's sports psychologist. I'd never heard of sports psychology, and in the house I'd grown up in, shrinks were for soft, privileged people incapable of solving their own problems. Alberto made me feel that struggling with pressure was normal, that it was part of being a pro athlete—not a sign that I wasn't one. His generosity and care felt sincere, and I started sessions with the sports psychologist he recommended right away, with Alberto's group footing the bill. Years later, I'd learn that Alberto's involvement in the health and lives of athletes he worked with had a deeply harmful side.

The next day, reading the news on LetsRun.com and the message boards below, I was reduced to the woman who heard voices, the butt of jokes, the head case, the classic crazy woman. The truth is, female athletes face this brand of criticism all the time. What I went through was minor compared to the treatment Simone Biles would receive during the Olympics in 2021 when she withdrew from an event for mental health reasons. Her professionalism and even patriotism were questioned, and she was subjected to overt racism and misogyny. When I was called crazy and unprofessional on the internet, I was embarrassed, but I was also ashamed of my own prior lack of empathy. I had never hidden behind an alias and thrashed another woman online, but I had thought these things about others before. I had made comments among close friends, piled on when someone else criticized a poor performance, referred to someone as a head case. I understood now how powerful the battle against yourself could be.

DARREN TREASURE, the sports psychologist Alberto introduced me to, met me in an office on Nike's campus. He taught me some skills around self-talk: basic but essential sports psychology tools that every single program should offer its athletes, given the forces around them and the vise they are placed in. These tools quickly made a difference for me. I'd thought that only weak people had negative thoughts, and that shame turned me against myself. He told me it was quite the opposite, with professional sports leagues and champions across sports having huge budgets devoted to sports psychology.

Darren started by making me write down the specific voices yelling in my head, and doing so made my pen shake. The voices reminded me I was bigger than my competitors, that I didn't belong at the top of the podium, that I was mentally weak. They went on. I made a long list, and beside each critical statement, I was prompted to write a counterstatement: what I *wanted* to believe about myself. From these, I picked my five favorite affirmations and wrote them in large letters on a piece of paper. *I belong*

among the best. I am confident. I am committed. I am a winner. I am relaxed.
Anytime a negative thought came back, I repeated these mantras
on a loop as a kind of shield. I recited them once in the mirror in
the morning, before, during, and after my run, and as I brushed my
teeth before bed. At first it felt like I was lying, but over time my
relationship to the words shifted. Even if I wasn't all of those
things, it felt better to spend time thinking I was than thinking I
was the alternative. The idea of all of this was that repeated
thoughts become beliefs, beliefs inform actions, and actions repeated over time create an identity. To change your identity, you
must start by changing your thoughts.

More than a decade later, I'd learn that Darren was reported by
other athletes to be operating without appropriate licensure and
violating HIPAA laws that protected the disclosure of patient
health information without their consent or knowledge. Darren
was on the Nike payroll, and all the Nike Oregon Project athletes
were required to work with him. He reportedly shared information with Alberto that athletes had told him in confidence, leaving
athletes with no safe place to report coaching abuse when it occurred. (I myself was a victim of their HIPAA violations in 2008
when Darren shared private information about my injury with Alberto, the coach of a competitor, but my remote relationship outside
of the Nike Oregon Project protected me from the other abuses.)
Darren played a key role in creating the environment of that professional group, an environment that young phenom Mary Cain and
teammate Amy Begley described in the *New York Times* as full of
body-shaming and other instances of verbal and emotional abuse. In
2021, Alberto was issued a lifetime ban for sexual misconduct by the
U.S. Center for SafeSport. Alberto has denied the accusations.

While it's horrifying to contemplate the harm that Darren and Alberto reportedly caused for so many female athletes, the introductory version of their mental training that I was offered was effective. With the benefit of hindsight, though, I can see how one could twist sports psychology to create a cultlike environment like the Nike Oregon Project, allowing an abuser to thrive. But with Vin as my coach, I was able to stay on the safe side of the line.

ANOTHER PERSON MADE an even more powerful impact on me that summer: a competitor out of New Zealand named Kim Smith. Over the past two summers of European racing, Kim and I developed a kind of summer camp closeness. Ray represented us both, and our race calendars were nearly identical. We requested one another as roommates, knowing that if we left it open to chance we could end up with someone who Skyped full volume with their boyfriend back home at 2 a.m.

Together again in the summer of 2007, Kim and I slipped into an effortless groove. We swapped trashy novels we picked up secondhand at charity shops and played at least 250 hours of UNO. We navigated every kind of public transit imaginable and moved our track workout days so we could overlap schedules as much as possible. I always loved being around Kim as a peer, but now I found myself looking to her for leadership. Kim was a fierce competitor and 100 percent herself, like I had been in college. Seeing her now, so embodied, so real, I could feel how far I'd diverged. I could feel how the chains of perfectionism had tightened around me when I stopped running for those thirteen seconds at Nationals. I remembered how different it felt to release it all and start running again. How amazing it felt just to experience the childlike joy of running as fast as I could, even with nothing external to gain. Kim represented a road not taken, a version of me who had never bought into the bullshit. Bolstered by her company, I won my first four races.

At Crystal Palace, the site of the prestigious Diamond League Meeting in London, I won my biggest international race yet. The positive mantras that used to feel uncomfortable to say felt true, and the whole time I was at the event, I was having fun. I felt gratitude for my opportunities and for my body. At the party after the event, I felt freer from perfectionism than I had in years. I took a drag on a stranger's cigarette. I danced to a busker's drums on the sidewalk. Way too early the next morning, Kim and I were seated across from one another in a food court at London's Heathrow Airport, trying to cure our hangovers with a full English breakfast. Kim was bent over her plate, a piece of back bacon in her hand, which was visibly dripping grease. The piece she was holding had a slab of slimy fat making up three-fourths of it. But instead of ripping that part off in favor of the leaner meat like I'd gotten in the habit of doing, she slurped the whole thing into her mouth, eyes closed in pleasure. Kim's ease around food once again hit me like a shock.

"I wish I could eat like that," I said.

She looked up at me from under her eyebrows, grease on her chin. "You can," she said.

"I'm not at race weight yet," I said.

"Who says?" She put her fork down. "You just won the fucking London Diamond League 3K. I swear all you Americans are way too obsessed with weight. You think you're eating healthy, but you're just obsessive. It messes with your confidence. You gotta let it go."

She skewered a fried egg whole, the edges brown and crispy like dirty lace. She wasn't worried about what it was cooked in. My first thought was, *Yeah, well, you're a freak, the exception.* And then my next thoughts were memories of other people saying that about me in high school and college. Back when I was unstoppable, confident, didn't worry about my weight, and loved to run. I knew she was right. Kim gave me a concrete role model with a healthy relationship with food and body, and her real talk was what made the biggest difference in challenging the beliefs I had internalized. She called me out, and built me up in the process. She got through to me in a way a health professional never could, because she was in the arena. After what Kim did for me, I fully understood the power a role model can have in this minefield if she is willing to say it straight, and I'd go on to do this repeatedly for others.

I finished my summer with a seven-second PR in the 1,500 in Rieti, Italy, outkicking the USA champion in the final meters. The 1,500 wasn't even my event. I'd never been prouder of a running season. Between all the marketing contributions, the "Objectify Me" campaign's success, and a flawless summer of lifetime bests and wins, I felt I had proven my value, despite my Nationals performance being one place behind acceptable. In the weeks since, I had managed to position myself as a favorite to make the Olympic team. My agent and I were confident I would make it through the year without a contract reduction.

Eleven days after getting home from Europe, on September 30, Jesse and I hosted 250 friends and family for our wedding at

Shevlin Park in Bend. My friends from the hide-and-seek days in Canyon Country drove fifteen hours and shared a house together. My best friends from high school and college and my old coach Dena Evans stood alongside me in the wedding party while De-Long officiated the ceremony. We used the envelope of cash my parents gave me to pay for a buffet of flank steak, salad, and bread. My mom and sister coordinated the invitations and photographer, and Jesse's family pitched in for beer and a DJ, and planned the event. Even with the unexpected rain, it was perfect—low on budget, but high on personality. My college teammates cheered as the DJ played requests for the top hits of past frat parties we'd attended, and I've yet to see more committed dancing at a wedding. Kids fell asleep on parents' shoulders in cookie comas. Someone passed out on the front lawn. Someone else went home with the photographer. It was exactly what we hoped for.

But even as I enjoyed newlywed bliss, stress and pressure awaited me. A couple of weeks before Christmas, I got a call from Josh, alerting me that Nike was going to reduce my pay. He was apologetic, stating that it was deeply unfair, and I could tell he meant it. This was the part of his job he hated, he said. In the end, Nike was a business, and it was going to make every reduction it contractually could to save money. He tried to go to bat for me since I'd had such a great summer and done so much for the brand, but a salary reduction was unavoidable.

I immediately panicked about the house. It was now worth half of what we'd paid. Jesse was spending down savings as an MBA student at the University of Oregon. Businesses were firing MBAs, not hiring them, but we had been covering our eyes, hoping things would get better. My friends and neighbors were losing their homes to foreclosure, along with millions of others around the United States. All the anxiety about money stress from my childhood came flooding in again: the arguments between my parents, the way my dad worked himself up to call around for a job, any job.

If I missed two USA teams in a row, I would get my salary cut in half from my newly reduced amount, and it could never be re-stored. Now, making the Olympic team in Beijing wasn't just a dream I hoped would come true—I *had* to make it, or our life would be knocked sideways. I *knew* I could do it. I had it in me. I needed to find a way to embrace this urgency without taking steps backward mentally. I scheduled regular calls with Darren to keep race anxiety at bay and made a season plan with Vin.

I took a Sharpie and wrote on a piece of notebook paper: *I am an Olympian.* Then I taped it to the wall next to my bedside lamp, where it would be the first and last thing I'd see every day.

12

WHAT YOU DESERVE

I was close to perfect in 2008. I hit just about every workout. Got my nine hours of sleep most nights. My diet was consistently good without being obsessive. My confidence was higher. I felt like I was finding a kind of maturity as an athlete. Jesse was out of the house most of the time, diving deep into his first year of his MBA in sports business and all its social events that revolved around alcohol and went way past my bedtime. I was lonely, and hungry for other interests, but I stayed focused.

Four weeks before the Olympic Trials, I flew to New York for one final test. The Diamond League, the premier track and field series contested across fourteen countries from May to September, was making a stop on American soil, and Olympic medalists from all over the globe gathered under the lights at Icahn Stadium. As I warmed up on the practice field adjacent to the stadium, I ran over my mantras to redirect my thoughts until I was calm. I watched athletes completing their pre-race preparations with deliberate co-ordination, like worker bees. The roar of the crowd stopped all of us in our tracks. The announcer's voice was tough to make out, but like a game of telephone, in a matter of seconds we all learned that the men's world record in the 100 meters had been broken. "This guy Usain Bolt is very good, Lauren," Ray said to me as I stretched. "A real performer. Bolt could save the sport." Getting good enough to win was hard enough. Being so good you could showboat before and after and back it up week after week, year after year, was unfathomable, but that's what it took to be a star. I couldn't see that happening in my event, ever. But I could maybe win today. I could maybe be an Olympian.

Bolt's record was quickly followed by actual bolts of lightning, and I followed the crowd of athletes indoors, layering up in our sweats to keep our muscles warm during the rain delay. We huddled in the halls with our backs against the wall, waiting for the signal. I was excited, and nervous, the kind of nervous that gives you the shits every twenty minutes and makes you marvel at the storage capacity of the human intestine. Across from me was my buddy Kim Smith, untangling her headphones cable. She looked nervous, too.

"Hey, Lauren," she said.

"Hey, Kimmy."

"This is the fucking worst," she said, and we both laughed. She put in her headphones.

Just seeing Kim, I was able to lower my shoulders a couple of inches. She knew how to feel nervous but not give the feeling too much power.

The race started steady, with the leaders on pace for the elusive fifteen-minute barrier. Kim moved into the front early and I tucked into her slipstream. I would follow her lead. My mind was clear as I threw myself into the front with a lap and a half to go, running a pace that promised to make anyone who dared to follow burn alive. I don't know if she followed. I never looked back. Not until the race was over, and we celebrated our 1–2 finish.

"Jesus, you've got a fast kick, Lauren," she said. "Well done."

"Thanks, Kimmy," I said. "You did most of the work."

"Yeah, thanks for that," she said, giving me a hard time, but smiling.

After the last runner crossed the line, we walked off the track together. Jesse was waiting for me in the cooldown area, and I walked toward him, smiling, still wearing my racing spikes. I had broken fifteen minutes for the 5K event, making me the eighth-fastest American of all time, a favorite to win the Olympic Trials on my home track. My finishing kick was the kind of rare talent that won medals. Even more exciting than that was the way I felt in my body: It had felt *easy*. After four years of battling my body and mind, the dream was coming true. I walked forward into Jesse's arms for a long hug that made it all the way to my heart. I felt more connected to him than I had all year.

"I'll go cool down, and we'll celebrate," I said, smiling.

As I turned away and tried to run, a stabbing pain in my foot caused me to gasp and stop immediately. I sat down and examined the bottom of my shoe to check if I'd stepped on a nail. I hadn't. I took off my shoe. Nothing. Using both hands, I mobilized the ball of my foot in case it was a cramp, but without weight on it the pain was gone. The thought of it being a legitimate injury was absurd. Every injury I'd experienced came on with some kind of warning, even if faint. I stood up gingerly, and as soon as my weight set in, the foot involuntarily lifted and dangled in the air like that of an injured dog.

I bargained with myself. "It's probably just a pinched nerve," I told Jesse. As the words left my mouth, I felt queasy. *Please don't let this be the end.*

MEDICAL CARE FOR athletes was fast in Ohio, but in TrackTown, USA, a month before hosting the Olympic Trials, it was instantaneous. Not two days later, an orthopedist in Eugene was reading my MRI report from his clipboard and pointing to a backlit image of my ankle.

"Increased blood flow around the navicular. Possible stress reaction."

The navicular is not a bone you want to break. It's one of the little stone-shaped bones clustered together in your ankle. Navicular fractures have a high likelihood of being "nonunion," meaning they refuse to stitch back together, and they often require a titanium screw and bone graft to fix. Navicular problems have ended a lot of careers, including Jesse's at the end of college.

"It's a common injury in racehorses," the doctor told me. "They don't heal well, and they usually shoot them."

"Good thing I'm not a horse."

The fracture was barely visible, a tiny, thin line on one edge, like cracked glaze on the edge of a teacup. The problem, I was told, was that continuing to pound the talus bone into that little crack could eventually split the bone in two. My only warning sign had been a stiff ankle, which I'd attributed to the new prototype spikes Nike had given me. The spikes may have contributed to the problem, I learned, as my doctor made a show of bending and flexing one in the air between us. "A shoe should naturally bend where your foot bends on takeoff," he said. "This spike plate is so long it flexes way back here under the navicular bone instead."

Maybe it was the shoes. Maybe my bones were still vulnerable from RED-S; there is a time lag between behavior changes and what the body needs to fully restore its health. Maybe it was both, or neither. There was no time to do a deep investigation. The Olympic Trials were in four weeks.

The medical team and Vin agreed that this injury was a shitty one, but we'd caught it so early that a couple of weeks in the pool could be enough to settle it down. I would lose some sharpness in the short term, and my goal of winning the Trials on my home track would probably be off the table. But if I could still eke out a top-three finish, a rested foot had a better chance of being able to make it to the Olympics without cracking in half.

"What's the other option?" I asked.

"Well," Vin said, "you give it a couple of days off, then train through it. I've seen athletes train on a cracked navicular for months. Let's say we do that and it all goes well and you win the Trials. Chances are it breaks before you get to the Olympics, and you stay home."

I thought about that for a moment.

"The point isn't to make the Olympics, Lauren. The point is to go there and *do something special*. Either way, it's a risk, but the option that protects your foot is also the best option to have a successful Olympics. Again, it's a risk. But I've seen what you've done this year. You're so fit, I think you can make this team at eighty percent," said Vin.

Just like four years earlier in Ohio, I was clicking off the final weeks of training in the pool. Rage would come in waves. *I worked so hard,* I would think. *This was supposed to be my year. I can't believe it's falling apart. I'm going to lose my house.* I leaned on Jesse for daily support, and used my positive mantras to believe. I tried visualizing myself digging deeper than ever, crossing the line, succeeding, and collapsing from the effort. But the image wouldn't come into focus. My instinct was telling me it wasn't going to happen, but I wouldn't listen. That wasn't the right answer. I kept at it every day, stubbornly adhering to the idea that a real professional could believe this into being.

I came out of the pool a week before the race and readjusted to land. And with each day that passed, more and more people descended upon TrackTown, USA, for the event. Incredible athletic specimens from around the country flooded my grocery store aisles and slowed the deli lines. Rental cars full of fans clogged up the windy road to Pre's Rock to pay their respects. I went to Pre's Trail to find my stride, and quickly grew self-conscious as dozens of unfamiliar faces examined mine in recognition as they ran past. When Vin and I met for a final tune-up on the track, it was clear from the workout that I'd lost the sharpness and sting of my finishing kick. But I was surprisingly strong, and my foot felt good. Maybe it would be okay.

The space Nike rented out for their hospitality suite was enormous, and no expense was spared. Vin and I were to meet here to decide on a race strategy, and I scanned the room. Beyond the pool tables and dining tables and beautiful food displays and bar, Cap was schmoozing and courting a new star, and I recognized the energetic engagement for what it was: conditional. A Nike employee behind a counter ran her pencil down the pages of lists, looking for my name among hundreds before fetching a swag bag for me and crossing my name off.

"What are you thinking for the race?" Vin asked.

"I don't know," I said. "My kick is gone. I don't know how it'll play out. I feel like we made a mistake taking that time off running to be safe."

There were two other top athletes rumored to also have navicular injuries, both of whom opted to take the risk and train through it somehow. They faced surgery when the season was over, but here they were, fit and sharp, not missing a beat.

"Maybe. I don't know, Lauren. But we made a decision with the information we had at the time. If the time off kept your injury from becoming serious, then it will pay off at the Olympic Games when you are back in peak form. Besides, you might not need to be top three to make the team."

"Are you sure?"

He reminded me that the top three don't make the team. It's the top three *with the Olympic standard* (a minimum time requirement achieved at some point over the course of the season). If this race went slower than the Olympic standard, the Olympic spots would go to the people who met the time standard earlier in the year, even if they finished eighth, ninth, and tenth. Heading into this race, only four women had the standard, and I was one of them. Two of them, Kara Goucher and Shalane Flanagan, had already qualified for the Olympics in the 10K, their primary event, earlier in the week. They were likely only entered in the 5K as a backup plan. Even if they qualified in both, doubling in the 10K and 5K at the Olympics was rare because it was a reach to medal in one event, much less two, against the best athletes in the world. We had a hard enough time making the final—it seemed logical to me to have a fresh squad in each race.

"Okay, so even if all three of the other women with the standard finish ahead of me, I could still make the team?"

"Yes, if one of them decides not to race the 5K at the Olympics. So if you can't finish top three, fight for every place, because the alternate would get to go in that scenario."

I started to believe maybe this was possible. Maybe.

As I stood up to say goodbye to Vin, Josh Rowe from Nike came over and put his hand on my shoulder, directing my line of sight toward the far wall. "Check it out," he said. There was a line of blown-up posters on the wall, and one of them had my face on it.

Nike had wanted to find a way to convey what the Olympic Trials are all about to fans and raise the stakes to make it more exciting, he explained. It wanted fans to understand that at this event, the excitement wasn't just about the winners, it was about that top three. It's ruthless, and exciting, and a huge accomplishment to qualify at all. The tagline of the campaign was "The Hardest Team to Make." I walked closer until I could make out the words: "One isn't the loneliest number, four is."

Kara Goucher's poster was right beside mine. It read, "Broken dreams hurt more than broken bones."

Josh handed me a stack of T-shirts with the same image as my poster on them. "We had these printed for your friends and family."

To them, this race was essentially just a marketing slogan. It was nice of Josh to include me, and maybe if I'd been healthy, it would have pumped me up, but holding those shirts felt like a jinx.

Every day was a battle to believe I had a chance. Jesse managed our extended families as they arrived in town, and I tried not to think about all the money they'd spent and the time they'd taken off work. He answered their questions, eased their worries, and protected my space. It was so much work just to keep believing. I couldn't spare an ounce of energy on anyone else I loved.

FINALLY, the day arrived, and Jesse drove me to the track for the race.

I'm sure we went through the usual checklist on the drive: spikes, uniform, race number, water bottle, credentials, probably followed by some nervous silence, but I don't recall any of it. I remember he parked outside the Bowerman building that bordered the final curve of the track, and we looked out my window at the security gate where he couldn't follow me. "I know it's not how you imagined it," he said. "But I know you, Lauren. You're a gamer. Nobody competes like you."

"I'm not sure it's going to be enough," I said.

"Maybe, maybe not. But you have a shot." I could tell he meant it, that he wanted it for me, and it made my chest hurt as I walked alone through the athlete entrance.

I'd watched Jesse's childhood dream of being an Olympian fall apart at the end of college when he broke his navicular running, and then later his neck, in a bike crash. I couldn't empathize at the time. Back then I thought those who succeeded deserved it, and those who didn't messed up. Now I knew better than ever. I deserved nothing. None of us do.

I walked onto the track behind the official, single file with my competitors. A pocket of people on the far side of the track screamed extra loud, and I knew it was my family. I gave them a glance and a small wave. My face was on my dad's new Nike shirt. And then I was ten, looking up at my dad, who was wearing a shirt with my school photo blown up on it, saying how proud he was to be my father. I took off my warmups, put them into my assigned basket, and strode out along the backstretch with everyone else—past the seats where Brad Hauser had given me a pep talk before my first NCAA championship, past the seats where we'd made music out of trash can lids and empty Gatorade bottles to cheer on the 10K competitors. This was my house. I lay down on its floor. I felt myself coming back into my body, ready to control what I could. I could feel the magic inside myself, still alive.

Jesse watched the race from the Bowerman curve, next to Vin, leaning on a strip of railing reserved for athlete support personnel. Later, he told me he couldn't watch it with the family, with all their emotions and questions. With a little less than a mile to go, the top three women put in a surge and I began to surge with them. This was it, the move that I'd imagined making since 2004 when I watched what it took from my injured place in the stands. I'd made it this far, and I was going to do it, no matter what it took, no matter how much it burned. For a moment, moving in synchrony with the fastest women in the nation, I felt a rush of destiny, of the rightness of all the struggles I'd had to get here. But at the faster pace, I began to labor. A space began to wrench open between me and the leaders, and I was helpless to stop it. The Olympic team was definitively running away from me when I passed Jesse on the rail, and I briefly looked his direction, just to remember not to throw it all away. Four years of work came down to this and I couldn't do it. I wanted to cry, but I knew any emotion would make breathing impossible. So I focused on my backup plan. I slowed the chase pack down slightly from the front, not wanting to lead anyone else to an Olympic standard. If the race stayed slow, I would still be the first alternate. Sara Slattery tried to pass, and I did my best to be in the way; I even poked my elbows out at one point to deter her, a blatant violation that should have disqualified me. I was racing like someone desperate, a version of myself I'd never seen before, and I didn't like it. On the final lap, Sara eventually got around me for fourth, but the time was slow. I was fifth, and the alternate to the Olympic team.

As I walked through the media zone, reporters baited me with questions for their heartbreak stories and were confused by my optimism. "I did my best; that's all you can do," I said. "I executed my race plan. And there's still a chance I could make the team," I said with a smile that was almost genuine. I hated being in that vulnerable position, waiting for other people's choices to determine my career trajectory, but I felt pretty confident someone would drop.

Leaving the wall of recorders, I walked up to the curtain door of the press conference tent and saw our top three women seated under the lights: Shalane, Kara, and Jen Rhines. From just outside the room, I watched the light falling on Shalane as she stated her plan to compete in both the 10K and 5K in Beijing, which stung but didn't come as a complete surprise. She did have the American record in the 5K, after all, and would want to see what she could do on the Olympic stage. And then someone asked Kara the same question. She said she planned to compete in both events, too.

That's when it hit me that my chance of going to the Games

had vanished. Kara's mouth kept moving under the lights, answering a different question, but I couldn't hear any sounds besides loud static in my head. I wandered out of the media zone into the darkness of the cooldown field. The first person who spotted me was Darren, the sports psychologist I'd worked with. "I'm sorry, Lauren," he said. "You'll make it next time."

Four more years. I wanted to kick him in the balls.

I sat alone under a flickering light on the outer edge of the field until the stadium had emptied and the warm-up field had only a few volunteers cleaning up. I couldn't get myself to leave. My sweaty clothes chilled me, and the brick wall behind my back felt like a slab in a morgue. My family, Jesse's family, the DeLongs—they were all waiting for me at a brewery nearby. I couldn't imagine facing them.

I love you. Just come see me, Jesse texted.

When I was the last person left, I walked out alone in the quiet night to a silhouette of Jesse waiting for me. I had wanted him to give up, but he hadn't. He put his arm around me and walked the long way to the bar. "They are still there," he told me. "They all love you."

He dropped me at the door, into the arms of my dad, who was cheery and loving, and he took me inside. Jesse would walk back out and sit on a curb and let the emotions finally release. I was in a kind of disassociated haze. The people who came to see me looked like cartoon characters, eyes big with concern, staring a little too long for answers I couldn't provide. I couldn't feel their love. I kept thinking about those last few laps, the way I impeded Sara with so little integrity. I didn't recognize that scared version of myself. This sport felt full of ways to lose yourself, and I felt like I was learning every lesson the hard way.

THE MORNING AFTER the Trials, I showed up to Olympic team processing as required. As alternate, I was to fill out all the same paperwork as an Olympian and try on the Olympic uniform so they could correctly record my size in case I was needed.

I ran my hand along every piece of the Olympic team kit hanging on the rack, and then went into a bathroom stall to breathe. I wondered if Kara or Shalane might reconsider if I appealed to them directly. And so, in the classic bargaining phase of grief, I wrote each of them a brief email, reiterating our shared dream of being Olympians, the heartbreak of facing four years of unknowns and aging out, and explaining the contract consequences of not making the team. They both turned me down.

At the time I hated them for it, and I went into my bedroom and paced alone, boiling over with jealousy I wasn't ready to own. *Fuck Nike for pitting us against one another with ruthless contracts. Fuck Kara. Fuck Shalane. Fuck them for hoarding something so impossible to reach. For leaving me at home, afraid.* By the end of it, I lay curled up on our unmade bed, pulled the blankets over me, and wept.

I stayed angry for a long time, but my anger wasn't about them. I was angry at my desperation and embarrassed for exposing it. I was angry that so much was leaning on one day out of every four years when everything had to go right. I was angry at how close I had been just a month ago and how quickly it had changed. I was angry that my living was so unstable. It was okay for me to ask

GOOD FOR A GIRL

them, to put it out there, but it was unfair of me to get angry that I didn't get the response I wanted. I can see that I placed a gendered expectation on them to put others first, to be selfless, which I wouldn't have expected from a male athlete. They earned the spots. They got to do what they wanted with them. We weren't even teammates, we just wore the same Nike kit. I can say all that and understand it intellectually, and make peace with my career and fully embrace my incredible life the way things turned out, and I have, but it still hurts every now and then because it was a death, the death of a dream.

During those six or so weeks as an alternate, I got so fit, so powerful, so fast that the grief couldn't catch up to me. I trained to delay the inevitable, my foot occasionally achy while handling the load. But nobody in the 5K field got injured, or sick, or changed their mind. When the start lists were published, it was officially over. I couldn't watch the Olympics. I took the boot and crutches out of the closet and rested my foot for six weeks, then eight, then twelve, with the goal of healing it completely. It didn't. The doctor recommended surgery. I had about a 50 percent chance of returning to form. I thought of the racehorses.

190

13

CHANGING THE GAME

How about Smithers and Mr. Burns?" Jesse suggested, pulling up some images from Google to show me.

He started laughing the kind of contagious laughter where he hasn't let you all the way in on the joke yet because he's not sure he can finish the sentence without laughing. Not much made me smile in those days, but that did.

"You've already got the wheelchair! It's perfect!" he said, enthusiastically gesturing to my new black sporty ride I got on Craigslist as I wheeled myself closer to the screen. "We just need a bald wig for you; I think I've got everything else. My hair is already weirdly perfect for Smithers."

It was our second year showing up to the University of Oregon's business school Halloween party in a couple's costume where we were both men. We'd gone as the "Dick in a Box" guys from *Saturday Night Live* the previous year, and being Justin Timberlake with a crotch box full of Halloween candy turned out to be quite interactive, especially for all the women at the party who thought I was a man. I loved it. Something told me Mr. Burns wouldn't generate the same enthusiasm, but Jesse was in love with *The Simpsons*, and I had no better ideas. So I leaned toward my wall mirror, licked the tip of my dried-out eyeliner pencil, and colored liver spots onto my bald cap.

My life was completely up in the air, and I would have followed Jesse anywhere just to avoid being alone with my thoughts. But I found myself lost in them anyway (cornhole and beer pong aren't great spectator sports). The titanium screw pinning my navicular together with bone graft was only a week old, and at least fifty-one more weeks stretched out ahead of me until I could hope to race respectably again. This time, I wasn't going to risk slowing down the healing process by cross-training excessively, and I allowed myself to truly rest, knowing I'd eventually have to start at the humble beginning. I considered the more aggressive return-to-run plans presented by some experts, but they weren't worth the risk to me. I'd already decided that a worst-case scenario wouldn't be missing the year, or even forced early retirement from pro racing—it would be losing the ability to run at all. The plan I settled on was the following: First, eight to twelve weeks of bearing no weight, using a wheelchair and crutches. Then two weeks with one crutch. Finally, four more weeks in a walking boot. And then, easy walk/jogs every other day, eventually inching my way toward normal mileage.

At first, the inactivity felt natural, probably because I felt depressed after the Olympic Trials and didn't want to do much of anything. But as the new year approached, when my clothes no longer fit and I smelled of stagnation, I itched to move my body again. One day, I finagled my wheelchair into the back of my Subaru and drove out to Dorena Lake, where there was a flat rail-to-trails bike path that went for miles. I set out on a one-hour wheelchair ride. Using my core, I drove my hands down along the rims of my wheels to propel me forward. Constantly drifting off to the right, I learned that the bike path wasn't flat as I'd previously thought, but arched, and going straight required riding in the middle, straddling both lanes. My chair pulled right still, but I learned to push a little harder with one hand to even it out. I pushed as hard as I could to get my heart rate up, searching for that familiar rhythm of breath. I missed running so much, and I wheeled harder. Every so often a scratch in the metal rim hit my hand just right on a rotation, making me wince. When my hands started blistering from the pressure points, I caved and took a break. My watch said I'd gone two miles. A runner passed going in the other direction. I wasn't sure I could make it home. I turned around, sweaty and deflated, and scooted my way back to the car at a crawl.

I wanted another chance at running at the highest level, but I also felt badly burned by the last five years. According to those who wrote the contracts and promoted the sport, I was a failure. USA Track and Field dropped my health insurance. In January, Nike notified me that they were exercising their maximum reduction clause in my contract. The new quarterly salary payment was so small I thought there must be a typo, but it turned out they back-dated the reduction to the previous quarter, subtracting what they overpaid me. I wouldn't get paid again for three more months. The inhumanity of backdating reductions with no warning enraged me. I would be okay—I had some savings to float me—but this had to be sinking so many vulnerable athletes.

I drove up to Portland and confronted Cap about it. He blamed it on accounting and said he'd look into it. Feeling the opportunity in front of me, I dug out a final burst of companionable charm, and asked very humbly for one more chance. I appealed for a reduction adjustment that would allow me to keep my home. He compromised, and I walked out with 50 percent of what I'd signed for, relieved but ill from the groveling.

With Beaverton disappearing into my rearview mirror, I thought about Nike's budget and how they used it. The big showy hospitality buildings filled with pool tables and big screens for watching the performances of underpaid athletes. Funding federations like Russia with state-sponsored doping programs, and paying users of performance-enhancing drugs like Lance Armstrong, Marion Jones, and others implicated in the BALCO scandal, who set an impossible performance bar for clean sport. Enacting ruthless reduction clauses, punishing women financially for so much as openly considering pregnancy, requiring athletes to work under the poverty line with no way out of their contracts when someone else offered them a living wage, as was the case for many of my Oregon Track Club Elite teammates. That man who had a budget of millions would be buying $250 bottles of wine at the next team dinner when he summoned athletes around him for this or that appearance. He would wave his company credit card to make our dinner bill disappear, the athletes at the table saying thanks with doe eyes, hoping his memory of their gratitude would grant them mercy next time their names came up to the chopping block.

Fuck that guy. Fuck that dance to please that guy. Never again. I put my middle finger up in the rearview.

With the wheelchair tucked into the garage and some basic contract security, I began letting myself dream of a fresh start. I helped OTC Elite hire a new coach, conducting athlete interviews with the final contenders that did not include any women. Mark Rowland, a British middle-distance coach with an unposh accent and a general distaste for the status quo, was my personal favorite. His nuanced training philosophy reflected his respect for individual differences, and the way he talked about coaching women made me confident he wouldn't coach based on a male athlete script. He could be painfully blunt, but he was humble, curious, and kind.

"Somewhere along the last twenty years, I've developed a knack for taking on the broken ones," he told me as I wrapped up our driving tour of Eugene's key training locations at Historic Hayward Field. We walked—or, in my case, crutched—through the gate onto the track where the 2012 Olympic Trials would be held in four years, and I felt my feet itch. "We'll start at the very beginning," he said with his gaze toward the iconic west grandstands. "You'll see. You're not finished yet, Fleshman."

It was March by the time I started running. While I was building up to three miles without a walk break, my teammates were beginning their outdoor seasons. Normally that would have made me feel behind and distressed, but I was building something new, filling my journal with reflections and ideas. I decided that if I was going to put my heart into this sport again, I would approach things differently. Making everything about winning, about the Olympics, about being the best . . . it felt *bad*. Not just when things went wrong, but most of the time. The industry's emphasis on outcomes placed no value on the things that made me fall in love with running in the first place: Sunday long run drives in Jesse's mushroom van, descending along a forest trail with my arms wide like wings, the ping of a rock I'd throw on a water tower at the end of my run, the simple pleasure of mastering a skill . . . any pursuit of excellence had to center these moments of joy, or it wasn't worth doing.

Jesse sat down with me to sort through my notebook scribbles and help me create an actual plan for this new vision of my career. Fresh off sports business courses that dove into brand-building and self-publishing tools, he suggested I start a website where I could control my own narrative and talk about what I felt was important. He showed me this new app called Twitter, and I made an account. "You can use it to get followers and let people know when you post new blogs." Scrolling through Twitter, I loved that all these untouchable famous people were right there, sharing their everyday thoughts, giving glimpses into their personalities.

The potential that social media presented for sports like mine was exciting, especially for women. You didn't have to wait for someone in traditional media to deem you story-worthy in the newspaper's sports section, which was something like 93 percent–dedicated to men's sports. You didn't need anyone to *give* you a platform. Tell a good story and add value of some kind, and you'll build your own.

Jesse proposed we begin by building a brand. I made a face.

"I don't feel like I've accomplished enough to have a 'brand,'" I told him. "It feels egotistical."

"You have a brand whether you cultivate it or not," he explained, while opening a document to take notes. "You're in the arena. People are watching. Having clarity around who you are, what you stand for, and how you want to be understood is not egotistical. It's a chance to take stock of things and be intentional. It's going to be good for life, too, not just sports. Let's get to the core of who you are and what you want."

The answers poured out easily.

"I want to find out how fast I can be without abandoning myself.

"I want to tell a sports story in a different, more human, more honest way, in real time, and not wait for someone else to tell it.

"I want to tell it as I go, and not wait to see if I'm 'successful' or not, because I want to expand the definition of success beyond traditional outcomes.

"I want to put my experience to good use with an advice column where I answer people's running questions, filling the chasm between professional and recreational runners.

"I want to see if my theory is correct that we are underestimating sports audiences. That humanizing elite athletes is the path to deeper engagement and investment.

"I want to leave the sport better than I found it."

Those were things I could do that didn't depend on my physical body being 100 percent perfect all the time. I could always tell stories and build communities. Maybe they would give people a story to follow, making the highs more exciting. Maybe they would make the lows a little less lonely and painful for me when they happened. And maybe storytelling and community building would make the transition out of sports easier one day. When it came time to retire from pro racing, I could potentially use my human biology and education degrees to become a trusted source for an industry publication like *Runner's World*, or work on reforming women's sport. I didn't know of any female "experts" or running advice columnists at the time.

In January 2009, we kicked off AskLaurenFleshman.com. My audience grew rapidly, and spanned a wide range of ages, demographics, and athletic abilities. It was a ton of work, but having a creative outlet after years of isolation was deeply gratifying. While my teammates were setting lifetime bests, I was sharing humbling stories of starting over. People were hungry for stories. Teachers, parents, doctors, students, and all kinds of people I didn't expect were seeing their emotions and experiences reflected in the pro sport world, submitting questions, and commenting on my posts. There were a few trolls, but for the most part, my website showed me the beauty and collective wisdom of everyday runners beyond the bright lights of the stadium. I learned things from my readers, and they learned things from me, and for the first time in my life, I felt like a part of the running community of everyday people who took a similar joy in the sport.

THERE WAS NO REASON to travel all the way to Europe to race an 800 that summer when an abandoned track down the street would have done perfectly well for a first maximum effort in spikes, but I was already over there. Jesse had taken up an interest in triathlon after six years of being a sedentary startup guy and then a business school guy minoring in beer pong. He was good at triathlon, as it turned out, and qualified for the age group world championships in Germany. While we were over there, I popped in a dinky race in the rain, finished last, walked away 100 percent pain free, and called it a victory. I was slow but healthy, and it was safe to dream big again. We ended our summer in Switzerland to finally celebrate our honeymoon—two years late, but right on time.

Of all the changes that time in our lives delivered, Jesse's diet turned out to have the greatest impact. Months of indigestion and room-clearing gas led to a revelation: He was being ripped apart by excessive gluten and dairy. Like any good partner, I went to the store to look for new snacks. Cyclists eat a lot of portable snacks, namely energy bars, and I searched the labels for one that matched Jesse's needs. The ones made of whole food ingredients that looked promising weren't balanced appropriately for exercise. Knowing they would sit in the gut like a rock or result in the shits, I decided I'd just make some myself. The result was a 9x13 cake pan cut into twenty-four even rectangles of mostly mashed-up fruit, nut butter, rice protein, and honey. They didn't look amazing, but they tasted good and they worked. Jesse used them in his training, and the problem vanished.

I didn't want to start a food business. I didn't even like cooking that much. But Steph insisted. Stephanie Rothstein and I had met sweating on neighboring spin bikes in a dim apartment gym over the winter when she buoyantly declared she planned to make the Olympics. I'd never heard of her. Steph's marathon debut of 2:40 was certainly solid, but not exceptional. Without a sponsor, she cleaned Airbnbs and nannied to fund her training. I admired her hustle. We grew friendly, encouraging one another and sharing snacks. The bars I gave her alleviated her digestive problems. Steph would later find out she had undiagnosed celiac disease.

Steph's childlike ability to believe in the unreasonable was catching. She believed in me, and she believed in the bars. She came over to learn how to make them. "People will buy these!" she insisted. "They can help so many people." I told her I didn't want to start a business. I didn't have time. "I'll help!" she said, and we partnered up. "You'll see," she said. "We'll be millionaires!" We brought them to the run club she coached on Thursday nights, and people started placing orders.

"You can't sell those for one dollar—you'll go out of business before you start," Jesse said, helping me hoist the used beaten-to-hell industrial mixer I'd just purchased onto the dining room table.

"Why not?" I asked.

"Because the ingredients alone have to cost more than that! And what about your labor?"

"We want them to be affordable," said Steph, unloading the grocery bags of dried fruits and nuts and honey and peanut butter we'd just bought at Costco.

"We don't need to pay ourselves to get this thing started," I added.

"Well, unless you plan to make them yourselves forever, at some point you'll need to hire help, and they won't work for free. And then what? You raise the prices and piss off your customers?"

Neither of us had an answer for that. Neither of us knew anything about business.

"You need a business plan," Jesse said. "And a way to calculate your cost of goods and margins. Also, can you even legally sell food you make in your house?"

These were all good questions. We asked Jesse to help. He made a Google Doc with a business plan. He applied for a home-kitchen license. He created Excel formulas that allowed us to calculate both cost per bar and nutritional facts! I bought an ingredient scale and adjusted the recipe to be precise and replicable. Together, the three of us named them "Picky Bars" after the picky eaters who inspired their creation. Impressed with Jesse's breadth of skills, Steph and I asked him if he wanted a job that paid in snacks, and the search for CEO ended before it began. "Chief eating officer," he joked. It was the perfect side gig to his budding professional triathlon career.

Almost exactly two years after missing the Olympics by one spot, I returned to the starting line of the National Championships feeling excited. With my readership growing as I blogged and answered questions about everything from motivation struggles to shoe inserts, I felt like I had an entire community behind me. Fitness had come slowly, early-season races were unimpressive, and only in the last month did Mark get a twinkle in his eye after a hard session. Mark's workouts were different from anything I'd done before, so it was impossible to compare them to the past, but I felt strong. I'd been away so long that nobody expected anything special from me, including me.

But once the gun went off at Nationals, I was delighted to find that the pace felt easy. I felt like I could make tiny adjustments in my body, as if I had access to all the dials, like that first time rounding the corner of my neighborhood when I realized that I was an animal first and foremost. I started near the back, invisible, and worked my way up over time. If you watch the broadcast, nobody talks about me. I positioned myself on the outside shoulder of the leaders with two laps to go, stalking them like the lion I was visualizing myself to be, and I heard the question in my head. *Here you are. Will you go for it?*

The move I made with six hundred meters to go was so extreme, nobody reacted immediately. Any fear I had about exposing myself out front was replaced by the rush of declaring my hand, of knowing I'd just committed to pouring every single bit of myself out onto the track. I didn't know if I'd pull off the win, but I knew I would cross the line with nothing left. I broke the tape in first and almost immediately dropped to all fours heaving, desperate for oxygen.

The on-field reporter from ESPN pulled me over when I recovered enough to stand and held out the mic.

"Tell me about that move you made with six hundred meters to go," she said.

"Oh my God, that was just balls," I said, unconsciously channeling my dad. "All that was was balls."

A flood of people reached out through my website and social media to congratulate me, many of whom said it was the first time they'd tuned in to a professional track meet. Having USA Champion next to your name gets you a lane in the best races in the world, and this time I could travel with Jesse as a fellow competitor. He watched my 5Ks, and I watched his triathlons. We both wrote about it.

All that writing turned out to be good for business. When we launched the website for Picky Bars with one flavor in late October, "Lauren's Mega Nuts" flew out the door. We hired more bar makers. Our "commercial kitchen" overflowed into the dining room. Jesse and I spent our winter nights on the sofa, carefully placing the sticker labels on poly bags while watching *The West Wing*. Most mornings, I'd walk downstairs and our employee Jenn would already be there, packing the orders in flat-rate envelopes, printing shipping labels, and restocking ingredients.

Traditional wisdom held that a professional athlete should remain focused, and pursuing outside interests or working a job were stigmatized as distractions that would prevent you from reaching your potential. I felt smug about debunking this until I got a mystery injury in my foot that evaded diagnosis. The old story, at once terrifying and impossible to shut out, came back to visit: that my voice didn't matter unless I was winning, and that I should disappear down the stress pit of despair until I was healthy again. But instead, I leaned into my larger story. I decided to blog about those fears one day, and it became my most-shared post. It was much harder for me to share the vulnerable moments than the victorious ones. People weren't used to athletes daring to show their faces when they weren't winning, so I experienced more trolling. But I found that the more honest I was, the more readers engaged positively, too. My blog gave me something to look forward to every day that wasn't running. And while I rarely talked about them—I didn't want to sound like a shill in my personal writings—it helped sell a ton of Picky Bars.

By the time my injury healed, I had only a couple of months to train for the 2011 USA National Championships. It wasn't enough time. When I finished eighth, a far cry from defending my championship, I decided to be proud of myself, even when the sport pundits called me out for my poor performance. Sometimes comebacks don't line up with the industry timeline. Normal people not brainwashed by elite sport culture understood that. That's life. I was on my own timeline, keeping my eyes on my own lane.

In the high altitude of Font Romeu, France, where my team was based for the summer, I went for solo runs in the foothills, my feet dancing around rivulets of runoff from the rain, feeling the company of ghosts that walked these ancient footpaths between villages before there were cars. I went on walks through the neighborhoods, stopping to feel the crepe-paper petals of the giant red poppies. Every other day, I went to the rubber-worn track to attempt the hardest workouts of my life.

One day when I showed up at the track, a tall blonde with a mechanical stride was cranking intervals behind her coach and husband, who was setting the pace with a bicycle. When I noticed her distinct head bob to one side, I knew there was only one person she could be: global distance running icon Paula Radcliffe, the British runner I'd looked up to my entire career. It was like showing up to a random soccer field in the middle of nowhere and stumbling upon Megan Rapinoe practicing penalty kicks. Even though we were both technically professionals in the same field, Paula was on another level, a multiple-time global champion, a household name, a Member of the Order of the British Empire. When she finished her workout, she walked over to introduce herself, and I had trouble finding my voice. She asked me about the hot springs I'd blogged about earlier that week, inquired about Picky Bars, and invited me to dinner. She ordered for the two of us in perfect French, and then we talked like old friends. Paula was brilliant, funny, and full of depth and curiosity. Over chocolate fondue, I confessed how I went off the deep end in 2004, comparing my own weight to the one listed in her bio. She asked what the number was, and I told her.

"I've never weighed that in my life," she said.

We talked about the dangers of comparison and the issues facing girls in sport in her country. In some ways they seemed even worse where she was from than they were at home. The NCAA had problems, but without a robust college sports system in the UK, young talent ran straight into the pressures of professional sport.

"Keep writing," she told me when she dropped me off. "It makes a difference."

I wrote about Mark. About developing a relationship with pain. About a failed 5K in Stockholm due to a horrible side stitch, and how dancing fixes everything. I wrote about London Diamond League being the last chance for someone to hit the World standard of 15:14 in the 5K, filling the one empty spot on the USA roster for the World Championships. I openly hoped it could be me.

As excited as I was to line up against a world-class field in London, I almost didn't race. On the warm-up, I got the same huge pain in my side that ruined my race in Stockholm. I felt I was in American-record shape, but I also knew my ability to express that hinged on the cramp.

"Look, love," Mark said when I found him in the warehouse near the call room. "You don't have to race. That's fine. But—you don't know."

"Know what?"

"You don't know. You don't know what will happen. Maybe you get the cramp, maybe you don't. You don't have to go out there and try to win. You can just go out there and be curious."

I used the bathroom one last time and looked at my face in the mirror. I backed up and looked at my body in my race top and buns. I stood tall and tried to visualize myself running powerfully. An unexpected wave of body criticism bubbled up when I worried about my buns riding up. But instead of spiraling out, I thought, *How interesting that a visual cue like these race buns could hijack the mind so easily.* These little briefs that only women were expected to wear were essentially designed for that purpose, to make female athletes objects of display. Feminine uniforms were created to assuage fears that sport and femininity were at odds, and as an entertainment consolation for audiences watching "inferior performances." Uniform guidelines mandating exposed skin and "formfitting" silhouettes for only one gender have been coded into rule books across many sports. In others, they have been internalized as symbols of professionalism by the women themselves—the high heels of the running world—but instead of back pain, you get body dysmorphia.

I dug into my bag, pulled out my regular running shorts, and changed into them. Looking in the mirror again, the negative voice disappeared. For so many years, if I felt self-conscious in my uniform, I thought *I* was the problem. A real pro wore buns, the logic went. The ability to wear a bathing suit confidently in a fishbowl packed with fans and while on camera was somehow the mark of true professionalism for the female athlete? No. I was the professional, with or without the outfit.

For the first two miles of the race, the pace was manageable, but only just. I kept waiting for the cramp to come, but it didn't. I made my move. When I crossed the line in first, fireworks shot into the air from either side of the finish line, delighting the full stadium. With a time of 15:00, I was going to the World Championships.

At dinner, I raised a glass of wine and praised Mark for his good coaching, for gently talking me into racing when I was about to quit. My earnestness made him squirm like I knew it would.

"Ah look, I didn't do anything but help you get out of your own way," he said, waving me off, putting down his glass.

"I'd be on a plane home if you hadn't. How'd you know what to say?"

He slowly turned his glass clockwise, thinking. "The best ones are always running from ghosts, love."

WE WERE ALL lobsters in a pot in Daegu, South Korea, the host city of the World Championships. The humidity was so thick it muffled the sounds of the cicadas that lined our running path. For two weeks, I watched the haze collect like forest fire smoke on the mountains outside the athlete village. But the weather didn't matter to me. The track was still four hundred meters.

A little whisper wondered if I could win a medal. The top runners in the world were much faster than I was on paper, but championship racing was often slow at the start and came down to a dramatic kick. There was a tiny chance the race could play out in a way that gave me a shot at something no American had ever done before in my event. And after smashing the final hard workout with Mark in Daegu, the whisper got louder. While I still knew it was a long shot, I allowed myself to enjoy the dream. I let myself visualize the whole race, and what it would feel like at every stage. I'd worked for fifteen years to get to this place. It felt incredible and freeing, giving myself this permission to dream among the best in the world.

When the official called us to follow him through the maze of halls toward the track for the 5K final, the hope was still with me. There was no part of me that felt the need to hedge or protect myself from failing. We were waved up a staircase toward a small rectangle of light that grew larger and more blinding as we ascended, eventually opening into the middle of the enormous stadium. As we walked toward the starting line, I took in the huge ring of packed seats towering above us, the fans specks of watercolor blurred by the haze of heat. Beside me, a young Japanese woman was shaking, clearly terrified, reminding me of how far I'd come. I reached over and put my hand on her shoulder. She looked in my eyes, and they softened. "It's going to be okay," I said, smiling. "Stay loose, try to enjoy it." I shook my arms out in demonstration, and she did the same, cracking a small smile.

There was no medal for seventh place, but I was proud. I'd done my best and actually *believed*, resulting in the highest finish by an American in history. The Olympics were one year away, and there were only four women in the world between a medal and me. I wanted it, but I didn't *need* it, which made the thought of chasing after it all the more fun.

Back home, I sat down to tackle a spreadsheet full of unanswered questions submitted to my advice column. There were so many young female athletes struggling with the same old issues: body image, eating disorders, depression, lost periods, stress fractures, mysterious injury cycles, anxiety. It seemed that things were only getting worse with social media. There were so many coaches and parents complicit in the harm, most of them well meaning. I felt that familiar urgency to help, but this time I didn't feel powerless. I partnered up with my friend Ro McGettigan, an Olympic steeplechaser from Ireland, and together we self-published a training diary for girls. Our template encouraged users to record not only the usual measurables like mileage, but also things girls are often taught to ignore, such as their menstrual cycles and moods. We included sports psychology techniques like the use of mantras and visual cues, as well as encouraging quotes from our peers. The goal was to create a tool that helped female athletes tune in to themselves in unsupportive environments and weather the periods of life when performance naturally dips or wanes. The first 1,500 copies sold quickly and appealed to a much wider range of people than we anticipated. We ordered 2,500 more. Ro ran the website and filled orders from her house in Providence, since mine was already a Picky Bars factory. We added our mantras and visual cues to T-shirts and jewelry and stationery and sold those, too. The sports psychology tools that helped Ro and I thrive under stress turned out to be applicable to life off the track, and our audience expanded accordingly.

Finding success as an entrepreneur was unexpected. I didn't even know what the word meant until I was twenty-eight and Jesse described me as one. I objected because many of the terms Jesse used in entrepreneurship didn't interest me: profit and loss, operational efficiencies, and the like. I was just identifying and solving problems, I insisted. It felt good to say "there, I did it!" just as it had when I'd mastered physical skills as a child. Creating things of value to others was an expanded use of those skills. Both writing and my bars business gave me confidence and an identity outside of athletic performance, making me better able to handle the times sport wasn't going well.

While making money was never my focus, money was coming in, and financial success gave me inarguable evidence that Nike's view of sports marketing was outdated. According to Nike, making the Olympics and medaling was what it took to sell shoes; by their definition, I was deemed a failed marketing asset. I couldn't help but laugh. The professional sports industry was still stuck on the traditional masculine ideals of aggression and competition that drove the creation of organized sports in the late nineteenth century, long before women were allowed to participate. Winning still mattered, of course, but it wasn't the only thing that mattered to sports fans. Being a whole person was powerful, but the economics of sports (defined and maintained by men) didn't leave much space for that. Contracts penalized the rocky road inherent to life, especially the one commonly traveled by women.

More recently, we've seen that begin to change, thanks to a movement across sports led by mostly women of color. When Naomi Osaka declined a mandatory press conference to prioritize her mental health, trolls raged—but other minds opened to the idea of an athlete's agency. When Simone Biles withdrew from certain Olympic events to protect her health and safety, people accused her of being less American than Kerri Strug, who embodied the iconic image of sacrificing yourself for the gold; Biles steadfastly stood proud in the knowledge that her well-being was worth more than any medal. The women of the WNBA have braided social justice work into their identities as professional athletes, refusing to shut up and play. And in 2019, Alysia Montaño, Kara Goucher, and Allyson Felix bravely tackled the forbidden topic of pregnancy and sponsorship with the *New York Times*, specifically calling out Nike's hypocrisy in advertising the power of moms in sport while cutting the contracts of pregnant athletes. In the running space, only one brand already had progressive protection policies: the feminist brand Oiselle, which released the contract language they used to make it easier for more brands to adopt consistent practices. As consumer pressure mounted, the major companies fell in line: Burton, Adidas, Salomon, Altra, Brooks, New Balance, and eventually, after a couple of false starts, Nike. And right now, many of the most famous women athletes are joining forces to stand against the wave of bills attacking trans kids, advocating for an evolution of sport that prioritizes inclusion over everything else previously handed down as sacred. In the process, all these women and many more who don't have the elite athlete spotlight aren't just changing women's sport, they're changing sport for everyone.

I didn't have these athletic role models yet, but I was trying, in my own way, to be one. When I broke my navicular and narrowly missed the Olympics, and was unsure if I'd return to what I loved, I looked for guidance everywhere online. What do you do when things fall apart? How do you continue trying when the likelihood of success is so slim? How do you make yourself vulnerable after heartache? I found these stories in literature, in the lives of fictional characters, but I couldn't find these real-time stories in sports. Athletes weren't telling them. They weren't talking unless they were winning, reflecting back on rough times long gone. I needed material that would help me take one more step forward without the promise of a happy ending. So I wrote it myself.

I made a commitment to grow up and win and fail in public in my little world of running, because I wanted to provide at least one person's accurate representation of chasing big goals for the next person who searched the internet during a low point. I hoped it would inspire other pro athletes to do the same, and it did. But the biggest winner in the short term was me. The more my life expanded off the track, the more satisfied I was on it.

14

C FOR COURAGE

Maybe if I'd have just flown home from South Korea and put my legs up for a few weeks, recovering like every other track athlete, I would have a tattoo of the Olympic rings on my ribs right now. Instead, I spent the next seven weeks training for the New York City Marathon.

I told people I was doing it to get stronger for the 5K, and that was partially true. I did need a huge strength-building block of pure endurance training to have a chance to compete with the runners from East Africa in the London Olympics the next year. But I could have done that without flying to New York. The real reason I did the marathon was the money. I had run eighteen miles for long runs in the past and now someone was offering to pay me $25,000 to run a few more? Run it fast—faster than two hours and thirty-five minutes—and I'd earn double, nearly a year's salary.

What's more, being invited to race in the elite field in New York was an opportunity only a handful of people in the world get each year. 5K track runners aren't normally among them, the marathon being over eight times our race distance and favoring different physiological strengths, but New York Road Runners, the huge organization that puts on the marathon every year, liked to assemble a field of interesting stories as much as exciting competition; since I had a whole website full of stories, I was the easiest runner for the media to get to know. The *New York Times* picked me out of the bunch to follow all weekend for a feature.

When I asked the reporter why he chose me, he cited my blog. "You make elite running approachable," he told me. "Trust me, that's not easy to do." While he stayed in the background as I obsessed over what to eat and how to avoid needing to poop during the race, I could tell he was nervous for me. Daring to show up in a place you aren't sure you belong, with 100 percent certainty of discomfort unlike any you've ever known before, is the story of first-time marathoners everywhere.

So is "hitting the wall," which I did—spectacularly. At mile nineteen, I was on pace for the big payday, methodically running 5:45 per mile, and then, out of nowhere, it was as if every spring in my body wore out, the impact of the asphalt underfoot tenderizing my thighs and rattling my vertebrae. I began to slow, but being five minutes ahead of big-money-pace, I didn't worry. Then I slowed some more. With two miles to go, I calculated that all I needed to do was maintain the pace of my typical morning jog to get the $50,000. Such a simple task. But one by one, the muscles of my body shut down like the lights in a warehouse, including the ones that held my eyelids open. Through tiny slits, I saw the walls of screaming fans leaning over the barricades in Central Park turn into one blob of sound. In my mind's eye, the only eye that worked now, thousands of dollar bills were being released into the wind behind me with every step. I actually laughed out loud at the absurdity of it all as the finish line finally approached.

I went home with $25,000 and a limp. A sore knee that had made itself known before the race was, unsurprisingly, not improved by racing a marathon. But it was nothing that rest wouldn't take care of, I thought. I spent the holiday season enthusiastically filling the influx of new orders for Picky Bars and Believe Training Journals from customers who'd discovered me through the *New York Times* or my *Runner's World* magazine cover. Our wild idea to start a subscription club with monthly deliveries, something we'd only seen from wine clubs and Dollar Shave Club at the time, revolutionized our business. Subscribers allowed us to predict our inventory needs each month with 98 percent accuracy, and unlike retailers who paid thirty, sixty, or even ninety days after receiving bars, subscribers paid first. We'd cracked the code for surviving as a food startup, Jesse was guiding us beautifully as CEO, and with bars being made in our home for ten hours a day by a fleet of mostly college students, we were selling nearly enough bars to meet the minimum order requirements of a contract manufacturer. Once someone else could make them for us, we'd have full use of our house back.

Growing Picky Bars served as an excellent distraction while I waited for my knee to improve. IT band syndrome, or "runner's knee," has no standard recovery timeline. A common injury for beginner runners with poor glute strength, it generally heals quickly through rest, massage, and physical therapy. Swimming didn't hurt, so I learned the crawl stroke, did my Jane Fonda leg lifts, and waited for it to turn around. Weeks turned to months.

Over that time, my goal changed from medaling in London to making my first Olympic team. Then maybe not making the team, but running respectably at the Trials. But eventually, I had to face reality. If I raced at the Trials, I would embarrass myself. The invincible athlete who was seventh in the world was gone.

"WHAT DO YOU want to do?" Mark asked me over pancakes.

"I don't want to quit," I said.

"Why not? You gotta accept the situation, love."

"I just have this feeling it will be my last Olympic Trials. I want to have a baby next year; my contract is up in a few months; I don't know what will happen. But I've earned a lane at the Trials, Mark. That still means something to me, even if I suck. I just want to find a way to get to the starting line and have an experience. I need your help."

This was a big ask. Mark was a self-proclaimed "elitist" in the sense that his coaching interest was purely in high performance. He laced his fingers together and surveyed me.

"If that's what you want, love. We'll think outside the box. *Way* outside the box. I have some ideas." He stuffed some pancake in his mouth and muffled out, "Women. I swear." His words were grumpy, but the smile lines around his eyes gave him away. He opened his notebook and started scribbling.

Strides—short bursts of faster speeds—created a knee angle that felt fine for some reason we couldn't pinpoint. So we extended my sprints longer and longer each week. My running total increased up to about seven miles per week, fewer than what I used to do in a day, but every one of those miles was at race pace or faster. The last big workout before the Olympic Trials, I was able to run a mile in 4:40, take a break, and then repeat that two more times, a workout nobody in their right mind would think could be achieved without a large base of conventional training. Those were some of the most fun times working with Mark. We continually surprised and delighted ourselves, anchored by curiosity. I managed to stay in the moment so well that I could forget that the race we were preparing for was one of the highest-stakes events in the world.

But then the temporary bleachers went up, turning my home track into a stadium for twelve thousand fans. NBC started setting up their aerial shot equipment. All of TrackTown, USA, transformed itself into the mecca for the Olympic dream with its bold billboards, its win or fail energy, its narrow view of success. A banner was hung over Cap's Corner, Nike's VIP seating, where spectators would watch the events with private catering. "Are you sure you want to do this?" my agent asked, pointing out that Nike was more likely to be forgiving if I missed a race due to injury than if I raced and recorded a terrible result. Without exception, people in my life were surprised I was still planning to race, and more than a handful tried to gently talk me out of it. They didn't want to see me fail.

At the press conference a few days before opening ceremony, the story the first reporter angled for was a life or death narrative of my last chance to make an Olympic team and be redeemed for 2008's failure. When I told them about my knee, my lack of formal preparation, and my goal to simply finish, another one said, "You've got to be the fastest 5K runner in history not to make an Olympic team. It seems you can't catch a break. How will it feel stepping out there, knowing that six months ago you were a favorite to win?"

My stomach turned over. "Four years ago, I bought into the idea that all that mattered was the Olympics. I lived like the running monk everyone told me to be, and it killed the joy of everything. Since then, I've defined success for myself and I do it my own way. I reject the idea that all that matters is becoming an Olympian. It's wrong, and it's a limiting belief that's not good for the sport, either. There are so many other good stories here. The fact is almost *nobody* traveling all the way here with their friends and family in tow will make the Olympics. Simply getting here is winning for most people."

"That's great, but that doesn't change the fact that the entire point of the Olympic Trials is to select the team," the reporter said.

"No . . . I get to decide what the point is," I said.

"I can't tell if you're being wise or delusional."

"Me neither."

A chuckle ran through the room.

"This isn't the ending I dreamed of, sure. But when you realize failing doesn't make you a failure, you give yourself permission to try all sorts of things."

"AM I DELUSIONAL?" I asked Mark at the track the day after the press conference. Despite my conviction at the time, the reporter's words swirled in and out of my mind throughout my final pre-race shakeout.

"You're bloody crazy; you know that, I know that, we all know that. Nothing new to report there."

Mark turned his attention to teammate and 800-meter specialist Nick Symmonds lining up for an interval and clicked his stopwatch. We both watched Nick power around the bend. He looked ready. Nick always managed to be ready to win at exactly the right time.

I sat down to change out of my spikes and fiddled with a knot for a few seconds before giving up. In two days, I'd be racing. All around the track were athletes in peak form, executing form drills, gliding over hurdles. It looked so easy, and I remembered what it felt like to be truly prepared. I felt emotions swelling up and walked off the side of the track into the weeds, the burrs scraping my ankles until I moved far enough away from the track to safely release whatever was coming. This could have been so different. It was hard to breathe. Somewhere, living in my body, was the alternate story where I won it all. I didn't want this story.

The last couple of nights, I stayed at a friend's cabin on the McKenzie River, where there was no offending grass pollen or people, a plan I had made for peak performance months before everything went wrong. From my little nest on the sofa, watching the fire, the idea of racing was making me squirm so badly, I told Jesse I wanted to stay here for the rest of the week and withdraw.

"Tell me why," he said.

"I am so much better than this. Nobody wants to see this. I don't want to see this. It's going to be humiliating."

"Who says?"

I just sat there, staring at the fire, biting my fingernail.

"Okay, just for fun, tell me why you should do it."

"Because I hate that I felt good about it until everyone else showed up. I hate giving that power to anyone. I've spent so much time writing about how *it's all about the journey* or whatever, and now I feel full of shit."

"It's easy to say it's all about the journey when you're winning," he said.

"With the arena and all the excitement . . . I do it for me, but I'm also a *performer,* Jesse. I wanted to show them what I can *do.*"

"You can still show them who you are."

ON MY PRE-RACE BLOG I made my intention for the race clear, and was honest about being scared. *If you're in the stands and want to show support, give me a sign when I walk out onto the track. Raise your hand and make a* C *for courage. XO, Lauren*

I knew it was cheesy, but I couldn't think of anything better, and I figured very few of my readers, if any, were actual ticket holders in TrackTown, much less for the midweek preliminary round of the women's 5,000.

Following the official onto Hayward Field, tucked single file among my competitors, I took it in. The iconic angle of the overhang above the sardined benches in the grandstands. The scoreboard and the towering lights. The track under my feet was clean, all dirt blasted free from the bumpy rubber. You could almost smell the fresh coat of paint marking the lanes. While everyone hopped nervously around me, I remained still.

Here I was, guaranteed to lose, but I looked at the stands, and saw people stand up, one by one: family, friends from the local running club, and so many people I didn't recognize, all smiling at me and making the letter *C.* They were all around me. I cried, and then smiled.

I shed my warmup layers, put them into my basket by the starting line, and thanked the volunteer standing guard over it. I lay on my back, feeling the track press against me, and closed my eyes. I listened to the sounds of the stadium. The rhythmic clapping increasing in speed meant a jumper was sprinting down the runway. The held breath and then the supportive but humble applause indicated an average mark. Sport was full of average marks and missed shots. It was still beautiful.

My preliminary round of the 5K turned out to be strategic, with a slow enough pace that I was able to keep up, even with my compromised fitness. The final sprint, though, was fierce, the leaders blasted off, and my mid-pack finish was hard-fought. I crossed the line with the same grit I summoned in the final of the World Championships the year before and was elated that I was able to stay present and positive the entire race. I'd done what I'd come for, and now I could go home proud. An eruption of cheers came from the area where my family was sitting, and I saw a little *q* next to my time on the scoreboard, which was somehow under 16:00! They'd posted the qualifiers who'd earned lanes in the final, and to my shock, I was one of them. Never expecting to make the final, I hadn't been keeping track of time or place. I was just focused on running the race as hard as I could.

ON THE DAY of the final, my body felt as though I'd been slammed against a wall like a dirty bath mat, and I walked onto the track laughing at how bad my legs felt simply walking while my competitors did last-minute explosive drills like it was nothing. But when I looked up toward the stands, the *C*'s were still there, held up by strangers and friends. People called out my name, and I gave them a wave and a here-goes-nothing smile. I wondered who they were, what their stories were, what we shared. And then I narrowed my attention to my body, and my breath, and my left toes just below the starting line.

The pity clap is a term used to describe the obligatory clapping given to the person who finishes "DFL"—dead fucking last. On my final lap of the Olympic Trials, all alone as I made my way off the famous Bowerman curve on wobbly legs in the final of the women's 5,000 meters, I heard clapping rise around me out of nowhere. I was confused, since the winners had crossed the line a good while back. It wasn't the rhythmic clap of a jumping event; it was softer and steadier. Kind, even. Then I realized it was for me. Surprisingly, it didn't sound like pity. It sounded like recognition. When the race was finally over, I felt completely spent and a little sad, but mostly in quiet awe of all I had experienced by giving myself a chance.

Everywhere I wobbled after my race, at the festival next to the track, in the bar afterward, people came up to congratulate me. Several of them were wearing a fan shirt with my silhouette on it. Nike hadn't made the shirt; it was a small women's running brand out of Seattle called Oiselle, I learned. The company had posted about them on Twitter, and a crowd of fans had apparently scooped up the freebies on a street corner. I was given my own T-shirt by Sarah Lesko, the organizer of the flash mob, along with an invitation to visit them the next day to meet their small team.

While Nike had taken over and decorated an entire building on University of Oregon's campus, the Oiselle house, called "the hippie house," was a vacation rental full of family artifacts that smelled of vintage hardcover books. It was so casual, so human. Dr. Sarah Lesko, a woman in her midforties who'd organized the fan shirts, directed me to a table full of snacks, and I dug in and plopped down in the living room where people were gathering. It felt so easy to connect, like I'd known them for years.

In a way, I had. For two years I'd been interacting with their brand on Twitter. Oiselle (which meant "female bird" in French, I learned, and was pronounced "wah-zell") was led by CEO Sally Bergesen. She ran the business's Twitter account herself, and our banter was turning out to be even better in person than online. In our interactions, I found myself wishing I could run for them. Being at the Oiselle house should have felt like a breach of contract with Nike, but they were so tiny that Nike didn't even know who they were. Nobody on the elite side of the sport did. I only followed them because they spoke to their audience of women runners so differently from anyone else, which made sense, of course, since the brand was run entirely by women. Sally and I also followed one another for more practical reasons. Oiselle, like Picky Bars, had originated during the recession, and we both used social media tools to build our brands in a scrappy, direct-to-consumer way. While Nike and PowerBar had millions to throw at traditional marketing, Oiselle and Picky Bars were out there rubbing sticks together to make fire, blowing on one another's flames from time to time. Sharing the love.

By the end of my time at the hippie house, Sally had invited me up to Seattle for a visit to "the Nest"—the company's headquarters. She dropped enough hints about money for me to know they had very little to offer, but I said I'd come up anyway. I needed to see what they were doing. I drove home high on creative energy, fantasizing about what was possible when women were not just tools for a campaign, but were also centered in every part of the business, from the inside out.

I took that energy straight up to Beaverton, Oregon, the next day. My business with Ro, making training journals and now T-shirts, had attracted the attention of a man at Nike named Aaron. With Lululemon on the rise, all the major sports brands were bleeding women customers, and Nike was on the hunt for ways to speak to women to win them back. Aaron invited us to pitch our concepts at a series of meetings to see where they fit. The inventory management business was not our strong suit, or frankly, our aspiration, and if Nike took on a collection based on our ideas, we could hand it off and have a far greater reach. How payment would work wasn't clear.

Ro and I worked our way through meetings on the Nike campus like levels of a video game. Public speaking makes me way more nervous than any race, but with each pitch I grew more and more confident, boosted by Ro's bravery and passion. She would hand off her new baby to her partner, Myles, in the hall and head into each conference room intent on making things better for the next generation. We told our stories from our days as athletes; we shared the big moments when we failed, and the ones when we lost our love of the sport due to fear and negative thoughts. We shared the research-based tools we used to turn things around, reach our potential, ride out the tough times, and experience joy.

Everyone has this inner critic sabotaging them, but women especially experience this, as we are squeezed from all sides. We presented a concept for a product line that helped women shift their mindset away from negative chatter and anchor it back onto themselves. It was a way to *stay* with yourself rooted in elite sport, but applicable to everyone. We delivered a case for a woman-centered marketing approach that diverged significantly from the norm. Nike Brand loved it. The women's category loved it. Girl Effect, the nonprofit affiliated with Nike that empowered girls through sport, loved it. Nobody seemed to know how we'd get paid, but the easiest business path would be if we were sponsored athletes on the roster. My contract with Nike was up in a couple of months. Ro's New Balance contract was up soon, too. Feeling so much support for our idea within the company, I felt confident when I walked into Cap's office that he would finally see the fullness of what I had to offer.

I was mistaken. He didn't seem interested in the meetings and appeared annoyed by the distraction. He asked if I'd recovered from the disappointment of the Trials, and I told him the story and explained that it was actually a really good day for me. He asked me if I planned to try again, and what my next four years would look like, and I told him the truth: that I wanted to have a baby and then make a comeback, but that I wanted to direct my racing schedule toward more community-based events, like road races, in addition to track.

He told me Nike didn't have an official pregnancy policy, but their standard was to treat it like a severe injury and suspend my pay for the year.

"If you get back to racing form, your pay resumes, no problem."

"It doesn't make sense," I said to Cap. "Kara Goucher and Paula Radcliffe had babies and their bumps were on the covers of magazines. They did appearances everywhere and got way more well-known. That experience made them more relatable." Nike had become the brand associated with pregnant running because of them. It hit me then that Kara, Nike's poster woman for pregnancy and running, had been required to do all that work for free.

"I can't pay women for taking a year off racing and not the men. That's not fair."

"Trust me, I wish my husband could carry the baby, but he can't. If you ask me, that's what's not fair."

Cap reluctantly offered me an annual salary of $25,000 to own me exclusively from head to toe for four more years, after the suspension year. One injury and it would be cut in half, or worse, and then what? A friend of mine had been reduced down to four figures a year, but Nike wouldn't let him leave for another brand offering him a living wage. The salary was insulting, and I said so. He said I could go seek a competing offer and bring it back, but they had the first right of refusal.

I knew my value was more than that. Picky Bars' revenue numbers had gone from $80,000 to $240,000 in one year, and we projected at least a half million in sales in 2013. (In eight years, we would sell it to Laird Superfood for twelve million dollars.) I wasn't done trying to win, but I also knew that my impact on the sport would be limited if I were only focused on winning random track races in Europe, or even going to the Olympics. I had so much more I wanted to give, and there were so many kinds of sports stories worth telling.

I was ready to burn the Nike campus down when I walked out to meet Ro in the lobby. As bad as Cap's offer was for me, he had nothing for Ro, who had a four-month-old baby. Once again, I found myself in CEO Mark Parker's office, imploring the brand to have common sense. I laid my samples on the coffee table and filled him in on the meetings. I relayed the discussion around pregnancy, expecting him to be horrified by Nike's pregnancy policy, especially the requirement for athletes to remain exclusive to Nike and do appearances while not getting paid. Instead of being outraged, he expressed support for Cap having his own philosophies and the necessity of letting his leaders lead. It was clear I'd reached my expiration date. I wish I'd fought harder, stormed out even, but the truth is that his lack of reaction made me doubt myself. Nobody I knew was fighting for pregnancy support in 2012. With my fertile years numbered, I felt like I had to choose between being a mother and being an athlete.

Most people in power, all men, acknowledged this sucked but then justified it with views similar to those around the underfunding of women's pro sports in general. This presumption of "lower market value" for all things female in the sports industry runs deep, and the least manly thing you can do in sports is get pregnant and breastfeed. Simply put, it's a career-ender. These fundamental experiences only the female body can have simply fell too far outside the male template, resulting in the discarding of so many women, all based on a myth that motherhood, like puberty, is an injury you can't come back from. Brand-new research, which Ro went on to help with years later, shows that elite female athlete performances are no worse post-baby than pre-baby when they are given time to recover from pregnancy and birth. Nothing can change until those in power see female-bodied experiences as deserving of their own norms.

When I left Mark's office, I walked back through campus toward my car. Everything felt so different than it had nine years earlier when I signed with Nike. As I walked on perfectly manicured paths with beautiful landscaping that ran around tall buildings with big windows and modern architecture, I thought about all they'd done that allowed them to pay for it. Lance Armstrong still had a building named after him then, but everyone knew he was cheating; other sponsors had dropped him, and he was only a few months away from confessing to Oprah. That building used to inspire me, but now it pissed me off. Who gets the benefit of the doubt at Nike? The most powerful sports brand in the world was saying cheating can be overlooked, but the fundamental realities of womanhood seemed insurmountable. For the first time, I felt the courage to leave it behind.

| 15 |

BIRD MACHINE

Watch out for the landmines," Sally said, pointing down at a splat of pink vomit on the concrete with one hand while jiggling a key into an old steel lock with the other. "Our downstairs neighbors leave something to be desired."

"The Little Red Hen," I read aloud. "At least the bar's name is on-brand."

"Indeed." The door finally gave way and Sally waved me in. "We take our birds *very* seriously around here."

She led me up a flight of stairs and opened the door to suite 201. "Welcome to the Nest!" I looked around. A budget office space from the '70s had been rendered borderline Pinterest-worthy with one stripe of fresh green paint around the walls, framed running campaigns, and yes, bird art. All I had to do was stand in the middle of the nine-hundred-square-foot room and spin to see just about every stage of the apparel business: design boards with clipped inspiration, a table strewn with fabric swatches and sketchbooks, factory samples stacked in clear plastic bins, a mannequin bust for adjustments, and a single clothing rack that held the entire fall line.

In a space that was barely twice the size of the Picky Bars office, I felt at home. The three employees, all women, were excited to have a visitor. The team possessed a youthful feeling of possibility that it could become anything it wanted to be. I picked up a pack of "rundies," underwear with days of training listed on them instead of days of the week: long run, fartlek, easy six, recovery. Sally had sent me a set as a courting gift, and the "fartlek" pair really stood out. Swedish for "speed-play," it's a term competitive runners would know, but certainly not everyone. "I love that you make things that speak to women who approach the sport from different perspectives. And there's whimsy and fun for both competitive and participatory runners."

"There's room for all of it," she said. "Speaking of running, wanna go for an easy six?"

Sally and I changed into some new running samples, hopped back over the vomit, and set out on the loop around Green Lakes, a busy park in northeast Seattle surrounded mostly by old craftsman homes and small businesses. As we ran side by side and navigated dog walkers and stroller joggers, we talked. I told her about the mantra designs Ro and I had been pitching at Nike, and the obstacle course of meetings with different groups of people who didn't talk to one another. The most common concern expressed by the men in the room was whether female customers would be turned off by our competitive backgrounds.

"Did you ask them if they felt that way about men?" she asked.

"Yes! They felt that recreational women wouldn't connect with professionals. I said that's on the storyteller. You don't have to be a competitive athlete to appreciate the thrills and lessons from competitive sport."

"That's true," Sally said. "And, your relationship with sport can change over time. Especially for women, with pregnancy, caregiving, career, etc. I know mine has. As a women's brand, we want to remind women of that. Things can change. You can change. We want to be there for women during all of it."

"Yes!" I said, feeling so happy to hear someone get it. "I'm just so tired of trying to explain to Nike why they should care about women. I get into these rooms, but I must not be articulating it well enough."

"They started as an innovative men's brand, and that's their DNA. If you're lucky enough to be successful as a startup, you become bigger. And bigger. And big ships are harder to steer," she said. "Women will always just be a category to them."

"Well, that leaves room for—you," I said, after almost saying "us."

When I first met Sally at the Trials, I was inspired by Oiselle's origin story. Finding that the bunched elastic that came standard on running shorts no longer felt comfortable on her postpartum belly, she designed something better: the first pair of flat-waisted shorts. Hers was a classic entrepreneurship story with a feminist bent. It was easy to believe she was a designer, but it took me a while to believe Sally was the CEO. That's how strong my gender bias was. Every major sports brand was led by a white man. She had been standing next to a man named Bob Lesko who'd introduced himself as an investor, and I'd thought, *I bet this guy* actually *runs things*. After all, Sally had two daughters—how would that work? Now that I was in Seattle running beside her, I felt embarrassed. In just a few miles, Sally changed my view of leadership, of the industry, of what was possible. She was forty-two; she knew who she was and what she wanted. I wanted her to succeed. I wanted to learn from her. I wanted to become someone like her.

We finished our run at a Starbucks and talked about family and business and running and our goals for all three. There was clear synergy and an obvious way for each of us to contribute. She had a brand that centered women and was nimble and authentic. I had professional athlete skills and an audience. We both had lots of ideas. When we talked about them, we had an alchemy that delighted us.

"I want to make this happen," I said.

"Let's make it happen," she said.

"Okay, there's just one thing," I said, and the feeling of pre-race nerves quickened my heart rate. "Jesse and I want to have a baby this year. I won't be able to race professionally for a year or so, but I still plan to run through pregnancy while I can, and write, and be in the community. I know I can contribute—" She cut me off.

"That's great!"

"What do you mean that's great?"

"I mean that's wonderful! We'll throw you a baby shower."

"Will there be a suspension?"

"Why would there be a suspension?"

I told her about Nike and she rolled her eyes.

"Here's the thing about women," she said. "Sometimes, we have babies."

I couldn't believe what I was hearing and felt empowered to write up a proposal for Sally as soon as I got home.

BOB AND SARAH LESKO, early investors in Oiselle, were my hosts for my night in Seattle. After they set me up in their basement room, we plopped down on the living room sofas to chat for a few minutes and didn't go to bed until well after midnight.

While Sally and I had talked about business, the Leskos and I nerded out mostly on running. Ex–elite runners who fell in love on the track team at Yale, Bob and Sarah left running behind for a while to get careers and kids going. Sarah went to medical school and residency and Bob got started in finance, and somehow in the middle of all of that, three boys were born. Track and field pulled them back in eventually as fans, and they watched the 5K the year I said "balls" on ESPN. They'd followed me ever since.

We got to talking about Mary Cain, the latest phenom, who at fifteen years old was breaking all the high school records. In Eugene, we'd all just watched her break the junior record in the 1,500 at the Olympic Trials. They wanted to know what I thought about Alberto Salazar coaching her, and I told them I was worried.

Together we listed off at least two dozen young phenoms over the years who'd disappeared from the sport. Mary Cain was going pro with Nike any day now, and I couldn't imagine a worse environment to go through puberty than the Nike Oregon Project under Salazar. "He's going to destroy her," I said. Alberto pushed every limit, stretched every rule, and clearly didn't know how to provide a safe environment for a developing girl. I'd been around one of the other young girls he'd isolated in Portland in a house sealed off and pressurized to ten thousand feet of elevation while she fell down the hole of an eating disorder. The night I spent around her in that house, I felt this mama bear desire to help, but didn't know how. I told Alberto about the laxatives and binging I saw, and he thanked me and said he had tried to help. I don't know what he did or didn't do, but it's hard to imagine it was a safe environment for her, given the public testimonies of athletes who came later. In NOP, a program iconic for its sink-or-swim mentality, the disposability of human beings was romanticized in the name of dreaming big. The teen girls in Alberto's care didn't stand a chance.

"Alberto coaching adolescent girls should be illegal," I thought aloud.

Sarah gave insights about female development and natural performance plateaus from a medical perspective, and we talked about how women really hit their prime in their late twenties and beyond. "Think of all the women in their early twenties who never find out how good they can be," she said.

"If I were a sports company," I said, daring to speak my dreams aloud to them, "I'd recruit the women other brands overlook. The ones who had talent when they were younger and haven't been able to capitalize on it. Talent doesn't go away. Maybe their environment didn't support them through puberty. Maybe they hit a slump at an inopportune time that made people give up on them. Maybe they fought their bodies for a while and didn't have enough time to come back from it. *Those* are the women I'd recruit."

"Would you ever consider coaching a group of your own?" Sarah asked.

I laughed. They didn't.

"I have no experience."

"Doesn't stop men from doing it all the time," Bob said, and I smiled.

"Well, I plan to coach myself from now on. Maybe in a few years I'll be ready to coach other people."

Sarah said, "If you trust yourself enough to do that, you could coach other people. You've had great mentors, some of the best coaches in the world."

"True."

Bob was getting excited. "Maybe Oiselle could sponsor it! It would be perfect."

"An all-female pro team coached by a woman. Does that even exist?" Sarah asked.

We got quiet while we mulled the potential in this idea. It wasn't too far off the training center concept I'd been scribbling about in notebooks since 2004, but I'd always imagined hiring a coach (and in my mind, that coach was a man). I thought about Sally and Oiselle. About what's possible when companies and teams put women at the center. She built shorts for women so they could feel good in their changing bodies, clothes that didn't get in the way of that feeling of unselfconscious flight. What if we did the same with sports? What would a team look like if we built it entirely around the female athlete and worked to remove the obstructive forces around them?

On December 31, 2012, Sally stood beside me and we posed for a photo in front of my contract offer. I was three months pregnant. Sally couldn't offer much salary to start, but it would grow, and she offered me stock and made me a partner, which was something Nike could not match. While watching my name roll in familiar curves onto the pages, I couldn't stop smiling. That night, we filled a local bar with people from the Oiselle community, my family, and a few close friends. Sally's partner, Alec, played his guitar, and as midnight struck, I was kissing Jesse on the dance floor and feeling like everything fit. We were moving to Bend, our dream location to train and live. Jesse was on his way to becoming one of the best professional triathletes in the world. Moving Picky Bars to Bend would provide jobs in his hometown, a childhood dream of his. I was joining a team I trusted, and carrying the beginnings of new life. I believe it was the first time a female professional athlete had inked a significant endorsement deal while openly pregnant. It felt like progress. I hoped that my being vocal about the support I was receiving over the next year would model a different way for the industry, inspiring people to demand more.

JUDE WAS BORN in June. I had been a good sport through pregnancy, but I never really felt at home in my body until its tenant left. The science nerd in me marveled at what the female body could do, breasts transforming into milk machines, hormones creating a letdown of milk without any personal control. I appreciated how miraculous it all was intellectually, but pregnancy and childbirth— for both Jude and my second child, Zadie, four years later—were experiences I wished someone else's body were having. As much as I loved my son, I often struggled to feel at home as a mother, and I resented the way my life was disproportionately affected by our choice to have a child. Mothering put the fact of my womanhood front and center in my life. For the first time in our relationship, Jesse and I found ourselves in highly gendered roles that took a toll on us over time and eventually required readjusting. But in the beginning we never questioned that Jesse would travel alone to focus on all his triathlon races and training camps, while I would power through all of my trips with a baby, two arms doing the work of twelve. Fortunately, at Oiselle, there were always a lot of hands to help hold a baby, freezers to store milk, and experienced moms to round up a running stroller or a babysitter. I felt supported and safe, feelings I had never associated with motherhood and professional sport before.

My first big work trip with Oiselle was to participate in a runway show at New York Fashion Week. Christy Turlington Burns, the maternal health activist and supermodel, was rocking a three-month-old Jude and giving runway tips while a group of us walked along a line of masking tape stretched across our Airbnb floor in front of her. The instruction to "just walk normally" was proving difficult for a group of runners to follow.

The idea was to put athletes on the runway alongside agency models, showcase activewear as you would fashion, and tell a story about it. Runners aren't models, and running clothes don't exactly scream "fashion." But Oiselle's clothes were different, intended to transition from sport to life and back again; we were on the front end of the incoming athleisure trend.

I'll never forget sitting in the green room before the shows with all the agency models drinking small sips of coconut water and staring at us while we ate breakfast sandwiches. Or filing through the hair and makeup stations provided by the event and watching women be transformed into art to match the aesthetic of different designers' visions. When it was our turn to walk, we had a blast, and for the finale I walked the runway in my competition kit. The event made running news and drew new eyes to Oiselle, and the *New York Times* covered our next show.

The picture of me in my racing uniform spread through the larger women's running community and created an unexpected reaction online.

"I can't believe she had a baby three months ago."

"This makes me feel like shit."

"How did she get her body back so fast?"

"What's wrong with my body?"

Women face immense pressure to experience pregnancy like leave-no-trace camping, with the goal being zero evidence on the body that it occurred at all. I felt sick that my photo reinforced that ideal, which was the last thing I wanted.

On my blog, I reminded people that the image of me on the runway was one of hundreds of photos taken during that twenty-second walk. It was selected for its lighting and angles and whatever other standards the industry valued, and most likely edited. I posted the runway photo alongside other photos taken around the same time at my home that showed my belly rolled over my waistband, a constellation of dimples on my thigh.

This was not a common image to post on the internet in 2013, and it was frightening to push the publish button. But when I did, over a million people around the world read the blog, and many engaged with the hashtag #KeepingItReal, posting their own photos of loose belly skin, thigh fat vibrating from impact, faces ugly with unselfconscious effort, cheeks drooping on their down step. People couldn't get enough, and the energy around this fifteen minutes of fame changed completely. It was yet another reminder that people are hungry for the truth, and that truth spurs liberation.

MANY OPPORTUNITIES OPENED after that. My blog expanded into a monthly column for *Runner's World* called "The Fast Life," and I was photographed for the cover. During the shoot, I was told that their creative guidelines required women to wear formfitting spandex shorts and expose their midriffs. Feeling more empowered now, I insisted I wear a short with a loose leg, the ones I felt best in, and after initially protesting, they conceded. It was a small victory, but a reminder that it was so much easier to resist with a flock of women behind you.

Back at Oiselle, after the issue came out, Sarah and Sally set me up at a table where I sat for multiple days, working my way through stacks of postal boxes filled with large manila envelopes. I had put out an offer to autograph any copies of *Runner's World* sent to the Nest with a postage-paid return envelope, and most people sent personal messages along with their magazines. Some were simple notes of encouragement and kindness that made me feel both shy and proud. I wasn't expecting the stories, the outpouring of honesty about the struggles people faced with sport and their bodies, stories from everyone from high schoolers to baby boomers. Readers I heard from were unwinding trauma from simply being women in the world, or their sport experiences, or their daughters' sport experiences; almost none of these athletes were elite. It helped me see how broad the problem was, how predictable, and it increased the urgency I felt to make sports a more empowering environment for women and girls.

I wrote a "Letter to My Younger Self" for a high school running website called MileSplit, warning my younger self against the shadow of the sport and the choices I'd be faced with, and encouraging her to embrace changes to her body with self-love and the long view in mind. The article blew up online and continues to be circulated in waves a few times a year. Oiselle printed five hundred paper copies and mailed them directly to high school coaches of competitive cross-country teams around the country. Unsure how to effect policy change, I tried to use honest storytelling as preventative medicine, and social media as zinc to stop a cold before it gets too bad. The Shorty Awards, an awards show that recognizes social media impact, gave me the award for best professional athlete, a huge surprise in a category with far more famous nominees like Kevin Durant.

Sally, the Leskos, and I worked well together and shared a passion for industry change. Through opinion pieces, media exposure, and direct advocacy, we tackled exploitation of athletes and noncompetitive practices by Nike and USA Track and Field, the national governing body of the sport. Nike's financial hold on the sport created a hostile environment for a women's brand, and for anyone who spoke out. I ran for a seat on the board of directors of USATF as an athlete representative, with a goal to divert the organization's hoarded funds into the pockets of athletes and increase accountability of the leadership, and I won. The toxic culture of political backstabbing made it the most miserable experience of my professional life, but there were a few wins for athlete revenue.

Kara Goucher, my old rival and one of Nike's biggest stars, saw the support I was getting from Oiselle and wanted to join us in 2014. I didn't want her to at first, convinced I didn't like her after

2008 when she rejected my plea for a spot on the team, but after thinking about it, I realized she was a stand-in for the grief I still hadn't worked through from barely missing the Olympics. Over the years, there were times I hadn't spoken highly of her, and now I felt ashamed of what that old bruise caused by jealousy brought out in me. Kara's interest in Oiselle became a chance to clear the air, so we set up a call. I was honest with her, and she showed me empathy, connecting with my feelings of powerlessness in a way that made us both cry. When she described the abuse of power by Alberto and Nike and her plans to hold them accountable, I wanted her to have a place where she could safely express her voice and her power. She joined the team.

Kara became one of the most outspoken athletes in the world against performance-enhancing drugs. She blew the whistle on Nike and Salazar for anti-doping violations and abuse, and has endured years of testimony and court dates and appeals in a battle that will protect future generations. I admired her as an advocate and a teammate, and watching the personal toll the advocacy took on her life was sobering. When she raced for Oiselle and finished fourth in the Olympic Marathon Trials, I was cheering her on from the sidelines, and when she cried from the anguish of missing the Olympics by one spot, my heart broke along with hers.

OISELLE HASN'T BEEN PERFECT. You can be by women, for women, and have plenty of blind spots and cause harm. Shortly after signing, my friend and former coach Dena Evans called me. "I love the shorts! And I love what you guys are doing. But looking at your website . . . it's pretty . . . white. Borderline Nordic. It almost looks like whiteness is aspirational." I was embarrassed about the website and embarrassed I hadn't noticed, and I shared Dena's observation with Sally. Then I started learning about intersectional feminism. I realized that during all my previous activism I had been centering people like me. Like generations of white feminists before me, I believed the most important thing was getting in the room with those in power; once rights had been secured for the group white men were most likely to cede it to, then it would be easier to expand those rights to others, or they would somehow miraculously trickle down. I couldn't have been more wrong. White feminism is laced with racism, intentional or not. If I had approached Mark Parker as an intersectional feminist, I would have advocated for true body diversity, not just the inclusion of muscles. The legacy of racism and redlining resulted in my communities being so homogenous that I didn't even know what I didn't know.

Oiselle has become more intersectional in its feminism over the years, reflected in storytelling, hiring, investing in extended sizing, building inclusive community, and more. But even though it's the most vocal and feminist brand in running and maybe sports, there's still plenty of room to improve. It's also a challenge to stay afloat. To run a business in a feminist way, you butt up against capitalism itself. You are far from the wet dream of the investment capital world. Your cost of goods is higher and your growth goals aren't sexy when you're building for longevity. You receive criticism and lose customers when you speak out against transphobia and racism in sports, but you educate some and gain others.

As the minority in an industry, you often face a choice. Wait to be successful before trying to change things, or speak up as you go, thereby risking your chance of succeeding at all. Advocacy can be exhausting: Some days are like hacking a new path through thorns with a spoon while naked. And it is undeniably more dangerous for those with multiple marginalized identities. But it can also be like running. There is a feeling of integrity in the daily work, exhilaration in taking the lead, and satisfaction in seeing an effort through to the finish line, even if the finish line keeps moving.

My racing life and my work life were finally in alignment when I partnered with Oiselle. *I* was in alignment. I had traded my obsession with being "the best" for being good. And I'm not talking about "good" in the normal sports term—"good" meaning "okay, but not great." I'm talking about *goodness*. I wanted more goodness in sport, in running. Not just in the recreational world where that idea was more naturally embraced, but in the professional world, too. If I was going to coach, I needed sports to be *good* for the athletes I coached. I needed to build the experience I wanted for my younger self. While that girl was grown up now, there were so many girls out there hoping that someone might holistically support them.

BEYOND THE LANES

I was six weeks postpartum when my first athlete recruit, Mel Lawrence, came to visit me in Bend. She had finished second, second, second, and fifth at Foot Locker in her four years of high school, arguably the greatest competitor the event had ever seen, and after one good year at the University of Washington, she'd spent the next four injured. In other words, she was exactly the type of athlete I wanted to mentor: talented, driven, and looking to make a comeback.

I'd known Mel for some time; I'd attended Foot Locker in 2003 and served as the pro athlete mentor for athletes from her region. Mel was so grounded then, even in the face of all the pomp and circumstance. Her years of injuries had eroded some of her belief in herself, but she was still the same person, and she made it clear a spark was still there. I told her that talent doesn't go away, that women often just need a longer runway and a healthy environment in which to develop it. I really believed that she could be one of the best in the world. She was in. So were a few other talented young athletes. Just like that, I was a coach.

Oiselle was the sponsor of the team, which we called Littlewing Athletics, and the Leskos and I made it work. Our approach started with health. Jay Dicharry, a renowned physical therapist and expert in biomechanical analysis, got the athletes on a state-of-the-art force-plate treadmill and identified the imbalances and root causes of the injuries the athletes had dealt with over the years, prescribed corrective work to achieve symmetry in their gaits, and performed regular follow-up tests. We advised preventative PT and massage on a weekly basis. A family doctor, dentist, and ob-gyn were on hand for general medical needs. We hired a registered dietician. Mental health care was available as needed at first and became strongly recommended within a couple years. We provided housing to those who needed it. The Leskos were the world's best support crew. They not only financed the club, but also provided emotional support and mentorship for everyone, including me. This allowed me to focus on coaching.

While I felt confident in our program's philosophy, I struggled to find confidence in myself at first. There were so few women in professional coaching. The idea was so foreign that when Littlewing was launched, a news story on LetsRun.com inaccurately named Jesse as the coach. It was apparently less of a stretch to imagine my triathlete husband—who had no coaching or pro running experience—in this job than me.

I also felt out on a limb because I wasn't using the traditional metrics of athletic success in my industry. I wanted to coach women to be the best in the world, but without subscribing to the dominant paradigm that athletes are disposable and that winning was worth just about any price. Success to me looked like developing the *empowered* athlete, not just the *winning* athlete. My priority was getting my athletes to stop outsourcing their key decision-making, to trust themselves, to take the wheel and drive their running and their lives. I hoped to teach them that they didn't need to override cues from their own bodies to please a coach or anyone else. It was crucial to me as their coach that they learned to listen to their bodies, respect what they hear, and act accordingly; I wanted sport to bring them closer to themselves, not further away.

I believed strongly that my athletes would improve in that kind of environment, and also that when it was time to move on from racing, they would be more likely to thrive and still love the sport. Since so many of my athletes arrived on the tail end of a rough patch, we had to build them up from scratch—in terms of fitness, yes, but also in terms of love of the sport, which sometimes gets lost in the frustration of injuries. Getting through the first year healthy, developing good habits, and having fun was our Olympics that first year. My own running started well, with some road races and a personal best in the 10K—a satisfying postpartum comeback—but a sore Achilles cut my season short. In some ways, I was relieved. Coaching took a lot of energy: I had logs to pore over, young women to mentor, and mistakes to learn from. My personal experiences in training and racing were proving to be necessary, but not sufficient. Every athlete was a case study of one, and I needed to pay attention.

IN THE OFF-SEASON after my first year of coaching, I attended a weekend retreat called Muse Camp, organized in Bend by Amanda

Stuermer, the founder of a nonprofit that focused on empowering women and girls to create social change. The program brought together women across any number of fields for conversations and workshops about fulfilling our personal, professional, and creative possibilities as women. For the first time in my adult life, I was attending an event entirely unrelated to sports.

In a writing workshop, I heard from total strangers sharing raw truths about motherhood, addiction, race, grief, uncertainty, and unfulfilled hopes. It was like tapping into the groundwater of the condition of womanhood, and I saw myself in all of them, an unexpected connection that shook me. So much of my life had been spent trying to be better than other people to feel worthy, and it had separated me from others and myself.

My last class was Dr. Melody Moore's Embody Love Movement workshop, which was devoted to body image. The description sounded a little kumbaya to me, with its "body liberation for all" messaging. But then Melody, a proud Texan brunette, walked into the center of the high-ceilinged library room of the main lodge, undeniably compelling and no-nonsense and experienced in facilitation. She drew me—and everyone else—all the way in.

We did a version of the line exercise common in team-building settings—with participants stepping forward with each answer of "yes" to a series of questions—except all the questions that day centered on our relationships with food, weight, and body confidence. It was impossible not to be heartbroken at how much shame people carry about the body that moves them through the world, and how ubiquitous those feelings are regardless of body size and shape. The twelve-year-old best friends who felt embarrassed in their swimsuits was a depressing story I'd seen before, but it was the women in their sixties who still felt at war with their bodies that made me cry.

As we sat in one big circle on the wood floor, Melody led us through a hands-on examination of popular magazines, asking us to rip out every page we came across that had images of those who were BIPOC and/or had visible disabilities, scars, acne, or larger bodies and put them in the center of the room. The collection was painfully small. And all of the photos of bodies larger than about a size 6 were accompanied by weight loss copy. Melody taught us about the economics of the global beauty industry, currently worth $511 billion, which depends entirely on women feeling that our bodies are wrong and must be fixed through consumer goods and services.

For the next exercise, we partnered up and wrote down the negative thoughts we had about our appearances on Post-it notes—the painful reactions that bubble up when we see ourselves in the mirror. When I wrote down statements like "Your thighs are too big," I felt a twinge seeing them on paper just as I had when confessing my athletic insecurities years before. Giving them space on a page is one thing, voicing them to a witness is another. When my partner read her negative self-statements aloud to me, I tried to swallow the emotion rising under my sternum, but choked sobs flooded out of me. I was able to hear these messages we tell ourselves for what they are: violence. Melody brought us back together and guided us toward action. I thought about all the pain women feel simply existing in their bodies, all their lives, because of a system of grossly skewed incentives. And how good people everywhere push diet culture in the name of health, not knowing they are complicit in the erosion of health on a much larger scale.

I understood now that the sports system itself was causing enormous harm to women by devaluing or denying their essential physiological experiences and emphasizing the wrong priorities at the wrong times. Every high school runner who starved herself to avoid puberty. Every woman who restricted her diet to reach an arbitrary weight her body didn't want to be. Every woman who lost time to broken bones and torn tendons. Every woman who lost confidence and self-worth for "failing" to progress. Every woman who couldn't eat without having "earned it" and turned to exercise as punishment to atone for indulgence. Ever since Title IX opened the doors to our participation, there have been countless women walking around carrying the wounds of their experiences in sport. When I thought about sports as one of the largest institutions in our culture, I saw the role it played in the bigger picture and knew we could and must do better.

Increasingly, I was looking back on my life as an athlete with an entirely new perspective. I had once felt angry with the women who developed eating disorders or made choices that hurt their health or our teams' prospects. Now I was angry that so many women and girls were blamed for not thriving in a system not truly built for them. I was angry with the coaches in charge. The athletic departments. The media for building up youth phenoms as they burst onto the scene, only to watch them crash. I felt haunted by the long list of girls whom I never heard about again.

IN MAY OF 2015, in the middle of my second coaching season, I flew to Los Angeles, leaving Jude at home alone with Jesse for the first time. My Littlewing athletes were competing in a track meet at Occidental College, and later that evening my dad had an important MRI to check on his liver tumors. He had been diagnosed with liver cancer right before Jude was born, and while the prognosis was bad—there was no cure, and he wasn't eligible for a transplant—he had responded to chemo reasonably well until recently.

The track meet was one of those mid-season poorly spectated races where America's finest athletes are trying to get qualifying standards out of the way. There was no frenzy here, no major media, no credentials or special access—just our community, doing our unsexy jobs. During each race, I paced the infield like all the other coaches under the lights. As the women's 1,500 ran ovals around us, I watched the newest phenom Mary Cain racing the older professional field and felt like I always did when her name came up: worried.

Mary Cain had signed an endorsement deal with Nike and moved out to Oregon to work with Alberto Salazar. Going pro right out of high school is highly unusual in American distance running, but male runner Galen Rupp had done it with great success working with Alberto, and now the coach was eager to build on that track record with Mary. Except things weren't going well for Mary. The Nike Oregon Project, or NOP, had grown into the best-funded and most prestigious professional running club in the world. Alberto had developed a reputation as something of a mad scientist, looking under every stone for that last .01 percent performance advantage. No one was more obsessed with performance than Alberto Salazar. I'd heard about how hard he pushed his athletes and observed how compliant they had to be to survive. Everyone who worked with Alberto seemed to become a little less human, outsourcing themselves to his decision-making, like a team of robots—not unlike Kerri Strug and the 1996 women's gymnastics team I'd watched on TV growing up.

When Mary Cain walked off the track at Occidental, dejected from another underwhelming performance in the 1,500, I resolved to talk to her to see how she was doing holistically and offer her mentorship if she wanted it. I began to walk toward her, but she was instantly flanked by Alberto and Darren, the team's sports psychologist with whom I'd worked myself several years earlier. They surrounded her as she changed out of her racing spikes, on the verge of tears. Neither of them offered her any comfort. To Collier, one of my older athletes who also served in an assistant role, I said, "Look at those guys, icing her out after a bad race. I want to fucking punch them."

Collier understood what I was getting at. "She doesn't look well."

"I'm going to find her when she's alone and give her my number. I want to make sure she has someone she can reach out to for help."

The sky exploded into lightning and hard rain without warning, the only way it seems to rain in Los Angeles, and everyone ducked for cover. All the athletes and coaches were cramming together under tiny tents, and soon I was even closer to Alberto and Mary.

He lit into her for her poor performance, blaming her weight. Nobody under the tent stood up for her. Nobody challenged Alberto's power. I felt too frightened to say something while Alberto was there—a shameful weakness of resolve I still regret to this day. In 2019, when Mary came forward in an opinion documentary for the *New York Times*, I would learn, along with the rest of the world, how dark that moment had been for her. Afterward, she had contemplated suicide and cut herself. It wasn't the first time she was verbally or emotionally abused by NOP coaches, but it was the first time it happened in front of anyone outside her team, and the silence that followed was an industry endorsement of her treatment. In 2021 Cain would go on to file a $20 million lawsuit against Nike and Salazar over the alleged abuse. She would also found Atalanta NYC, an elite women's running group in New York City that focuses on creating a healthy, positive training environment, while also providing mentorship to local, underserved girls. But first she would need to get out of NOP.

DRIVING ON THE LA freeway to the medical imaging center, I thought about Mary. I wished I could coach her. Mary was nineteen years old, and her body was developing. The performance dip she was facing was entirely predictable, and yet like every other situation I'd seen like it, it was being received as something to grieve—or, to Alberto, something to punish. Alberto reportedly treated Mary like she was faulty, undisciplined, and unworthy of care unless she "fixed" herself, essentially by not being a developing woman. The reason Mary was so depressed wasn't because her times were slower. It was because she felt scared, alone, and trapped in an environment that was deeply hostile to normal female body experiences. She needed her differences acknowledged, respected, supported, and built around. That's what every developing female athlete deserves.

The medical center glowed against the night sky as I walked through the wide wall of glass doors to meet my mom in the waiting room. The wheelchair surprised me. My dad's beanie-covered head hung down like he was asleep on an airplane, and when I took over for the nurse who was pushing him, I was shocked by how much of his spine was showing out the top of his too-loose T-shirt collar. My mom kneeled in front of him.

"Frank, how did it go?"

"Not good, Joysst," he slurred, never opening his eyes.

My mom and I exchanged a look.

"Let's get you home," I said.

Unable to rouse him the next morning for his medication, we called 911, and a team of EMTs came into the house. I remember the booming voice of one of them shouting, "Frank! Can you hear me, Frank!" and feeling hope when my dad yelled back, "Yes, sir!" I ran into the room as the EMT yelled, "Frank! How old are you, Frank?"

With his eyes still closed, he yelled, "Thirty!" He had just turned sixty. He didn't answer the next question, or the next.

Twenty-four hours later, my mom, sister, and I stood in his hospital room next to his untouched tray of food as he labored for air through crackly lungs. It was horrifying to watch, even after doctors tried to assure us that the coma he was in prevented him from suffering. This man was the strongest person I knew. He would plant his feet like the roots of a redwood tree and let my sister and me climb all over him. He built homesteads and spaceships and playhouses and could carry anything by himself. It was physically painful to see him shrunken like this, a whisper of himself. Hoping it would somehow make it end sooner, I walked over to him and placed my head on his bony sternum and told him I loved him and that it was okay to go. My sister came over, and I made space for her as she bawled over his laboring body. When my mom walked over to him, I felt myself wanting to cover my eyes to avoid the way his face was contorted with the effort of breathing, but I made myself watch, even though it was terrifying, knowing it was the last time I'd see him. Eventually, mercifully, there was no air left to find.

My dad's brothers and a couple of his closest camping buddies gathered in our backyard within hours. On their way to say good-bye in the hospital a little too late, they shared stories about him over a campfire instead—about a life with rough edges, and the joy he'd taken in simple things. I listened, standing beside my first childhood friend, Gina, and her son, wishing I was holding my own in my arms.

ABOUT A YEAR LATER, in 2016, I made it official and announced my retirement. When I did, I felt completely at peace. Every run for the rest of my life would be entirely my own, I resolved. Now, I could fully embrace the title of coach, and I filtered as much of my work as possible through a broader feminist lens. I absorbed as much as I could about not only physiology, but also patriarchy, diet culture, racism, transphobia, sexual abuse, and the other societal forces that disproportionately affect women. At the center of my coaching was the development of the empowered woman. If I was successful, each of the athletes I worked with would become the kind of competitor only she could be.

Over the next five years, I made plenty of mistakes, but I built on the best things I learned from my own coaches, the work of other experts and leaders scattered around the country, and my own intuition, and eventually found some answers to the questions

I had been asking. What does it look like to center women in the creation of an alternative professional model? Can you do it that way and still be successful? I don't measure my success by traditional standards of times and podiums, but even by traditional standards, the answer is yes. Of course there was also good luck involved, but we certainly set ourselves up well to run into some. In the 2021 season, all six track athletes on Littlewing ran lifetime bests, and all qualified to compete in the Olympic Trials. More importantly, none of them broke their bodies irreparably, or jeopardized their fertility and bone density, or engaged in self-harm, or fell out of love with running. All of them developed a deeper understanding of themselves, learned to listen to and use their voices, regained good menstrual health, trained in a body-positive environment, were active participants in the decisions that affected their lives, and left my team as stronger people.

Mel, my first athlete, worked her way back from four years of injuries in college to become a world-class steeplechaser over the course of eight years, finishing as high as third in the USA Championships and achieving a top-twenty ranking in the world more than once. In 2021, our final year of working together, I watched as she took the wheel of her career, stepped into a leadership role with the younger athletes on the team, and put herself in a position to be a contender for the Olympic team. She didn't qualify, finishing seventh. That's what outsiders might see—a binary notion of success. But what I see, and know, are the years of work she put in to believe that achievement was possible, the courage she summoned to give herself a real chance, and the maturity she possessed to feel her disappointment deeply while remaining undefined by any one result.

I know I am not the best coach in the world, and Mel may have achieved even more with someone else. There are better physiologists, workout wizards, and people with more time to give their athletes than I can. I'm grateful for every athlete who has trusted me with their career while I learned on the job, like every other coach. What drew me to coaching was an attempt to repair something that was broken in the system, and in me. To make right the things that hurt teammates I loved, and strangers I never met. To try to build a safe place in the mess. And we did. But even if I were to do this forever in my little bubble in Bend, and band together with all the other coaches doing right by women, it's not enough.

Title IX opened a door fifty years ago that can never be closed again. But equality doesn't end at the equal right to play. True equality in sports, like any other industry, requires rebuilding the systems so there is an equal chance to thrive. I'm just one person telling a story to bring an embodied experience of the female athlete to life. I can't create policy, or NCAA best practices, or medical guidelines. But I have some ideas of where to start.

We need policies like those created around concussions that specifically protect the health of the female body in sport. We need to create a formal certification to work with female athletes that mandates education on female physiology, puberty, breast development, menstrual health, and the female performance wave. We need to be able to monitor menstrual health and educate people about RED-S. We need to draw boundaries preventing race weight and body composition from being emphasized in high school or college, or any time before it is developmentally appropriate. We need eating disorder literacy, so we know how to identify, prevent, and talk about them. And we need eating disorders to be treated like self-harm, requiring coaches to immediately report and refer someone suffering to a specialist, because the likelihood of making a full recovery is strongly correlated to the length of time before intervention.

We need to require the measuring of things that actually matter in school programs, such as menstrual health, injury and mental health statistics, athlete satisfaction, and attrition rates, and use these values to create an alternate ranking system for college sports programs that would hold schools accountable and empower recruits with information that's imperative to their future well-being.

We need coach job descriptions to be compatible with having children so fewer women leave coaching, and so coaches of all genders have the ability to be active partners and parents. We need breast education and a free sports bra for every middle schooler who wants one. We need adults to deal with their own issues around food and body so they don't pass them on to the children and young adults in their care. We need to comb through the rule books of all the sports and eliminate existing rules mandating uniform styles known to increase self-consciousness and lower body satisfaction, and explicitly permit alternative options designed around optimizing movement and body confidence.

There's so much more, but really it all begins with a willingness to *see* women as human beings worthy of thriving. The problems women and girls face need to be seen as *human* issues that everyone takes responsibility for changing.

I'm not a doctor or administrator or researcher. Maybe you are, and if so, we need you. We need passionate leaders of all genders to take women's sports into the next fifty years and beyond. But we also need stories. A flood of them. The invisible and the forbidden. The small stuff that adds up to big change.

THE MORNING AFTER my father died, I woke to the childhood sounds of kitchen cabinets opening and closing behind my bedroom wall. I opened my eyes slowly to the sunshine-lit room and saw my dad, young and slim, in jeans and Red Wing boots, leaning the back of his white T-shirt against the closet door. I blinked a few times, smiling with him, and after one of the blinks, he was gone. When I told my mom, she told me she had a similar experience as a child, after her brother had died by suicide. The idea of ghosts bent all logical reasoning, but I had no choice but to accept that at a minimum, my subconscious put him there, knowing I would be facing my first day without him.

I put on my running clothes and headed out the front door. I found myself running the two-mile route toward my high school track—it was a Sunday, and nobody would be there. I tried to find peace in the familiar neighborhoods, the stucco houses, and all the things that hadn't changed. Running hadn't changed. Running was still my own. But then the labored rhythm of my breath had the same cadence as my dad's the day before, and my chest tightened so quickly I had to stop and bend over with my hands on my knees to grab any air at all. I sobbed in the middle of the sidewalk until I was ready to run again.

Slowly, I worked my way up to the track and hopped the fence. I ran eight laps in lane eight, with a small rest between each. It was something simple and familiar that could remind me that running was still mine, not a reminder of death. But on the second lap, when the breathing got hard, I saw him again on the top of the curve, leaning against the fence, and I dropped to my knees and covered my head with my hands. With my lips two inches from the rubber track, I whispered, "How will I do this without you?" and the words surprised me. I didn't think I was doing anything for him anymore. But the truth of it hit me: part of me still was.

I remembered sitting on my trundle bed in eighth grade, writing a letter to my dad on recycled notebook paper, searching for the right words to get him to stop drinking. I closed it with, *I love you so much, Dad. I want you to be alive until you're old, to play with your grandkids. If you really love me as much as you say you do, more than anything in the world, you'll quit.* After he went to bed, I placed it on the bar, right where he would have his coffee at 4:30 in the morning before work. When I woke up for school, it was gone. He never replied or brought it up, and I never mentioned it again. He never quit drinking.

So much of my running was trying to feel his love. But I'd grown up a lot since my earliest days of competing and hearing Dad's voice in my head, spurring me on. While it had taken me some time to realize it or call it by its name, my whole life I had been engaging in the hard work of learning to run for myself, not for others. I had been learning how to return to myself, again and again, in a world full of forces that consistently pull us away. I wanted to hold tight to that knowledge; even more strongly, I wanted to pass it on. I stood up from the track and began to run home.

ACKNOWLEDGMENTS

Due to significant unforeseen global, national, and personal circumstances, this book kicked my ass. When I started writing it, I didn't know I'd have to become a homeschool teacher, lose childcare for huge stretches of time, and be pulled into a never-ending square dance of COVID isolations and track meet postponements. And I certainly didn't know I'd have a mental health crisis, though looking back on it all now, it certainly makes sense. This book would have kicked my ass anyway, because it's a book. People who write them always say, "I couldn't have done it without a lot of help," but I guess I never believed them. But literally, without help, I couldn't have done it, and I would have quit. Which would have been unfortunate because I needed to get this book out of my body for myself, as much as for anyone else. And now that I have, I have some final notes.

I have done my best to accurately represent the events in this book, but I acknowledge that memory isn't perfect, and others may have different recollections of the same events. A few people's names and identifying characteristics have been changed. Dialogue is exact sometimes, and other times I improvised based on the substance of the conversation. The language I use in this book surrounding gender and sex is mostly reflective of how I experienced it at the time, which was binary, and it is not indicative of how gender language should be used culturally, or in future policy.

I really want to acknowledge some people, so I'll start with the countless advocates and early sport pioneers who paved the path so I could have access to sport, as well as all the current researchers and coaches and allies working to create healthy environments worthy of the diverse array of athletes participating in women's sports. Your work inspires mine.

My personal support team for this book begins with my agent, Daniel Greenberg at Levine Greenberg Rostan Literary Agency, who helped me turn an impassioned phone call into a book proposal and served as a sharp reader, trusted adviser, and skilled negotiator. Ann Godoff, Scott Moyers, and Emily Cunningham at Penguin Press asked all the right questions, nudged me more toward literary memoir, and invested in me, for which I am deeply grateful. Rose Tomaszewska and the team at Virago, thank you for investing in this book's potential in the UK and beyond. Caspian Dennis, thanks for the assist.

Emily, my editor, took on the project when I was healthy, passionate, driven, and organized, and the author she ended up with was, well, me in a crisis. She championed the book when I was unable to, always knew exactly what the assignment was, offered skill and softness when I needed it, and never once wavered in her conviction that I would finish with something I was proud of, even when it took twice as long as expected. Victoria Lopez, Danielle Plafsky, Colleen McGarvey, Megan Buiocchi, Carla Benton, Linda Friedner, and the rest of the team who played important roles in making this a real book and finding readers for it, thank you for all your hard work.

I relied on scientists and doctors to help me with key parts of this book. Dr. Sarah Lesko spent several days with me gathering research and strategizing structure, after several years of being the best ideahasher-outer and co-conspirator for female athlete health. Dr. Trent Stellingwerff, Dr. Kirsty Elliott-Sale, and Dr. Kate Ackerman provided helpful articles and suggestions on my manuscript. Rachel Vishanoff compiled research on Title IX and aesthetics in media, and Traci Carson collected research to support the existence of a female performance wave.

I have also leaned on other writers. My book coach, Jennifer Louden, threw me the ladder that helped me climb out of the pit, breaking the book into smaller steps. She also helped me recover from the devastating realization that I wasn't Ann Patchett about halfway through the first draft, reminding me that most writers must learn to tolerate long periods of writing absolute garbage. Laurie Wagner's "Wild Writing" practice helped me go deeper and be more honest in my work. Marianne Elliott showed me how to apply the lessons learned from my running to my writing. Liz Weil coached me on narrative arc and gave me a North Star to look toward. Eva Moss brought their screenwriting and filmmaking expertise to help with tension. Michelle Hamilton and Lily Raff McCaulou provided generous mentorship and, alongside Sarah Cyr, taught me the incredible value of a local writing community. My early readers include some of the above, but I also want to thank Jessie Dale, Sally Bergesen, Alysia Montaño, Laura Winberry, and Dr. Melody Moore for providing feedback that made this book better.

As for family of origin, mine had its tough bits, but there is no doubt I was incredibly fortunate to have the love and support I had growing up. My mom and sister don't get much attention in this book because it's about running, and I didn't really let them into that part of my world because I didn't know how at the time. But along with my dad, their love moves through absolutely everything, and I wouldn't trade my family and all our adventures for anything. My mom is a private person, and there were parts of this book that are uncomfortable to own but important to tell. I want to thank her for being a gentle guide who always made me feel I had agency over my life.

My coaches have been some of the most impactful figures in my life. DeLong, McCauley, Vin, Dena, Terrence, Mark, and many more who worked in assistant roles, all have played critical roles in how I saw myself and the world. There is vulnerability involved in being a part of a story in which you aren't holding the pen, and I want to thank them, along with everyone else who shows up in the book, for their humanity and everything I've learned from them. Coaches are always learning in public, and I realize a book takes this to the next level. I want to thank the athletes I have coached through Littlewing. I admire each of you so much. Thank you for trusting me, for making coaching so rewarding, and for telling me when I screwed up. Making mistakes, getting new information, taking accountability, changing your mind and your behavior, these are things my coaches modeled for me. Thousands of people doing just that will change sports for women and girls more quickly than any policy change ever could.

I want to acknowledge my teammates for shaping some of the most meaningful memories and experiences of my life. A special thank-you to those who shared their memories, experiences, and reflections. They helped me so much. Julia, thank you for sharing the details of your accident, for being someone I look up to even *more* outside of running, and for your empowering life outlook. This book focuses mostly on the struggles of female athletes for a reason, but there could easily be many books written about the joys and adventures. It makes me uncomfortable not to be able to make full people out of everyone who is in the book, but that's the nature of memoir. Everywhere in my life I see the mark of my teammates on me— my career, my hobbies, my interests, my baby names, my preferences, everything—even though we rarely see one another in person. I guess in some way I am you, and you are me, forever.

I couldn't have done this work without childcare support beyond me and Jesse. Thank you to our neighbors dubbed the "Quaranteam" during the dark days, Bailey and Megan for your many hours of childcare and household help, and our active grandparents, Joyce,

Carol, Jeff, Gary, and Janna, for all the pinch-hitting when it was safe to do so.

To my family and friends who have listened, showed interest, and offered support, thank you. To Oiselle, Salomon, and Laird, thanks for your committed partnership during the weirdest of times. Special thanks to Sally, Sarah, Jessie, Alan, Nicole, Stephanie, Christine, and Meredith for the multitude of ways you have shown up, and the depth of your love and care. Eva, thank you for being such a bright light in my life and helping me relocate my strongest self when I needed her most. Thank you to my therapist, Rhyver Rudick, and thank you Wellbutrin. Thank you to my kids, Jude and Zadie, for supporting this book in ways that frankly amaze me for how young you are: the coffee and breakfast deliveries, the hugs, the encouragement, all of it. And to Jesse, my lifelong teammate, my spouse, co-parent, business partner, early reader, and resident cutie, thank you. This was a heavy load for us to carry the last few years, and you have shown up for me and for our kids in so many humbling ways. I thought my title of "Most Supportive Spouse," earned during your professional triathlon career, would remain safe from a challenger forever, but I think you *may* have eclipsed me. I love you.

And you.

Yeah, you.

Thanks for reading.

I love you, too.

SOURCES AND RESOURCES

In addition to my personal experiences, stories of others, and formal education, I relied on the work of many researchers, writers, and organizations to create this book. I want to share the sources and resources that influenced my thinking, organized by theme, for those interested in learning more. This is of course not an exhaustive list of all the great work being done.

On the theme of body development and girls' sports participation, University of Portsmouth's 2016 comprehensive survey of more than two thousand schoolgirls from ages eleven to seventeen provided critical insights into breast development as a lived experience. Bras for Girls is a nonprofit providing breast education and sports bras to middle schoolers, a simple intervention you can support that has enormous impact. A free sports bra should be standard-issue equipment in middle school for every person who needs it. For comprehensive information about girls' sports participation, the Women's Sports Foundation is a great resource. They use research, advocacy, and community impact to maximize girls' sports participation, and they identify what a lot of the barriers are.

Analysis of performance development for male and female athletes through puberty was presented in a digestible way by Espen Tønnessen et al.; their 2015 paper published by *PLOS One*, "Performance Development in Adolescent Track and Field Athletes According to Age, Sex and Sport Discipline," provides data about when performance paths diverge, why they do, and for how long. The charts in this paper are the visual representation of my experiences in chapters two and three. The book *Roar* by Dr. Stacy Sims provides an incredible overview of female-specific performance variables. Emma Hilton and Tommy Lundberg's 2021 paper called "Transgender Women in the Female Category of Sport: Perspectives on Testosterone Suppression and Performance Advantage" published in *Sports Medicine* is where I got the specific percentages for sex-based performance differences across sports and activities. While the science of sex-based differences as they relate to testosterone exposure throughout puberty is widely accepted as fact, this is not a justification for trans athlete exclusion. Rebecca Jordan-Young and Katrina Karkazis wrote a fantastic piece in *Scientific American* in 2019 called "4 Myths about Testosterone," highlighting the ways testosterone is misinterpreted and misused in sport policy.

The menstrual cycle and female athlete health and performance have been historically understudied, but there is a body of exciting new research. For historical context on the evolution of female physiology and sport, check out "The Question of Rest for Women During Menstruation: The Boylston Prize Essay of Harvard University for 1876" by Mary Putnam Jacobi. Dr. Kirsty Elliott-Sale has done a ton of recent work on the intersection of menstruation, the female reproductive axis, and performance, and has coauthored many papers used for this book. Some include "The BASES Expert Statement on Conducting and Implementing Female Athlete-Based Research" in 2020 from *The Sport and Exercise Scientist*, "Period Prevalence and Perceived Side Effects of Hormonal Contraceptive Use and the Menstrual Cycle in Elite Athletes" published in the *International Journal of*

Sports Physiology and Performance in 2018, and from *Sports Medicine* in 2022, "Evolutionary Biology Meets Exercise Science: A Comment on the Application of Life History Theory to the Study of Low Energy Availability in Athletes." The 2021 paper published by the *Journal of Athletic Training* called "Presence and Perceptions of Menstrual Dysfunction and Associated Quality of Life Measures Among High School Female Athletes" by Aubrey Armento et al. shows the huge number of adolescent athletes who view losing their period as "normal" and links menstrual dysfunction to anxiety, fatigue, and pain interference. The connection between impaired ovarian function and decreased performance is illustrated by Jaci Vanheest et al. in a 2014 paper called "Ovarian Suppression Impairs Sport Performance in Junior Elite Female Swimmers," published in *Medicine & Science in Sports & Exercise*. Ignoring period loss works against the performance aims of coach and athlete, which I experienced in chapters nine and ten, and these papers are important for considering how to address these problems in the future.

The 2020 paper "Prevalence of Female Athlete Triad Risk Factors and Iron Supplementation Among High School Distance Runners: Results From a Triad Risk Screening Tool" by Paige Skorseth et al., published in the *Orthopaedic Journal of Sports Medicine*, shows the high rates of menstrual dysfunction, bone loss, and disordered eating in high school were even worse than I feared. Katherine Rizzone led the 2017 paper in the *Journal of Athletic Training* titled "The Epidemiology of Stress Fractures in Collegiate Student-Athletes, 2004–2005 Through 2013–2014 Academic Years" that provided the statistics on stress fracture rates in females versus males. Anne B. Loucks influenced my thinking that the risk of RED-S and menstrual dysfunction are influenced by age, giving more shape to the female performance wave and making an even stronger case to protect developing female athletes; her 2006 paper "The Response of Luteinizing Hormone Pulsatility to 5 Days of Low Energy Availability Disappears by 14 Years of Gynecological Age" was published in the *Journal of Clinical Endocrinology and*

Metabolism. Jill Thein-Nissenbaum's 2013 paper in *Maturitas*, "Long Term Consequences of the Female Athlete Triad," is part of what got me thinking that the NCAA's lack of adequate action on eating disorders, menstrual dysfunction, and RED-S has consequences in a similar manner as concussions, which can lead to chronic traumatic encephalopathy years later.

With regards to RED-S and low energy availability, the published work and insights of Kathryn Ackerman and Trent Stellingwerff completely changed how I look back on my entire career, and their work should offer a basis for policy changes and new best practices. Their 2020 article (coauthored by Elliott-Sale, Amy Baltzell, Mary Cain, Kara Goucher, Margo Mountjoy, and me) in the *British Journal of Sports Medicine* titled "#REDS (Relative Energy Deficiency in Sport): Time for a Revolution in Sports Culture and Systems to Improve Athlete Health and Performance" is a strong statement for the future. The 2018 paper "Low Energy Availability Is Difficult to Assess but Outcomes Have Large Impact on Bone Injury Rates in Elite Distance Athletes" by Ida Heikura et al., published in the *International Journal of Sport Nutrition and Exercise Metabolism*, is another I leaned on, as is a 2020 paper published in *Nutrients* by Danielle Logue et al. titled "Low Energy Availability in Athletes 2020: An Updated Narrative Review of Prevalence, Risk, Within-Day Energy Balance, Knowledge, and Impact on Sports Performance."

To bolster my understanding of support—or lack thereof—for athletes' mental health, I referenced "The American College of Sports Medicine Statement on Mental Health Challenges for Athletes" from 2021. The NCAA's failures were covered well by Wendell Barnhouse in the *Global Sport Matters* article "NCAA Faces Uphill Battle Getting Mental Health Care to Student-Athletes." The NCAA's website contains a statement of its mission as well as bylaws committing to athlete health, which holds them accountable. The NCAA includes an article on its website called "Mind, Body and Sport: Eating Disorders," which is an excerpt from the Sport Science

Institute's guide to understanding and supporting student-athlete mental wellness; written by Ron Thompson, that guide is basically a starting point for what should become best practices and policies. The NCAA's "Concussion Safety Protocol Checklist," also available online, is a great reference for future health legislation for female athletes. See also NCAA Bylaw 3.2.4.17: Concussion Management Plan—Bylaw 16.4.2: Mental Health Services and Resources is the closest bylaw covering the issues in this book, and it is not being fulfilled adequately.

On the theme of femininity and sport, my influences include Deborah Brake, Patricia Clasen, and Mary Jo Kane. Dana Voelker and Trent Petrie's work with the program Bodies in Motion highlights the health fallout from the conflicting identities of the female athlete. Sports scholars Leslie Heywood and Shari Dworkin's discussion of the "babe factor" in their book *Built to Win: The Female Athlete as Cultural Icon* made a strong impression on me. Chris Mosier, Schuyler Bailar, Nikki Smith, Alex Showerman, and Joanna Harper helped me understand the ways sports are important gender-affirming spaces for people other than cis women, and the cost of exclusion not just for trans athletes but for everyone.

The influence of male bias on women's lives is central to this book. Caroline Criado Perez's book *Invisible Women: Data Bias in a World Designed for Men* is useful in understanding just how much is built upon the default human in our modern society, how we got there, and how consequential this is for women's lives. *Unwell Women* by Elinor Cleghorn dives into how this is playing out in the medical system and in women's health. Neither of these books focuses on sports, but they clearly show that the assumption of sameness, once a key strategy in the women's movement for gaining equal rights, has consequences. Thinkers who have contributed to my understanding of feminist history more broadly include Kate Manne, Kimberlé Crenshaw, bell hooks, Mary Beard, and Mikki Kendall, among others.

Studying the history of women in sports that led up to Title IX, as well as those first politically turbulent years, was an essential part of my research. The historical analyses of Jaime Schultz, Lucille Adkins, Deborah Brake, Welch Suggs, Victoria Jackson, Alison Mariella Désir, and Amira Rose Davis influenced my thinking about the intersections between the larger women's movement, the civil rights movement, and the women's sports movement, as well as which stories get erased. Davis is one of the hosts of the *Burn It All Down* podcast about sports and culture, which is aptly self-described as "the feminist sports podcast you need." On the topic of Title IX compliance, Nancy Hogshead-Makar does a good job in her legal advocacy work for athletes illustrating how far we still have to go. Alia Wong's 2015 article "Where Girls Are Missing Out on High-School Sports" in *The Atlantic* shows where Title IX compliance and noncompliance are located geographically in the United States and how that intersects with race. The University of Minnesota's Tucker Center for Research on Girls & Women in Sport is the go-to resource for gender in coaching and administration. "What Gender Inequality Looks Like in Collegiate Sports" by Terrance Ross for *The Atlantic* in 2015 has great information on coaching inequality. On the theme of female athlete abuse, the documentary *Athlete A* about women's gymnastics was incredible. Mary Cain's short documentary for *The New York Times*, along with several published articles about Alberto Salazar and the Nike Oregon Project, were important sources. The United States Center for SafeSport is a critical resource for athlete safety and reporting abuse.

For an understanding of body image in sport, Peiling Kong and Lynne Harris's 2015 article in the *Journal of Psychology*, "The Sporting Body: Body Image and Eating Disorder Symptomatology Among Female Athletes from Leanness Focused and Nonleanness Focused Sports," shows that female athletes have worse body image than non-athletes, and it's far more than leanness-focused sports. Sixty percent of female athletes experience body-shape pressure from coaches.

When it comes to understanding the forces that impact women's body confidence more broadly outside of sport, Sonya Renee Taylor's book *The Body Is Not an Apology* and her interview on Brené Brown's podcast *Unlocking Us* are a fantastic read and listen. Jean Kilbourne's TED Talk "Killing Us Softly" does a brilliant job condensing the harmful gender differences in media representation into just a few minutes. Dr. Melody Moore and I had a great discussion on Julia Hanlon's podcast *Running on Om*, which is useful for anyone trying to create a sport environment that reduces negative body image and disordered eating.

The National Eating Disorders Association (NEDA) is a critical online resource, and I dove into many of the scholarly articles linked on the site. It is the first place I send parents, coaches, and athletes who express concern for someone struggling with disordered eating and is a great place to get curious about your own eating habits and body image story. *Eating Disorders Review* is an online source for the shockingly high ED rates among athletes. Their findings that nearly 70 percent of athletes have disordered eating patterns confirmed the general feelings I had in the book as I experienced sport culture. The outstanding documentary *Light*, directed by Caroline Treadway, covers eating disorders in climbing. The film includes great insights by Dr. Jennifer Gaudiani that inspire a behavioral understanding of people suffering from eating disorders, which is absolutely critical for anyone who hopes to identify and prevent them. Gaudiani's statement that the number on the scale becomes more important than family, God, and life itself was so arresting and familiar to me that I included it in chapter six. Other books I'd recommend that highlight the role of sports culture on mental health are *Little Girls in Pretty Boxes* by Joan Ryan, *The Silence of Great Distance* by Frank Murphy, *What Made Maddy Run* by Kate Fagan, and *Running While Black* by Alison Mariella Désir.

2198232060291q